A SHORT HISTORY
OF ROME

A SHORT HISTORY
OF ROME

FOR SCHOOLS

BY

E. E. BRYANT, M.A.

Assistant Master at Charterhouse. Formerly Fellow of
Emmanuel College, Cambridge

Cambridge:
at the University Press

1924

CAMBRIDGE
UNIVERSITY PRESS

University Printing House, Cambridge CB2 8BS, United Kingdom

Cambridge University Press is part of the University of Cambridge.

It furthers the University's mission by disseminating knowledge in the pursuit of
education, learning and research at the highest international levels of excellence.

www.cambridge.org
Information on this title: www.cambridge.org/9781316601662

© Cambridge University Press 1924

First edition 1914
Reprinted 1917, 1918
Second edition, enlarged 1924
First paperback edition 2015

A catalogue record for this publication is available from the British Library

ISBN 978-1-316-60166-2 Paperback

PREFACE

THE study of Roman History is not as a rule commenced before a student has gained a fair knowledge of the history of his own country. By that time he should have learnt that historical facts and dates are useful, not as disconnected fragments of information, but as the necessary basis for a knowledge of the tendencies and influences which have been at work in the developement of a nation.

This book attempts to tell the story of Rome as the growth and decay of a living organism, till it is born again in the new form of an empire. With this aim, stress has been laid on the developement of Roman character, on social and political tendencies, on the state of Italy and the Provinces and their relations to Rome, and on the steps in the revolution during the last century of the Republic. Maps and illustrations have been added, and a list of the most important dates and events has been placed at the end of almost every chapter.

The book is intended primarily for the use of middle and upper forms in Public Schools. It is hoped that it may serve to introduce a boy to Roman History and to give him a clear general view, which shall help him when he goes on to work in detail at a special period. If it arouses in the minds of some boys an interest in the subject and a desire to read further for themselves, it will have fulfilled its purpose.

E. E. BRYANT.

CHARTERHOUSE,
Sept. 1914.

PREFACE TO SECOND EDITION

Four chapters have been added, carrying the story down to the death of Constantine. It has been necessary to omit much, but an attempt has been made at the end of Chapters XXVII and XXVIII to call attention to some of the main features of the world of the Roman Empire. The new departure under Diocletian is described at somewhat further length.

E. E. B.

Jan. 1924

CONTENTS

ILLUSTRATIONS

MAPS AND PLANS

CHAPTER I

THE FOUNDING OF ROME

Introduction. Why are you asked to read about the history of Rome? The Romans are only one of many nations which have perished, and why do we read their history rather than that of other peoples? History, whether ancient or modern, is the tale of men like ourselves in their nature but different from us in their circumstances and surroundings; and it is only by seeing the same human nature under far different circumstances that we understand what human nature is and what it is capable of, how much of our ways and methods of living and acting as members of a state is due to natural inborn qualities and how much is due to environment.

The history of Rome is one of the few which we can read. For the Romans wrote of their own doings and have left us in the pages of Livy and Caesar and Tacitus a fuller and more interesting account of themselves and their deeds than we have of almost any other nation. The history of Rome has too a special interest for the Modern World, because many of our laws and institutions are based on those of Rome. When the barbarians, our ancestors, at last overthrew the power of Rome in 410 A.D., they did not destroy all her influence but slowly learnt her spirit and adapted her institutions to their needs, so that the civilization of Western Europe is still largely based on the civilization of Rome. But perhaps the greatest interest of our subject lies in the fact that the Romans at their best were men of strong resolute character with the deepest sense of duty and patriotism, ruling themselves and therefore born to rule the world. Their example of strength and duty and determination is not one of which we can afford to be ignorant. To the Jew the world is indebted for Religion, to the Greek for all that is beautiful in Thought and Art, to the Roman for Law and Order and the sense of Duty. Vergil gives the true spirit of Rome when he writes :

> Tu regere imperio populos, Romane, memento,—
> Hae tibi erunt artes,—pacisque imponere morem,
> Parcere subiectis et debellare superbos.

The history of Rome may be divided into five periods, of which the last looks forward to modern history:

- (*a*) 753–510 B.C. A small state under kings.
- (*b*) 510–270 B.C. Establishment of the Republic. Conquest of Italy. Struggles of Patres and Plebs.
- (*c*) 270–133 B.C. Conquest of Mediterranean Coast. Rule of the Senate.
- (*d*) 133– 23 B.C. Break up of the Constitution. Power of great generals.
- (*e*) 23 B.C.–410 A.D. Empire. Luxury and decay.

Italy and its inhabitants. Italy, as we know it, is bounded on the north by the Alps; but to the Ancient World the Apennines, where they come across from the Gulf of Genoa to the Adriatic, formed the Italian frontier ; and the basin of the Padus or Po between the Apennines and the Alps was regarded as part of Gaul. Southward the Apennines form the backbone of this peninsula, which measures roughly the same number of square miles as England, Scotland and Wales together. There are many easy passes from west to east in the mountains,

while the widest stretches of fertile lowlands are found
on the west in Etruria, Latium and Campania.   As
moreover the chief harbours lie on the western coast,

Italy

the growth of civilization was in this district first.   Italy
looks westwards, turning its back on Greece which faces
east with Athens and the Aegean as the centre of its life.

The inhabitants of the peninsula were of three main stocks—Iapygian, Etruscan, and what for lack of a better name we will call Italian. Of the Iapygians little can be said. They were a dark race, the aborigines of Italy, akin perhaps to the Iberians of Spain and the Ligurians of the north-west coast of Italy. The origin of the Etruscans is uncertain. They were unlike the Latins and stand apart in history as a people whom we cannot connect with any other. The fragments of their language which remain cannot be translated. Yet they were great sailors and traders, rich and skilled in architecture and art, especially in vase-making. Their religion was dark and gloomy, dealing with sacrifice and offerings for the dead ; and from them the Romans learnt the art of divination and the custom of gladiatorial shows, which in their origin go back to the primitive idea of providing a dead chieftain with servants to bear him company in the other world. From Etruria too the Romans derived their twelve lictors, the purple-bordered *toga*, the curule chair of ivory and many other of their marks of office. The Etruscans were not a single united nation but separate communities linked loosely together in leagues of twelve cities. Volsinii was the metropolis of Etruria proper, but at the height of their power the Etruscans included in their dominions the valley of the Po and the coasts of Campania.

The Italians were a branch of the great Aryan family, to which almost all the peoples of modern Europe belong. These Aryans or Indo-Europeans seem to have wandered over Europe and parts of Asia, off-shoots of them settling, as they went, in India, Germany, Greece and Italy ; and the kinship of one branch with another is shown most clearly in similarity of language and customs. When the particular branch which settled in Italy broke off from the main body is not known, but the Italians were at

any rate very close relations of the Greek branch.   Coming
into Italy they divided into two families; the Latins
occupying the western lowlands of Latium; the Sabellians,
from whom came the Sabines, Volscians, Umbrians and
Samnites, turning to the more mountainous centre of the
country.   The Romans were one section of the Latins
and their gradual conquest of their cousins is the union
and consolidation of all the Italian stock under one head.

In addition to these three main races there were
Greek colonies in Italy.   Cumae on the Bay of Naples is
said to have been founded in 1050 B.C. and to have given
the Romans their alphabet.   But the chief Greek colonies
were in South Italy and Sicily, and from them this district
got its name of Magna Graecia.   Tarentum, founded from
Sparta before 700 B.C., caused an important war at a later
period, but the Greeks in Italy were outside the Roman
world for the first few centuries.

The Beginnings of Rome.   The Latins were a race of
farmers, living to the S.E. of the Tiber in small cantons or
country districts round a stronghold, to which they could
retire with their cattle on the approach of an enemy.   This
arx or stronghold was also the centre of their religion and
on it was the shrine and altar of their god.   The cantons
were independent of one another but were loosely united
round the central stronghold of Alba Longa on the Alban
Mount, where yearly sacrifice was offered to Jupiter
Latiaris, the god of the Latins, and matters relating to the
whole league were discussed.   Tradition tells us that in
753 B.C. a colony from Alba Longa was founded on the
Palatine hill, overlooking the Tiber and about fifteen miles
from its mouth, and received the name of Rome.   The
place was well chosen in spite of the unhealthy marshes
which extended round the Tiber.   It was sufficiently far
from the sea to be safe from the raids of pirates ; the hilly
ground was a refuge from robbers and at the same time

commanded the ford, which crossed the river by way of
the Tiber island and was the means of communication
with the rich industrial cities of Etruria; the river was
at once a defence against northern neighbours and the
natural outlet for the produce of Latium, while up the
stream from Ostia sailed small sea-going boats bringing
in exchange the merchandise of Campania or Magna
Graecia and salt, one of the chief necessities of life, from
the salt pans near the mouth of the Tiber.

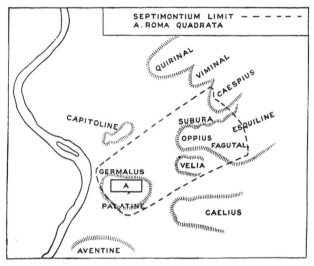

SEPTIMONTIUM LIMIT — — — — —
A. ROMA QUADRATA

QUIRINAL

VIMINAL

CAESPIUS

CAPITOLINE

SUBURA

ESQUILINE

OPPIUS   FAGUTAL

GERMALUS   VELIA

A

PALATINE

CAELIUS

AVENTINE

Roma Quadrata and the Septimontium

The Alban settlement was but small, situated on the
Palatine alone and known as *Roma Quadrata* or square
Rome from the shape of the hill-top. But it soon grew
and took in six other districts, the Velian hill, the Esquiline with its three summits, the Germalus and Subura;
and the festival of these Seven Mounts, *Septimontium*,
recorded the formation of this sevenfold city, though we
must remember that the name of the festival does not

refer to the " Seven Hills " of Rome. It was later that
a union was made with the Sabine settlements on the
Quirinal and Capitoline hills and Rome at last was the
" City of the Seven Hills "—the Capitoline, Palatine,
Aventine, Quirinal, Viminal, Esquiline and Caelian.
The Capitoline as being the steepest was chosen as the
arx and seat of worship for the united city ; the marshes
of the Tiber were drained ; a wooden bridge, *Pons sub-*

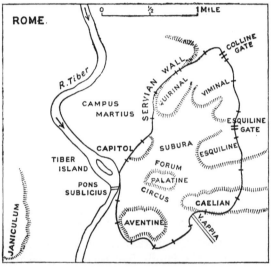

" The City of the Seven Hills "

licius, was built across the Tiber, and the Janiculum on the
further side was fortified to guard the bridge. Between the
Palatine and Quirinal the low ground became the *Forum*
or place of business, and part of it was set aside for the
Comitium, the meeting-place of the Assembly or *Comitia*
of the People, with the *Curia* or Senate House close at
hand. This gradual extension of Rome and incorporation
of other settlements are to be traced in the three primitive

tribes of the city, the Ramnes, Tities and Luceres. Probably the Ramnes were the original Palatine settlers, the Tities the Sabine settlers from the Quirinal ; the origin of the Luceres is quite uncertain, though they may have been Etruscans.

Early Organization of Rome. Our city of Rome is now founded. How was it organized ? Like all other Latin or indeed Aryan communities the state was just a family on a large scale. Very strong was the idea of family life among them. The father was the head of the family with power of life and death over his children; he decided whether the new-born babe should be reared ; and when his sons grew up, their property belonged to him, though they might be allowed to enjoy on sufferance some little *peculium* of their own. He was a priest too, responsible for the worship of the *Lares* or family ancestors, whose number he would join at his death. As in succeeding generations the family broadened into the clan or *gens*, the chief honour belonged to the head of the *gens*. He was the father of the clan. These clans or *gentes* were combined in wards or *curiae* under one headman, and from the *curiae* were formed three tribes under the father of the nation or *rex*. The *Patria Potestas* was the foundation stone of the organization of the Roman state.

The father of the family had been expected to consult the grown-up sons on important questions ; so too the King by custom asked the advice of the old men of the nation, the *Senatus*, originally the *patres* or fathers of the different *gentes*, though he was not bound to do so. And to the Assembly of the People voting by *curiae* (*Comitia Curiata*) questions were submitted on which they could only vote Yes or No. We have thus a King, a Senate and an Assembly. The King was nominated by his predecessor or by an *inter-rex* appointed by the Senate, and the *imperium* or supreme power was conferred on him by the Assembly. He was supreme judge, the leader in war, head in all matters of religion and civil administration, but head as a father not as a despot.

Wars were frequent, raids made on or by a neighbouring town, and every *juvenis* or man between 17 and 45 fought in the *legio*. Each tribe furnished 100 horsemen and the men of each tribe were under their own tribe officer or *tribunus*.

Religion was a family matter with the Romans. The interpretation of the flight of birds (*avi-spicium, auspicium*) and the inspection of the entrails of victims may have come from Etruria, but the real religion of the Romans consisted in the worship of Lares and Penates and Vesta, the Spirits of Ancestors, the Household Gods and the Home. The hearth was an altar on which the fire must never go out ; the offerings and gifts to the ancestors must never be omitted. Every occupation of the home life had its own special god, and all the real deep feeling of a Roman centred round his hearth and home, in whose worship none but members of the home must share. There lay the real strength and bond of union in Roman life. Each *gens* too had its common worship, and Jupiter Latiaris, the god of the Latins, was the All-Father of the race, the god of the Latin family. Later the Romans identified many of their gods with those of the Greeks and took over with the Greek gods the stories of Greek mythology. But the worship of ancestors and the power of the family bond were the inspiration of Rome at her best.

The position of strangers in Rome. With its close family life Rome could not admit strangers into an equality with the citizens or into the old *gentes*. Yet many came attracted by the strength and commercial importance of the new town. They formed a new class called, as time went on, Plebeians as opposed to the Patricians or

sons of a true Roman father. These Plebeians were of
mixed origin. Some were members of towns which had
been conquered by Rome ; others were traders and crafts-
men attracted to the place ; others were refugees and
outcasts of other towns who had fled to the *asylum* of
Rome as to a cave of Adullam ; others again were slaves
who had been granted their freedom. Many put themselves under the protection of a Patrician family, as
clientes under a *patronus*, getting protection in their business in return for certain services ; others were loosely
under the protection of the king. Probably in course of
time the bond connecting them with their patron often
grew weak, and children did not feel the same debt of
gratitude, which their fathers had felt towards the Patrician who had befriended them ; or the family of the
Patrician, to whom they owed their welfare, may have
been exterminated in one of the many wars. But at any
rate the Plebeians grew into a distinct class, large in
numbers but regarded as outside the state, not allowed
to intermarry with the Patricians or to share in the
government. In time Rome came to be almost two
cities in one, the Patrician city, or community of true
citizens, on one side, the Plebs on the other. We shall
see later that it took two centuries of wrangling before
the two bodies could be blended into a united whole.

Legends of Early Rome. Livy gives us a graphic
account of the early years of Rome, full of names and
incidents, stories which will never be forgotten ; stories
of Romulus and Remus, the ' she-wolf's litter ' ; of the
Rape of the Sabine women, of Tarpeia and the joint rule
of Tatius the Sabine king with Romulus ; of Numa Pom-
pilius and the laws which he learnt from the nymph
Egeria ; of the fight of the Horatii and Curiatii which
decided the supremacy question between Rome and Alba.
What truth is there in them ? Livy was in some ways a

poet, though he did not write verse, and even as a historian
he is more inclined to make an interesting story than a
true one.   What he tells may be a faint echo of a truth
far away, confused by time and patriotic tradition.   The
story of Tatius may echo the fact that Sabines, the men of
Cures or Quirites, combined with the Palatine settlers to
make Rome ; the story of the Horatii and Curiatii may
be the memory of some quarrels between Alba and its

The She-wolf with Romulus and Remus

colony.   But the importance of the legends lies in the
fact that they were what the Romans believed about
themselves.   They were sprung from Mars the War-God ;
the she-wolf had suckled them ; they had fought hard and
lived hard and died hard ; their laws and institutions
were divine.   It is as if the stories of King Arthur and his
Knights of the Round Table were known and believed by
every English child ; as if King Arthur and Lancelot and

Galahad were our ancestors and we felt we must not disgrace their memory. The legends are not historically true but they make us know what a heritage the Romans claimed. Read, if you can, Livy, Book I, and Vergil, *Aeneid* VI ; or if that is too much, Macaulay's *Lays of Ancient Rome* will give you some idea of what a Roman felt about his city.

CHAPTER II

THE LAST KINGS OF ROME.

The Legends. With the last three kings of Rome the legends have a more solid substratum of fact though it is not easy to disentangle the truth even here. The stories tell us that Lucumo, son of a Greek and married to an Etruscan called Tanaquil, left the town of Tarquinii owing to the hatred of his fellow-townsmen and migrated to Rome. Marked out for greatness by an eagle, which swooped down upon him on his way, he won the favour of Ancus Marcius, the fourth king of Rome, and on the death of that king was chosen as his successor, taking the name of Lucius Tarquinius, the Romanized form for Lucumo of Tarquinii. He was a conqueror, extending the Roman dominions at the expense of Latins, Sabines and Etruscans, while inside Rome he looked for the support not of the Patricians but of the Plebeians, one hundred of whom he admitted to the Senate. He also drained the low-lying parts of the city between the Palatine and Aventine hills, where he built the *Circus*, instituting the *Ludi Romani* and also beginning the temple of Jupiter on the Capitoline.

This Tarquinius Priscus was succeeded, so the story

goes, by Servius, originally a slave boy round whose head, as he slept, a flame had been seen to play in token of the great destiny which awaited him. Tarquin had given him his daughter in marriage, but he did not succeed to the throne without a conspiracy on the part of the sons of Ancus Marcius to recover the royal power for their own house. Servius was the greatest of all the kings both at home and at war. He defeated the Etruscans and altered the relation of Rome to the rest of Latium, so that Rome was no longer one city of the Latin League but standing outside the league made a treaty with it as a whole, discussing common affairs with the members of the league in the temple of Diana on the Aventine. He enclosed the city with a wall, though the so-called ' Servian Wall ' is of later date, and increased the tribes to four in place of the three tribes of Romulus's day. Then he went on to remodel the army, calling upon Plebeians to serve as well as Patricians and thus going outside the close circle of Patrician *gentes*. For this purpose he divided the people into classes according to the amount of their property and sub-divided the classes into *centuriae* or companies of 100 men. Now this new organization of the army was made the basis of the Comitia or Assembly. The people voted by their centuries in the *Comitia Centuriata*, and so through Servius's action the Plebeians began to have some share in the management of the state. Such a change made the Patricians discontented, and a conspiracy was formed under the son of Tarquin to murder Servius and set up the Tarquin family again in royal power. Servius was murdered by Tarquinius's servants, and his own daughter Tullia, Tarquinius's wife, drove her chariot over her dead father, as his body lay in the *Vicus Sceleratus*, the Accursed Street.

Thus young Tarquinius became king, called from his character Tarquinius Superbus and ruling as despot,

consulting neither Senate nor Comitia and banishing all who
opposed him, but extending the power of Rome till Latium
acknowledged her sway. And he was a great builder,
finishing the temple on the Capitoline and building the
great drain of Rome, the *Cloaca Maxima*. But he had
offended all classes alike by his arbitrary rule, and at last
a brutal outrage committed by his son Sextus upon
Lucretia and his cruel treatment of his sister's family,
the Junii, brought matters to a crisis. Led by L. Junius
Brutus and Collatinus, husband of Lucretia, the people
rose and drove out Tarquinius and with him the power of
king from Rome.

The Etruscan Kings. To get at the truth under-
lying these stories is difficult, but some main ideas may be
gathered from them which are fairly certain. The story
of the arrival of Tarquinius Priscus in Rome and his
subsequent election as king is probably the Roman way
of admitting that Rome passed at one time under the sway
of Etruria and submitted to Etruscan kings. This would
not necessarily involve much real submission to Etruria.
The Etruscan cities were leagued together in very loose
confederations, largely independent in their internal
politics and government and uniting mainly for purposes
of war against a foreign foe. But the name Tarquinius
is the Latinized form of Tarchon, the name of an Etruscan
prince in Vergil's *Aeneid*, and Lucumo was the title of the
nobles of Etruria which was changed into the familiar
Latin Lucius. The bundles of rods, the *fasces*, carried
by 12 lictors in front of the king were a recollection of the
12 cities of the Etruscan League, and the *sella curulis* or
state chair of ivory for the king and his *toga praetexta* with
its purple border and the other marks of royal power were
derived from the same source. The three main facts,
which we gather about the period, point in the same way
towards a foreign dynasty ruling strongly and increasing

the material prosperity of the city but relying within the state on the support of the lower classes rather than of the aristocracy which hated its rule. The three facts you must remember are their building, their conquests and their encouragement of the Plebeians.

(i) **Their building.** From the time of the Pharaohs in Egypt or Nebuchadnezzar in Babylon or the so-called ' Tyrants ' of early Greek history, rulers who have felt themselves above and apart from their people have left memorials of themselves in the buildings which they set up. The Etruscan kings were no exception from the rule. We have seen that Tarquinius Priscus built the Circus and began the temple of Jupiter Capitolinus, which his son completed. Tarquinius Superbus built also the Cloaca Maxima, but the most striking feature of the building of the Etruscan kings was the wall of Servius. As the Pharaohs forced the Israelites to build their great monuments, so too the Etruscan kings exacted the labour of the Romans for their building. The forced labour, which they performed in the construction of Servius's wall, finds its echo in the word *moenia* (walls), which comes from the same root as *munera* (tasks). The burdens, which the kings put on their people, were not light but the task above all was the taskwork at the walls.

(ii) **Their conquests.** It is not easy to trace the steps in the growth of Rome through the twilight of legend, but it seems clear that under the Etruscan kings Rome ruled over an extent of territory which she hardly regained for a century after their expulsion. Tullus Hostilius, the legendary third king of Rome, is said to have destroyed Alba, but this is not likely to have meant a substitution of Rome for Alba as ruler of the Latins. Rome may have been the most important city of Latium before the time of the first Tarquin, but she certainly had no real dominion wider than a circle of five miles round the city with perhaps

control of the banks of the Tiber down to its mouth.   In
the time of Servius Rome's position is stronger.   She is
the equal of all the rest of Latium taken together and
forms an alliance on equal terms with the Latin League.
Tarquinius Superbus is said to have forced the Latins to
acknowledge Rome as their head, and the fact that he
came into collision with the Volsci shows that he ruled
over territory at some considerable distance from Rome
to the south and south-east.   The Latins had to wait

The Environs of Rome

for the expulsion of the Tarquins before they could make
a determined attempt to regain their freedom at the battle
of Lake Regillus in 496 B.C.   But of the action of the
Latins at that time we shall have to speak later.

(iii)   **Their encouragement of the Plebeians.**   The
establishment of a foreign dynasty naturally offended the
Patricians, from whom a native king would otherwise have
been chosen.   To the Plebeians the substitution of one
master for another made little difference except that a
stranger would be less likely to be bound by custom and

prejudice in favour of the Patricians. We are told that
Tarquinius Priscus added 100 Plebeians to the number of
the Senate, and it is at least probable that he used the
right, which the king possessed, of summoning whom he
would to his council in favour of the more prominent
Plebeians. Servius's action in calling on the Plebeians to
serve in the army was intended to make them share in the
burdens of the state rather than in its government. But
it proved a step on the path of granting them the position
of full citizens, though many years passed before they
were on an equality with the Patricians, as we shall see
later. There were no doubt large numbers of Plebeians,
many of whom had made money and owned property in
Rome. Servius wished that they should share in the
defence of the city and therefore superseded for military
purposes the old organization of the state. Abolishing
the old tribal distinctions of Ramnes, Tities and Luceres
he made four new tribes from all owners of land, whether
Patrician or Plebeian. Of these the richest men supplied
18 centuries of cavalry; the rest he divided into five
classes according to their property and the classes into
centuries, the units of the Roman army. This gave, with
the addition of extra centuries at the bottom of the
list, a total of 193 centuries arranged as follows:

Equites				18 centuries
1st class, property worth	100,000	asses	80	,,
2nd ,, ,,	75,000	,,	20	,,
3rd ,, ,,	50,000	,,	20	,,
4th ,, ,,	25,000	,,	20	,,
5th ,, ,,	11,000	,,	30	,,
'Capite Censi' i.e. counted by heads ,, less than	11,000	,,	1	,,
Musicians and engineers			4	,,
			193	centuries

(The 'as' was a copper coin and 100 of them were in old times
the price of an ox.)

This new organization of the people as an army superseded the old organization in *curiae*, the *Comitia Curiata*,
for ordinary business, and became as the *Comitia Centuriata* the regular assembly of the people for voting.
Each century had one vote and was only nominally 100
men, the 80 centuries of the first class being very much
under the 100 and those of the fifth class above that
number. And as the combination of 18 Equestrian
centuries with 80 of the first class would give an absolute
majority in the total of 193, it is clear that the votes of

Roman As.   Circular Aes grave

the poorer Plebeians counted for little and that the change
was in no sense the establishment of a democracy.   It
was rather in the direction of making wealth the basis
of power instead of birth.   But it was a beginning of
giving the Plebeians a voice in the government of the
city.

In 510 B.C. the rule of the kings came to an end.
The general dissatisfaction with the arbitrary rule of
Tarquinius Superbus came to a head owing to some act
of brutality or stupidity; Tarquin was driven out and

the Roman Republic began its five centuries of marvellous growth, prosperity and decay. It was greatest in character and stability and all that makes for true greatness, when its great men lost themselves in their devotion to their country. When the city means less and the names of great men stand out on the pages of her history, the day of her decline has begun.

CHAPTER III

THE EARLY REPUBLIC TO THE TIME OF THE DECEMVIRI

Struggles for existence. On the expulsion of Tarquinius Superbus in 510 B.C. Brutus and Collatinus became chief magistrates under the name of Consuls or Praetors. But so great was the hatred of the Romans for the house of Tarquin that Collatinus, who was a cousin of the king, in deference to the wishes of the people laid down his office and withdrew from Rome. He was succeeded by Valerius Publicola, 'friend of the people,' who with Brutus had to face a conspiracy inside Rome for restoring the kings, in which Brutus's own sons were involved. The father was compelled by his office to condemn his own sons to death and to witness their execution:

> Natosque pater nova bella moventes
> Ad poenam pulchra pro libertate vocabit.

Soon after he met his death in an indecisive battle against Tarquin's forces. Tarquin now applied for help to the Etruscan Lars Porsena, king of Clusium, who came with a large force and shut up the Romans in the city, almost taking the city by his swift advance, had not Horatius Cocles and his two comrades held the Etruscans at bay,

while the Pons Sublicius was cut down. Porsena then
blockaded the town, till C. Mucius made his way into the
Etruscan camp and only failed to assassinate Porsena by
mistaking the secretary for the king.   Thrusting his right
hand into the fire to show his contempt for the torture
with which he was threatened, Mucius so moved the king's
admiration that he was allowed to go free ; in return for
Porsena's generosity he warned the king that he was only
the first of 300 who had sworn to kill him.   For this deed
Mucius received the name of Scaevola or ' left-handed,'
and Porsena, unable to crush the Roman spirit, withdrew
from Rome and gave no more help to the Tarquins.

In 496 B.C. the thirty cities of the Latin League taking
advantage of Rome's weakness resolved to free themselves
from her control.   In the battle of Lake Regillus near
Tusculum Castor and Pollux, the Twin Gods, are said to
have fought for Rome in white armour :

> White as snow their armour,
> Their steeds were white as snow.

Then at evening, when they had won the day for Rome,
they washed off the stains of battle in the spring by
Vesta's temple and vanished from human sight.

We may believe that the Tarquins made every effort
to regain their kingdom and that the Latins saw their
opportunity in Rome's weakness.   It is supposed that
the Latins were fighting to restore the Tarquins, and they
may have felt the rule of an Etruscan stranger less heavy
than that of a native Roman oligarchy.   But it is hardly
likely that their real aim was anything but independence.
Rome's power extended no more than five miles beyond
the walls, and it is stated by Tacitus that Porsena actually
took the city.   If he did so, he was unable to induce the
Romans to take back the Tarquins, and the friendly
feeling, which Romans in later times had for his name,
tends to show that he was a generous, if successful, enemy.

Political results of the Expulsion. The Plebeians perhaps thought that by helping to drive out Tarquin they had improved their own position, but they soon found out their mistake. The change was similar to that which occurred in many Greek states when the rule of a king changed into the rule of a close oligarchy. A king was far above the Plebeians; his rivals could only be the Patricians from whom he had sprung. But the Patricians stood to the Plebeians in the natural class-opposition of the ' haves ' to the ' have-nots,' and their efforts were directed to keeping the ' have-nots ' in their place, while the latter had lost in their king the Patron who could protect them from oppression. To see how entirely the power was in the hands of the Patricians we must look at the chief factors in the Roman state.

(i) **Magistrates.** The absolute power, which had been the king's, was not abolished in 510 B.C. but changed in form. Two Praetors, or Consuls (colleagues) as they were afterwards called, appointed by the Comitia Centuriata each year, took over the power of king and the only theoretical limitations of their power were that they held it for a year only and that one consul had the right of *intercessio*[1] or veto against the other. In case of great danger the consul nominated a dictator, supreme over all magistrates but limited to a six months' term of office. Consuls and dictator were alike Patricians.

(ii) **Senate.** In theory the Senate had no power. It was the council of old men, whose advice the king formerly and now the consuls asked, though no obligation rested on either to follow that advice. Remember that the magistrates were the only executive authorities and

---

[1] Every magistrate could veto the acts of an equal or inferior magistrate. It is a most important principle in Roman History, especially in the case of the Tribunes of the Plebs, of whom we shall hear.

that the Senate could only advise. But a consul would
be an ordinary senator after his year of office and the
leaders of his own class were senators ; so that a consul
was likely to be very chary of opposing the ablest men of
his own class, in whose ranks he would soon stand. And
if he did, the opposition could only last for one year at
most and even within the year the Senate could generally
induce the other consul to veto his colleague's acts. The
result in any case was that a *Senatus Consultum* or advice
of the Senate given in answer to the question of the
magistrate had all the force of a law. Now it is true
that there were Plebeians in the Senate ; the name
Patres Conscripti, if it means *Patres et Conscripti*,
Patricians and others enrolled to make 300, reflects
that fact. But the Patrician part was a united body
and the Plebeians of the Senate, as they had held no
office, had no capacity for, or knowledge of, the carrying
on of public business. Thus the Senate was in effect
Patrician no less than the magistrates whom it controlled.

(iii) **Comitia Centuriata.** In this the principal business was the election of the chief magistrates and the
passing of laws. Plebeians voted here, but we have seen
that the system of voting gave much the strongest influence to wealth ; the rich men were largely Patricians ;
and accordingly the Comitia Centuriata was Patrician.
Moreover no proposals for laws could be made except by
the Patrician magistrate and no one could stand for
office except a Patrician. The Plebeian, we can see, had
small chance of getting much for himself out of the Comitia
Centuriata.

Grievances of the Plebeians. In a general way the
grievances of the Plebeians are clear enough. They were
in the same city as the Patricians, they fought in the
same army, but they had practically no say in anything

and no prospect of fair treatment from a rival class. If we try to analyse their troubles we find they come under two main heads which we may call *Social and Political grievances*. Social questions are those which concern a man's everyday life in his relations to his neighbour, what chance he has of making a living, what protection he gets from the laws and so on. Political questions concern a man's rights and power to affect the government of the state, to change the laws or elect the magistrates. Political reforms can wait. Often they are needed only as stepping-stones to social reforms. Social grievances touch everyday life and press for settlement. It is the latter with which we have to deal chiefly now. The settlement of political grievances will come in a later chapter. But for convenience we may put them side by side here.

A. Social grievances:

>   (i)   The pressure of debt.
>   (ii) Unfair division of conquered land.
>   (iii) Ignorance of the laws.

B. Political grievances. Exclusion of Plebeians from:

>   (i)   Intermarriage with Patricians.
>   (ii) Holding office.
>   (iii) Making laws.

To remedy these grievances the Plebeians took a very modern line. They formed a kind of Trade Union of their own with their own officers and went ' on strike.' Let us see what the point of each grievance was and how it was dealt with.

The pressure of debt. In the early stages of most societies the laws of debt are very severe. Interest is high and when a man has exhausted other means of raising money, he pledges himself. This was so in early Rome. The class of *nexi*, men who had bound themselves

as slaves to their creditors, was numerous. In the frequent wars men were called away from their farms to
serve in the army. They left their land untilled and on
their return found themselves without means of living
through the year, or perhaps their homesteads had been
burnt by the enemy and their cattle driven off. So
borrowing, debt and slavery followed in due course.
Soon after 510 B.C. such cases were very common. Campaigns to keep off the Tarquins or the Latins called out
the farmers year after year, creditors extorted their
interest mercilessly and distress was acute. In 495 B.C.
the Plebeians refused to go out against the Volsci, unless
enslaved debtors were released. Pacified by the consul
Servilius for the moment, on their return from the
campaign they were treated as cruelly as ever by the
other consul, Appius Claudius. Amid growing discontent
M. Valerius was made Dictator, and under his promise
of protection for debtors they defeated the Volsci, only
to find on their return that Valerius could not carry
through the Senate his proposals for the relief of debt.
Then the Plebeians went ' on strike,' the *First Secession*,
494 B.C., withdrawing in a body to the Mons Sacer three
miles from Rome at the fork of the Tiber and Anio. The
Senate in alarm sent Menenius Agrippa to them, who by
his story of the ' Belly and the Limbs ' showed them that
Patricians and Plebeians alike were helpless unless they
supported each other[1]. A compact was made between
the two orders, whereby existing debts were to be cancelled and free grants of land given to poor Plebeians.
But above all the Plebeians were to have the right of
electing two of their own class annually as their protectors
against the Patricians.

Tribuni Plebis. These two Plebeian officers or tribunes were increased to five in 471 B.C. and to ten in
457 B.C. Their power lay in the fact that it was agreed

[1] Cf. Shakespeare's *Coriolanus*.

that they should be *sacrosancti*, i.e. it was the gravest
religious offence to hinder them by any violence, and that
they had the right of *intercessio* against any magistrate
except the dictator. They had also the *ius auxilii* or
right of setting free any one wrongfully arrested and they
presided in the *Concilium Plebis*, or meeting of the Plebeians, taking their opinion by *Plebiscita*. At the same
time two Plebeian Aediles were appointed to help the
Tribunes. Their principal work lay in the markets of
Rome to see that fair weights and measures were used.
By the appointment of Tribunes the Plebeians had a
lever which could exert tremendous influence on the
state, when they learnt to use it. They could stop all
public business and throw all the machinery of government out of gear till wrongs were put right. The laws of
debt were not altered by the Secession of 494 B.C. but a
greater thing was secured in the Tribunate.

Unfair division of conquered land. In 486 B.C., eight
years after the trouble about debt had come to a head,
the question of the sharing of conquered lands caused a
crisis in Rome. Land won from a foe was known as *Ager
Publicus* or State land. Some of this was left as common
pasture land, on which all citizens had a right to graze
their cattle on payment of a tax called *scriptura* ; other
parts might be occupied by squatters or *possessores*, who
were expected to pay rent. Naturally the rich had an
advantage here, as they alone would have enough capital
to permit of their waiting till uncultivated land could be
made productive. But after the expulsion of the kings
the Patricians claimed the right to both sorts of land for
themselves alone, even excluding the cattle of Plebeians
from the pastures. In 486 B.C. the consul Spurius Cassius,
who had won fame by his successes in Latium, proposed
an Agrarian law giving the Plebeians allotments free of
charge. They had fought as well as the Patricians to

win the land and might fairly be entitled to their share.
This first *Lex Agraria* caused great resentment on the part
of the Patricians, and though it was passed, Sp. Cassius
was prosecuted next year, 485 B.C., on the charge of aiming
at royal power by courting the people and was put to
death. The land question rested for some time after this.
There was not much land yet to distribute, and the Plebeians were on the whole too poor to occupy what there was.

Ignorance of the Laws. Early law was often hedged
in with forms whose origin was forgotten but whose
observance was insisted on. This was the case in Rome,
where the Patricians regarded the exact observance of
the forms as a religious matter but kept the knowledge
of these forms from the Plebeians. As the magistrates
also who administered the laws were Patricians, Plebeians
stood little chance of getting justice ; and a vigorous outcry arose from them for laws plainly published, which all
might understand and the magistrates would be forced to
observe. For many years the Patricians resisted the
demand, but in 454 B.C. yielding to the tribunes they
appointed three commissioners to examine the legal codes
of Athens and other Greek cities. On their return in
451 B.C. a commission of ten *Decemviri* was appointed for
one year to draw up a code for Rome, and, that they might
have a free hand, they were to be the only magistrates for
the year and there was to be no appeal from them. They
were all Patricians, Appius Claudius their chief ; but they
ruled well and drew up ten tables of laws which were
welcomed by all. As their work was not completed,
Decemvirs were again appointed for 450 B.C. Appius
alone was re-elected and the rest were men under his
influence. They finished the code by adding two new
laws and the *Twelve Tables* of the Decemvirs became
the ' fountainhead of all law in Rome.'

But when the work was done, Appius and his

colleagues seem to have made up their minds to become Tyrants. They enrolled 12 lictors each as if they were ten kings and refused to resign at the end of the year. Their tyranny culminated in two outrageous deeds. L. Siccius Dentatus was a gallant centurion who had been wounded many times in battle. Chosen tribune in 452 B.C. he had opposed the nobles, and the Ten were resolved on his death. He was sent with a company of their men to reconnoitre the enemy and these men fell upon him when they were alone. He slew many before he fell and the rest returned with the tale that they had fallen into an ambush.

The second deed took place in Rome. Verginia, a daughter of a centurion, Verginius, was betrothed to Icilius, a leading Plebeian. Appius Claudius had seen her, as she went with her nurse to school, and in his lust waited till her father was fighting against the Aequi and then, sitting in judgment, sent his freedman to claim her as the daughter of his slave. Fearing the outcry of the people Appius did not dare to decide the matter in his own favour at once but postponed it till the morrow. Then when Verginius had come, Appius gave judgment that she was his freedman's slave. And Verginius, begging leave to speak apart with her, caught up a butcher's knife from a stall hard by and crying, " There is no way but this," stabbed her to the heart rather than leave her to Appius. Pity for Verginius and indignation against Appius caused the *Second Secession* to the Sacred Mount in 449 B.C. ; the Decemvirs were driven out, Tribunes and other magistrates restored and an agreement made between the two orders by the *Leges Valeriae-Horatiae* [1] 449 B.C. which provided :

[1] Cf. *Leges Publiliae* of 339 and *Lex Hortensia* of 287. In the account of the legislative powers of the Concilium Plebis I have followed the views expressed in Prof. J. L. Myres's *History of Rome*.

(i)   that there should be a right of appeal to the Comitia Centuriata against any magistrate on a capital sentence. This was a repetition of the *Lex Valeria de Provocatione* of 509 B.C.

(ii)   that *Plebiscita* or resolutions of the Concilium Plebis should have the force of laws passed in the Comitia. This needs explanation. We have seen that the tribunes had the right of taking the opinion of the Concilium Plebis ; the *Lex Icilia* of 456 B.C. had allowed the consuls to bring such Plebiscita before the Comitia Centuriata and the Senate. If both these bodies approved, the Plebiscita became laws. Probably in 449 B.C. the consuls were *compelled* to give the Plebiscita this *chance* of passing into laws.

Wars and foreign politics. So much for the first struggles of Patricians and Plebeians. What of the relations of Rome to her neighbours in the period ? Rome was hard pressed after 510 B.C.; but the defeat of the Latins at Lake Regillus 496 B.C. secured her independence and three years after in 493 B.C. Sp. Cassius made a treaty (known as the Latin League) between Rome and her Latin cousins on equal terms. This was a great advantage to the Romans. The Aequi and Volsci her most troublesome neighbours lay to the east and south, and the Latins served as a buffer between Rome and her enemies, leaving Rome to grow while her neighbours exhausted themselves. A few years later in 486 B.C. the Hernici, wedged in between Aequi and Volsci, joined in alliance with Rome, thereby preventing the union of Aequi and Volsci and securing for the Romans a road southwards when they were ready to use it. For the rest there were wars and raids innumerable against Etruscans, Volsci and Aequi, of which three episodes will suffice.

(i)   **The Fabii and Etruscans, 477 B.C.** Rome was being harassed by raids from the neighbouring Etruscan town of Veii, till the men of the Fabian Gens undertook at last to free the city from this danger. Issuing from Rome they built a fort on the R. Cremera in Veientine territory and harried the land for a year. But as they returned to Rome for the religious festival of their Gens, the men of Veii fell on them in an ambush and slew all the Fabii save one lad who had been left in Rome. From him in after years the house of the Fabii was sprung. But Etruria was on the wane. The Gauls were already pressing on it from the north and the Syracusans by sea. We shall hear of other wars with Veii, but the danger to Rome was not from there.

(ii) **Coriolanus and the Volsci,** 488 B.C. C. Marcius, who by his valour at the siege of Corioli had earned the name of Coriolanus, offended the Plebeians by his pride, bidding the Senate in time of dearth starve the Plebeians unless they would consent to give up the tribuneship. But the tribunes brought him before the Concilium Plebis and would have killed him, had he not gone away in anger to the Volsci. So Coriolanus with Volscian troops and Tullius, their king, came against Rome, and no embassy might soften him. Then Volumnia his mother and Virgilia his wife with his little children and the women of Rome went out to meet him ; and when he would have kissed his mother, she would know first whether she was his mother or his prisoner. Then Coriolanus moved to tears said, " Mother, thou hast saved Rome but destroyed thy son." He led away his army, and they say that the Volscians slew him, because he had failed them. The story, which you may read in Shakespeare, makes it clear that the Volscians were formidable foes, against whom the Romans could make little headway.

(iii) **Cincinnatus and the Aequi,** 458 B.C. In 458 B.C. the Aequi, coming down from their highlands to the east of Rome, trapped the consul Minucius at *Mons Algidus* close to Rome. Then the Senate named L. Quinctius dictator, called Cincinnatus from his curly hair ; and the messengers found him ploughing on his farm, whither he had retired because his son had been unfairly banished. Now he obeyed the Senate, and starting at nightfall with his men carrying 12 stakes each he encircled the Aequi, who had hemmed in Minucius's army on the hill, with a trench and a palisade.   So the Aequi were caught between two Roman forces and were sent under the yoke.

These stories are half legendary, drawn from the family annals of the Fabii, Quinctii and Marcii, and we cannot believe them implicitly.   But Rome was at any rate holding her own.   She was a city with an organized government and was learning slowly how to unite Patricians and Plebeians into one body and to use their combined and disciplined strength against the ill-organized and ill-disciplined tribes who surrounded her.   Meanwhile the Latins were a useful barrier, on which the force of raiders could spend itself.

DATES	INTERNAL	DATES	EXTERNAL
510.	Tarquin driven out.	496.	B. of Lake Regillus.
494.	First secession. Tribunes.	493.	Sp. Cassius's Latin League.
486.	Sp. Cassius.	488.	Coriolanus and Volsci.
451–0.	Decemviri. xii Tables.	486.	Alliance with Hernici.
449.	Second Secession.	477.	The Fabii and Etruscans.
449.	Leges Valeriae-Horatiae.	458.	Cincinnatus and Aequi.

CHAPTER IV

THE EQUALIZATION OF THE ORDERS

WE will leave for another chapter the wars of Rome between 450 and 350 B.C. and follow for the present the political developments within the city during the same period.   Hitherto the quarrels inside the city have chiefly concerned social questions, the relief of debt, the sharing of Ager Publicus and the need of a fixed and known code of laws. To this end the Plebeians had secured the power of expressing their needs in Plebiscita and the election of tribunes for their own protection. The wealthier Plebeians with means and leisure enough to hold office were now to realize that the organization of their own class with its own officers and the strike or secession in the background was able to open up all the magistracies to them. Towards the close of the period the distress caused by the Gallic invasion brought up questions affecting rich and poor Plebeians alike ; and by a union of both kinds of Plebeians final equality with Patricians was obtained. We may repeat here the political grievances under which the Plebeians laboured, as they will form the groundwork of the chapter. They were :

Exclusion from—

    (i)   Intermarriage with Patricians.
    (ii)   Holding office.
    (iii) Making laws.

Their social grievances, as far as they depended on economic causes, could hardly be settled by the passing of laws. Evil results which follow from very uneven distribution of wealth have lasted to the present day. Political grievances may be redressed by laws, and it is this process which we have now to trace.

Leges Canuleiae, 445 B.C. Marriage between Patricians and Plebeians was not recognized by the state. In case of such unions the children, even if their father was Patrician, were counted as Plebeian. The first step towards the Equalization of the Orders was to break down this absolute barrier between them, which kept them apart as if they were two separate cities. It was clearly not a question which would affect poor Plebeians directly, but they joined forces with their richer comrades and made a *Third Secession* in 445 B.C., this time only as far as the Janiculum   But it produced its result.   The Plebiscitum of C. Canuleius, a tribune, was agreed to, providing that children of mixed marriages should belong to their father's Gens.   The Plebeians won the *ius connubii* or right of intermarriage with the Patricians, and the possibility of fusion of the Orders was thereby admitted.

The same Canuleius proposed that Plebeians should be admitted to the Consulship.   A compromise was arrived at.   The Patricians maintained that religion required Patricians as consuls for the due taking of the auspices, but for the next year agreed to the substitution of *Military Tribunes with Consular Power*, who might be Plebeians, instead of consuls.   These Military Tribunes, who were originally officers of the legions and varied in number from two to eight, must not be confused with the Tribunes of the Plebs.   They were to have the authority but not the prestige of consuls, being unable to take the auspices or enjoy a triumph.   For the next 80 years there was constant wrangling whether the officers of the year should be consuls or Military Tribunes, and in the years when the Plebeians secured the appointment of Military Tribunes they could not always in the Comitia Centuriata elect one of their own number to the office.   Manipulation of the votes or rejection of the Plebeian nominations by the presiding officer delayed the election of a Plebeian till the year 400 B.C.

Patrician monopoly of office breaking down.   The Leges Canuleiae sanctioning the intermarriage of the two Orders and opening in a modified form the highest office to the Plebeians were an irreparable breach in the defences of Patrician monopoly.   But the Patricians had means of postponing the evil day.   Seeing that the Consulship was doomed as a preserve of their own they cut off from it some of its more sacred duties. The duty of keeping the *Census* or roll of citizens in tribes and centuries according to their wealth, revising the list every five years and holding then the *lustrum* or solemn purification of the state, was transferred in 445 B.C. from the consuls to Patrician *Censors*, appointed once in five years and holding office for a year and a half. Again, the Quaestorship, an office partly financial, partly legal, was put on a new basis. The *Quaestors* had been assistants to the consuls in these two departments ; they were made a separate office in 421 B.C., and such financial business as did not come before the censors was transferred to them in the hope that the control of the money might remain in Patrician hands. But the tribunes intervened ; the office was thrown open to Plebeians in the same year, though some years passed before in 409 B.C. the first Plebeian quaestor was elected. An important result followed. It had been the custom and afterwards became the rule that the Senate should be filled up from ex-magistrates. Thus through the Quaestorship the Plebeians secured a way of entering the Senate in the ordinary course.

Spurius Maelius. The advance of the Plebeians was not made without outbursts of resentment on the part of the Patricians. In 439 B.C. Sp. Maelius was their victim. In time of dearth he had bought corn from Etruria and sold it cheap or even given it away that the poor might have bread. The Patricians raised the cry that he was ambitious for the position of Military Tribune, that so he might raise himself to be king. They appointed Cincinnatus, now grown old, as Dictator, and he sent his second-in-command or Master of the Horse, Servilius Ahala, to bring Maelius before him ; and Ahala with his own hand slew Maelius, when he refused to obey the summons. Blame in these quarrels belongs to both sides. The Patricians were fighting jealously for vanishing privileges; the Plebeians, inexperienced in politics, were not unlikely to give their support to a possible tyrant. In 433 B.C. a *Lex de ambitu* against 'corrupt practices' in elections was passed, and neither in the case of the Patrician oligarchy nor of Plebeians such as Maelius were its provisions superfluous.

Marcus Manlius. The long siege of Veii, 406–396 B.C., and the capture of Rome by the Gauls, 390 B.C., turned the minds of both parties for a time from domestic disputes. But the poverty and distress which they left behind hastened the conclusion of the struggle of the Orders. In 384 B.C. M. Manlius, of whose gallant co-operation with the geese we shall read in the next chapter, met in the Forum an old comrade-in-arms, who was being dragged off in chains by a creditor. He paid the man's debt and vowed that he would spend all he had before any fellow-citizen should be so treated. Winning the confidence of the Plebs, he accused the Patricians of appropriating the gold collected to buy off the Gauls and so came into conflict with Camillus, the general at the time of the Gallic invasion. Accused like Cassius and Maelius of aiming at royal power he was brought to trial in the Campus Martius; but none would condemn him, when he showed his scars and pointed to the Capitol which he had saved from the Gauls. At the adjourned trial, held where the Capitol could not be seen, he was condemned and thrown from the Tarpeian Rock.

The Licinian Laws, 367 B.C. But the distress continued and united the poor Plebeians who felt the pinch of poverty with the rich Plebeians who were as yet only half-way to victory in the struggle for political equality. In 376 B.C. two tribunes C. Licinius Stolo and L. Sextius Lateranus brought forward three proposals:

    (i)   That existing debts should be reduced by

deducting interest already paid and three years allowed for clearing off any balance.

(ii)   That Consuls should always be appointed instead of Military Tribunes but one of the Consuls *must* be a Plebeian.

(iii)   That no one should occupy more than 500 *jugera* (i.e. 300 acres) of Ager Publicus nor keep more than a fixed number of cattle on the public pastures.

Ten years' struggle followed.   Other tribunes were induced to veto these proposals and in return Licinius and Sextius vetoed the holding of Comitia for election of consuls.   For five years Licinius and Sextius were re-elected tribunes and maintained their veto.   Affairs were at a deadlock till the veteran Camillus was appointed dictator in 367 B.C. and induced the Patricians to bow to the inevitable.   The spirit of practical common-sense, which was after all stronger in the Romans than party-spirit, prevailed.   The Licinian laws were passed in 367 B.C. and Camillus vowed a temple to Concord to mark the close of the long struggle.

Results of the Licinian Laws.   The passing of the Licinian laws in 367 B.C. was the most important event since 510 B.C.   They abolished for purposes of practical politics the distinction between Patricians and Plebeians. Henceforward these names have an antiquarian interest ; men knew which they were, and members of the old families prided themselves on being Patrician by descent, as we might do on our ancestors having come over with William the Conqueror.   But for practical purposes there was soon no distinction.   Patricians and Plebeians alike held the higher or curule offices, and the families in which a curule office had been held were known as *nobiles*.   Gradually there grew up a new aristocracy composed of these noble families, Patrician and Plebeian alike, which in time became exclusive and tried to keep all offices within a narrow circle of a few Gentes. But for a century and a half they governed well and were a splendid source of strength to Rome in times of the greatest danger. The tribunes of the Plebs were still Plebeian, but their opposition was less needed and less used than of old. They were soon given a seat in the Senate and power to summon meetings of that body, and they became in many ways the officials of the Government rather than of the Opposition.

Some minor victories had still to be won but they followed almost as a direct consequence of the Licinnan laws. The Patricians in 366 B.C. handed over the judicial duties of the consul to a Praetor who must be a Patrician; but in 337 B.C. the Praetorship was opened to Plebeians. In 366 B.C. again they appointed Curule Aediles to balance the Plebeian Aediles; but an arrangement was soon made whereby the office was held by Patricians and Plebeians alternately. In 356 B.C. the Dictatorship and in 351 B.C. the Censorship were opened to Plebeians, and by 300 B.C. the last inequality was removed in the admission of Plebeians to the Collegia of Pontifices and Augurs.

What real advantage the poor Plebeians had gained from the latter half of this struggle is not clear. The Licinian laws gave them a temporary relief from the pressure of debt and a prospect of sharing in the Ager Publicus by the restriction of the amount which any one man might occupy. But the limit of 500 jugera was high, a restriction on the rich in favour of the middle class rather than of the poor. And for any *possessio* or occupation of uncultivated land capital would be required beyond the means of those who needed the opportunity most. The opening of Magistracies too did not concern those who had to work hard with their hands to make their living. The poorest class indeed seem to have been rather left in the lurch; their only relief came through the foundation of colonies, to which they were drafted and where they made a new start. Of these we shall hear when we deal with the wars of the period.

Powers of Legislation. We have seen that the Comitia Centuriata was the recognized body for making laws but that decrees of the Senate in course of time practically gained the force of laws. Besides this Plebiscita or resolutions of the Concilium Plebis, if they were approved by the Comitia Centuriata and the Senate, became laws binding on the whole community. Such was the position after the Valerio-Horatian laws of 449 B.C. How the Plebeians came to have an equal or greater share in legislation than the Patricians must be told now as a part of the story of the Equalization of the Orders, though it belongs to a period 30 to 80 years later than the Licinian laws. We must begin by noticing that besides the *Comitia Centuriata*, which has been explained in Chapter II, and the *Comitia Curiata*, which was used for purely formal business, there was also a *Comitia Tributa* or Assembly by tribes. This Assembly was used from very old times for purposes of assessing the amount of property-tax, which was due from the land-owners of each tribe. Later the Quaestors, as financial officers, and the Aediles were elected by it, and with the advance of the Plebs it was consulted on general matters of legislation as expressing more correctly the wishes of the whole community than the Comitia Centuriata. You must remember that the same people would be present in both Assemblies, but in the Comitia Centuriata they were so arranged by centuries that the votes of the rich always carried the day, while in the Comitia Tributa the votes of rich and poor counted equally. But both Comitia were assemblies of the *whole* community, whereas the *Concilium Plebis* was a meeting of the *plebeian* section of the state alone.

In 339 B.C. Q. Publilius Philo carried the following laws :

(i)   That Plebiscita should be binding on all citizens without the sanction of the Patres.

(ii)   That the sanction of the Patres *must* be given beforehand to all laws proposed by a magistrate in the Comitia Centuriata.

(iii)   That all proposals put before the Comitia Tributa by a Praetor *must* be submitted to the vote.

The first of these did away with the necessity of the sanction of the Senate for Plebiscita.   Such resolutions of the Concilium Plebis now became law, if the Comitia Centuriata alone approved.   The second aimed a blow at the control of the Senate over the legislation of the Comitia Centuriata, which it had exercised through its practical hold over the magistrates.   The third confirmed the Comitia Tributa in the legislative functions, which we saw it had gradually assumed.   Proposals put before it by the praetor could not be shelved, but a vote must be taken on them.

In 287 B.C. after the *Fourth and Last Secession* Q. Hortensius carried the *Lex Hortensia*, which gave Plebiscita passed in the Concilium Plebis the force of laws without need of sanction by any other body, making *the resolution of a purely Plebeian meeting binding on the whole state.* This is good proof of how completely the distinction of Patricians and Plebeians had been forgotten for practical purposes in the 80 years which followed the passing of the Licinian laws.   Most of the legislation however of the next century and a half, in which Rome was engaged in her great wars with Pyrrhus, Carthage, Antiochus, Macedon and Greece, was passed in the Comitia Tributa which was more fairly representative of the whole state than either Comitia Centuriata or Concilium Plebis.

DATES

CHAPTER V

THE DECAY OF ETRURIA AND THE
INVASION OF THE GAULS

THE history of the external growth of Rome during
the century, which followed the passing of the Valerio-
Horatian laws of 449 B.C., has for its main feature the
invasion of the Gauls. They captured Rome in 390 B.C.
but for all that their appearance in Italy was a great
advantage to the city. They did not stay long in Central
Italy and perhaps had little wish to hold much land south
of the Apennines ; their attack on Rome was a raid provoked by Roman folly. But they reduced Etruria to
helplessness and so freed Rome from the fear of her
dangerous northern neighbours ; while the commotion
caused by their appearance on the northern Apennines
forced the tribes of that district southwards along the hills.
Thus the Aequi and Volsci, threatened in the rear by the
hill-tribes, whom the Gauls were pushing south, and
already weakened by the attacks of Rome, had their
hands full and ceased to be dangerous.

Movements of the Gauls. The Gauls were the fore-
runners of the Goths, who just 800 years later put an end

to Ancient History by the second capture of Rome. Pressed westward and southward by other tribes behind them or by some instinct, they had come across the Rhine into Gallia Transalpina, the modern France, some centuries earlier ; and thence their tribes had found their way to the south of the Alps, the Insubres founding Mediolanum or Milan, the Cenomani settling round the head of the Adriatic and the Boii between the Padus and the Apennines. The later stages of these migrations, which gained for the district the name of Gallia Cisalpina, were taking place from 500 B.C. onwards ; and the Gauls in effecting their settlements broke the power of the northern Etruscans, who inhabited the valley of the Padus. Etruria proper south of the Apennines was still unharmed, when some time after 450 B.C. fresh arrivals, the Senones, in default of other land moved down the Adriatic coast and finding the soil and climate not to their liking began to press westwards through the passes of the Apennines into Etruria. The military strength of Etruria was turned to meet these formidable invaders, and Veii in the south was left to face Rome without any assistance from Northern Etruria.

Veii and Rome. In 437 B.C. Veii, which forty years before had destroyed the Fabian Gens at the Cremera, endeavoured to check the advance of Rome northwards by encouraging the revolt of Fidenae. But in the war which followed Lars Tolumnius, prince of Veii, was slain by Cossus, who thus won the *Spolia Opima* or spoils taken in battle from the enemy's leader, an honour shared by Cossus with Romulus alone before him and Marcellus about 200 years later. Veii was glad to make peace with Rome in 425 B.C. for two hundred months ; and in 424 B.C. the Etruscans suffered another loss, being driven out of Campania by the Samnites. On the expiration of the truce Rome with no fear now of Aequi or Volsci started

definitely on her career of conquest by commencing in
406 B.C. the subjugation of Veii.   The task took ten years ;
for Veii was as large a town as Rome and strongly situated.
But with Northern Etruria hard pressed by the Gauls the
Veientines had to depend on their own resources and such
help as they could get from the neighbouring towns of
Falerii and Capena.   They were gradually driven within

Rome and Etruria

their walls, but their long resistance compelled the Romans
to adopt continuous military service winter and summer
alike instead of the short summer campaigns to which they
were accustomed.   To make this possible pay for the
soldiers had to be raised by means of the *tributum* or tax
on land, that the men who were now unable to attend to
their farms might receive compensation.   In spite of this

the siege dragged on, and in the ninth and tenth years of the war the troops of Falerii and Capena inflicted great loss on the Romans and once almost captured their camp.

From this point onwards the story becomes interwoven with legend. Portents alarmed the Romans. The waters of the Alban Lake in Latium overflowed and an old Veientine seer was heard to cry out that the Romans would never take Veii till the Alban Lake was drained. Enticed by a trick into the Roman camp the seer repeated his words before the Senate in Rome; and the Delphian oracle in Greece gave the Romans the same warning. Then they set about draining the lake and appointed M. Furius Camillus Dictator. He routed the Etruscan allies in the field and being unable to storm Veii dug a tunnel under the town as far as the temple of Juno in the citadel. When all was ready, he summoned all who wished to share in the spoil to come from Rome to Veii, and a company of his men were at the end of the tunnel ready to break through. As the king of Veii was about to offer sacrifice that morning in the temple, the priest in the temple was heard by the Roman soldiers, waiting in the tunnel beneath, to declare that whoever offered the sacrifice would win the victory. Then the Romans burst through, offered the sacrifice and seized the citadel, while Camillus amid the confusion and panic carried the walls. The Veientines were slain or sold into slavery and their land distributed to the Plebeians, and the image of Juno bowed her head in assent when Camillus prayed that she would take up her abode among the Romans.

Thus in 396 B.C. Rome destroyed Veii, and with Falerii and Sutrium surrendering to her she had by 390 B.C. secured the south of Etruria as far as the Ciminian Hills. But Camillus, accused of unfairness in the distribution of spoils taken at Veii, went into exile with the prayer that the citizens might soon feel the need of his help again.

The Gallic Invasion. Camillus's prayer was soon answered. We have seen that the Gauls were pouring through the passes of the Apennines into Northern Etruria. In 391 B.C. they laid siege to Clusium and the Etruscans in despair appealed to Rome their old enemy. The Romans sent ambassadors to bid the Gauls return, but the latter continued fighting and the Roman ambassadors, outraging the law of all nations, joined in the conflict on the side of Clusium. Brennus, the Gallic chieftain, thereupon applied to the Senate for the surrender of the men who had done this wrong, but the Romans far from making amends elected the ambassadors among the Military Tribunes for the next year, 390 B.C. The Gauls in fury raised the siege of Clusium and marched on Rome. Unprepared and not realizing the danger the Romans allowed the Gauls to advance unopposed as far as the point where the Allia flows into the Tiber from the Sabine hills, eleven miles from the city. There the Gauls with their huge stature, their yellow hair streaming behind them and their blue eyes flashing as they charged with terrifying shouts, made short work of the Roman levies. The *Battle of the Allia*, 390 B.C., was long remembered and its anniversary kept as a day of mourning by the Romans. A few only of their soldiers escaped and the way to Rome lay open to the Gauls. The able-bodied citizens retired to the Capitol, the priests and Vestal Virgins with the sacred fire were sent away to Caere, and the rest of the people fled far and wide into Etruria, while only the old men of the Senate waited the end in the city. The Gauls, amazed at their victory and fearing an ambush, came slowly on ; finding the city unguarded at length they entered, and as they roamed the streets they came to the Forum, where sat the aged senators like the statues of the gods silent in their chairs, clad in official robes. But when a Gaul in wonder began to stroke the beard of Papirius, he smote him with his staff; then the Gauls in anger slew all the old men together and sacked the city.

The Capitol still held out, and the Roman fugitives in Etruria were appealing to Camillus to come back from Ardea and help them in their need. He would not return from his exile without leave of the Romans in the Capitol, and to obtain their consent a messenger was sent from Etruria to swim the Tiber and scale the cliff of the Capitol. But the Gauls saw his footsteps and by night they climbed where he had made his way. Neither guards nor dogs heard their approach; yet the wakeful geese gave the alarm. M. Manlius was roused and with his shield, which he caught up as he sprang from his bed, he thrust back the foremost Gaul who was just setting foot on the top of the rock. He, as he fell, bore down the next behind him, and the defenders being awake now to their danger repulsed the attack and saved the hill. For this exploit Manlius won the surname Capitolinus.

But no relief came and the Romans in sore straits bargained with the Gauls, who agreed to depart on payment of one thousand pounds' weight of gold. And when, as they were weighing it, the Romans complained that the weights were false, Brennus threw his sword into the scale crying out, '*Vae victis*,' 'Woe to the conquered! Lo, with this sword I weigh your gold.' The story goes that Camillus came up in time to drive off the Gauls without the gold. But though there is little likelihood of this being true, certainly the Gauls withdrew. They wandered about in North Italy for some time. In 360 B.C. they were encamped on the Anio and a great Gaul, a second Goliath, with a collar of gold about his neck came out as champion of the host; and young T. Manlius ran out against him and slipping in under his guard slew him and took the collar from his neck and for this deed earned the name of Torquatus. Again in 349 B.C. M. Valerius in conflict with another Gallic giant was aided by a raven, which settled on his helmet and beat its wings in the Gaul's face, so that Valerius slew the Gaul and was thereafter called Valerius Corvus. But gradually the Gauls settled down in the north and were content to leave Central Italy unmolested for a time.

The Recovery of Rome. After the withdrawal of the Gauls from before the Capitol, a proposal was made to transfer the city to a new site at Veii. But Camillus wisely opposed the scheme, and the work of restoration began. But since there was no general plan of reconstruction and each man built as he thought fit, Rome became like London after the Fire, a tangle of mean buildings and crooked streets. But she recovered her strength speedily and was a match for her old enemies who thought that their opportunity had at last come. The Aequi in the later years of the 5th century B.C. had been crushed by the capture of Labicum and Bola, while the Volsci were kept in check by the Roman colony at Ardea and had even lost Tarracina on the coast beyond the Pomptine marshes. Now both these tribes took the field again, and for 13 years Rome had to wrestle with them, while even the Latins and the Hernici stood neutral or sided with the foe. But under Camillus the city emerged successfully from her troubles, and the capture of Antium from the Volsci in 377 B.C. may be taken to mark the end of the struggles of Rome for sovereignty in Latium. No doubt the Aequi and Volsci had suffered from the presence of the Gauls and from pressure of mountain tribes whom the Gauls had set in motion. From this time we hear little more of them ; they were swallowed up in the Roman dominions.

In 356 B.C. Rome had some trouble in the south of Etruria, where Caere and Falerii with the help of Tarquinii rose in revolt. But Tarquinii was captured and the two rebel towns reduced. By 350 B.C. Rome ruled over all the land west of the Apennines from the Ciminian Hills in Etruria to the R. Liris in the south of Latium and had begun the system of planting military colonies to secure the territory which she had won, Sutrium and Nepete in Etruria, and Satricum Antium and Tarracina in the Volscian district being some of the earlier outposts of Roman power. With the growth of her dominions Rome had closed the Latin League[1] in 385 B.C., refusing to admit any new towns on the old footing of equal alliance. On the reduction of Caere in 351 B.C. its inhabitants were put on a new footing. They were compelled to pay the Roman property-tax and serve in the Roman army and were given the rights of intermarriage and trade with Rome (*connubium* and *commercium*), but not allowed the right of voting or of holding office in Rome, while a *praefectus* was sent out each year from Rome to govern the city. Caere thus treated became a model for the treatment of later conquests in Italy. Rome would for the future make conquests ; she would establish colonies and incorporate among her own citizens those whom she conquered or rule over them as subordinates ; but she would not permit the growth of any separate organization within her dominions. All must be closely and directly linked with herself.

DATES

437–425.	War with Veii : Cossus.
406–396.	Siege of Veii.
390.	The Gauls : B. of the Allia (July 18).
385.	Latin League closed.
377.	Capture of Antium.
360.	Gallic war : T. Manlius Torquatus.
351.	Caere reduced.
349.	Gallic war : M. Valerius Corvus.

Camillus

[1] Cf. p. 28.

CHAPTER VI

THE THREE SAMNITE WARS AND
THE LATIN REVOLT

WHEN the Romans had made themselves masters of Latium, they came into contact with the Samnites, the strongest among the other Italian nations, and the wars which followed during a period of 70 years gave Rome the dominion of Italy. The prize was not won without a tremendous struggle. But the Samnites were not supported till too late by the other tribes of Italy whose battle they were fighting, and the organized strength and bulldog tenacity of Rome carried her through. The period, which will cover more than one chapter, includes the First Samnite War and the Latin revolt, 343–340 B.C., the Second Samnite War and the rising of Etruscans, 327–304 B.C., the Third Samnite War and the final effort of the combined Italians, 298–290 B.C., and lastly the invasion of Pyrrhus and the conquest of the Greek cities of the south, 282–272 B.C.

The Samnites. The men of Samnium formed the strongest branch of the mountain stock which extended over the whole length of the Apennines. Tradition said that they were Sabines by origin who had moved southwards under pressure of the Umbrians, and led by an ox had founded Bovianum, the town of the Ox, just as their kinsmen the Picentes led by a woodpecker (*picus*) had turned to the shores of the Adriatic and the Hirpini (*hirpus*, Sabine for *wolf*) had followed a wolf as far as the borders of Lucania. Whatever the origin of these names, which seem to point to something like the ' totem ' (animal-god) of Red Indian tribes or the crest of a mediaeval knight, it is likely that the Samnites had been pushed forward into the valleys and uplands of the Central Apennines by invaders from the north. They were divided into two tribes, the Pentri and Caudini, but the name of Samnites was sometimes vaguely used to include also the Marsi to the north and the Hirpini in the south. They were first-rate fighters but, being isolated in their mountain valleys, they had never grown into a united nation and for this reason they fell victims to Rome.

First Samnite War, 343–341 B.C. In 424 B.C. one body of Samnites had overrun the plains of Campania and, intermarrying with the Etruscans and Greeks of Capua and Cumae, had formed a new nation, the Campanians. But the wealth and luxury of the district and its fertile soil spoilt the character of the invaders and they settled down into an easy-going and weak people far different from the mountaineers from whom they had sprung and who now began to make raids on their degenerate kinsmen. In 343 B.C. the Samnites attacked Teanum close to the Liris, and the other Campanians, finding themselves helpless to protect the town, appealed to Rome. The Romans were on friendly terms with the Samnites, but when the Campanians offered them the city of Teanum as a price for their help, the temptation was too much for them. They ordered the Samnites to withdraw and on their refusal declared war. M. Valerius Corvus marched along the coast road towards Cumae and Neapolis and won a great victory on Mt Gaurus; the other consul, Cossus, moved up the Volturnus and becoming entangled in the hills at the back of Mt Tifata was only saved by one of his officers, Decius Mus, who seized an unoccupied hill and inflicted an unexpected defeat upon the Samnites. The campaign proved that the Romans would find the invasion of the Samnite hills too dangerous for the present; and a mutiny of the legions in Campania induced the city to make peace in 341 B.C. The contrast between the

wealth of Campania and their own poverty had stirred
the discontent of the soldiers, and they were not pacified,
till Valerius Corvus was made Dictator and promised
them better terms of service with improved chances of
promotion from the ranks and a fairer share in the spoils
of war.

The Latin Revolt, 340 B.C. When the mutiny of
the legions was bringing the First Samnite War to a close,
the Latins and Campanians for part of the year remained

Latium, near the Alban Mount

in arms and continued the war on their own account. As
a natural result they began to think of the olden times
when they had been in an alliance on equal terms with
Rome, and to contrast their former and their present
positions. Since 385 B.C. the Latin League had been
closed, i.e. there were to be no new allies on equal terms
with Rome, but all new extensions would be made in boa-
constrictor fashion by incorporating the newcomers in
the Roman state. Even inside the league the same process was going on ; towns which revolted from the alliance

were on their reduction swallowed up in the Roman community with the grant of full citizenship as in the case of Tusculum or of partial citizenship as in the case of Caere. Now Latin troops were fighting for the riches of Campania, and all they won would belong not to themselves but to Rome. Accordingly they sent an embassy to Rome demanding that Rome and Latium should be united into one nation on equal terms, while half the Senate and one consul should always be Latin. The Senate at once rejected the proposals and the Latins and Campanians rose in revolt. The Hernici however remained faithful and the Samnites, hating their Latin neighbours and engaged for the moment in disputes with Tarentum, allowed the Romans a passage through their territory and thus enabled them to take the Latins in the rear and drive them down to the coast. The decisive battle was fought at Veseris near Mt Vesuvius and shattered the hopes of the Latins. In the same year 340 B.C. the remnants of the Latin army rallied at Trifanum near the mouth of the Liris, and with their defeat at the hands of Manlius Torquatus the consul the revolt practically came to an end.

Two stories of the battle of Veseris illustrate what the Romans meant by discipline and patriotism. While the armies lay facing one another, Manlius had forbidden any irregular single combats. His own son went out and killed a Latin who had challenged him ; but when he came back rejoicing in his spoils, his father like another Brutus put him to death for disobedience. And in the fight when the Romans were hard pressed, the other consul, P. Decius Mus, with head veiled devoted himself to the gods below ; then he rushed to his death where the battle was fiercest and at the price of his own life won the victory. The *Manliana Imperia* and the self-sacrifice of Decius were not soon forgotten in the Roman army.

Dissolution of the Latin League, 338 B.C. After the

revolt was over, Rome took in hand the final settlement of Latium. Little punishment was meted out to the rebels and their loyalty to Rome in the days of Hannibal proves that they were not unfairly treated. But the old League was dissolved and *in place of a general confederacy each town was carefully isolated from its neighbours and bound by a tie to Rome alone.* Thus Rome was to be the only centre of Latium ; between other towns there must be no bond except through Rome, not even the right of intermarriage or trade with one another. Two Latin towns might be within five miles of one another, but the only bond between them was henceforth to be that they were both bound to Rome. Beyond this the details are not very important. Tibur, Praeneste, and some others were to remain independent, bound only to follow Rome in war. Other towns were given full citizenship, but most received the inferior citizenship, i.e. *connubium* and *commercium* with Rome, but not the right of voting or holding office in the city (*ius suffragii et honorum*). Thus Latium became a compact state with Rome its only centre ; and for additional security colonies were sent out to serve as military outposts. In 338 B.C. Antium was colonized and the Volscian inhabitants compelled to surrender their ships of war, whose bronze beaks (*rostra*) were fixed to the orator's platform in the Forum, which was called from them the Rostra. A few years later Cales and Fregellae on the Campanian frontier received colonies ; and with the building of the Via Latina and the Via Appia in the same direction before the end of the century, the network of roads and colonies was begun whereby Rome held fast her conquests.

Appius Claudius. It was Appius Claudius, a descendant of the Decemvir of 450 B.C., who was responsible during his Censorship in 312 B.C. for the building of the Via Appia, the Queen of Roads, across the Pomptine

Marshes and thence to Capua, one hundred and twenty miles in all, while the Via Latina ran in the same direction but closer to the hills. Appius also provided Rome with a supply of good water, constructing the Claudian Aqueduct from the Sabine hills on the east into the heart of the city. But what is more to our purpose for the present, he showed favour to the Latins. Many of these had settled in Rome and their numbers increased rapidly when Rome became the only centre of Latium. These settlers together with the *libertini* or sons of freed slaves Appius in 312 B.C. admitted to the tribes, which had increased with the growth of Rome to the number of thirty-one, and so gave them a vote in the Comitia Tributa. But it was found that their influence was too great, and a few years later they were restricted to the four city tribes, so that they could not carry more than four votes at most out of the thirty-one.

Appius also enrolled undistinguished Patricians and even *libertini* in the Senate and held his office of Censor for the unprecedented time of two and a half years. It is difficult to see how far he was a man of go-ahead notions who really wanted to get things done and how far he was ambitious for himself. Like most of the Claudii he was rather ' bad form ' in the eyes of the more respectable Romans. The constitution did not provide definitely for every point ; there was for instance no power to compel a magistrate to resign when his year was ended. Much was left to the good sense of the average man; and not in vain, so long as Rome was surrounded by foes. Appius Claudius had the pushful modern attitude rather than the dignity and patriotic self-effacement which marked the true Roman character.

Second Samnite War, 327–304 B.C. The First Samnite War had been but a preliminary skirmish compared with what was to follow, and the Samnites had

Remains of the Claudian Aqueduct

(A conduit in the masonry above the arches carried the water from the Sabine Hills in the background.)

acted unwisely after it in helping Rome to suppress the
Latin revolt ; but their attention had been turned to their

Campania and Samnium

southern frontier. The Greek cities of the south of Italy
had outlived their effectiveness and Tarentum alone
was of much account among them. Hard pressed by

Lucanians and Bruttians, Tarentum had called in help from Greece, and first Archidamus of Sparta and after him Alexander of Epirus had come over to Italy. The latter defeated the Lucanians so completely that they appealed to the Samnites for assistance. But Alexander was a match for both together and seemed likely to found a kingdom of his own in S. Italy, till some time before 330 B.C. he was assassinated by a Lucanian.

The Samnites now had leisure to note their danger from Rome. They resented the colonization of Fregellae on their borders; and the struggle between the two great stocks of Italy, the Latins of the lowlands and the Sabellians of the hill-country, was ready to break out at any moment. Where now lies the city of Naples there were then two small towns, Palaeopolis the old city and Neapolis the new. Being threatened by the Romans because they had molested Roman settlers in Campania, they appealed to Samnium and after useless recriminations the war broke out in 327 B.C. The Romans under Q. Publilius Philo, who was continued in his command beyond his year of office with the title of *Proconsul*[1], soon reduced Palaeopolis and Neapolis and, by generously admitting these towns into equal alliance, won to their side the governing aristocracies of all the Campanian towns. The Samnites fought unaided; for though the Lucanians nominally joined them for a time, they never gave any real help and soon became neutral, while the Apulians through jealousy of their Lucanian neighbours became firm friends of the Romans and thus gave them a means of assailing the Samnites in the rear. During the first five years of the war the Romans were everywhere successful and in 322 B.C. the Samnites sued for peace, their general Brutulus Papius killing himself in despair. But

[1] The practice of prolonging the term of office led to important results. Cf. pp. 135 and 180.

the Romans thinking they had the Samnites at their mercy refused to make peace.

The Caudine Forks, 321 B.C. In 321 B.C. with C. Pontius as general of the Samnites fortune changed sides. The Romans under Veturius and Postumius were in Campania near Calatia waiting to advance into Samnium. Pontius caused a report to reach them that the whole Samnite army was away besieging Luceria in Apulia. The Romans, thinking that the loss of Apulia would be a most serious matter and that the way through Samnium was undefended, set out for Luceria. Near Caudium the road led through the Caudine Forks, a long gorge which broadened out about the middle enclosing a stretch of meadow land, but an unbroken line of wooded hills on either side ran from end to end of the pass. The Romans made their way through the meadows in the middle, but where the pass narrowed again they found the road blocked by the enemy and, turning round to retrace their steps, they found that the Samnites had by this time blocked up the defile by which they had entered. They were caught in a trap and after a hopeless struggle they surrendered. The story goes that Pontius sent to ask his father what he should do with his prisoners, and the old man sent back word, "Let them all go free." Not understanding the advice Pontius sent a second messenger and the answer came back, "Kill them all." The father meant that his son must either win the lasting goodwill of the Romans by his generosity or inflict on them a blow from which they could not recover. Instead Pontius forced the consuls to agree to restore all the Roman conquests in Samnite territory and to make peace on equal terms ; and when this had been agreed to and 600 hostages given him as sureties for the ratification of the agreement, he dismissed the Romans sending them under the yoke with the loss of all their standards and arms.

Pontius acted unwisely. The Romans felt humiliated and disgraced by the surrender; but they were not weakened by it and wanted vengeance. Pontius had made an agreement with officers who had no authority to speak in the name of the whole state. It is true that he had a promise of peace which would be enough to bind one honourable man in his dealings with another ; but nations are more thick-skinned than individuals and honour counts less with them than material advantage. The Senate at once repudiated the treaty and thought that it satisfied honour by surrendering the officers who had sworn to the treaty. Postumius, when the *fetialis* or sacred herald surrendered him to the Samnites, went through the farce of solemnly and effectively kicking the herald, saying that by his surrender he was now a Samnite and by the kick had given the Romans just cause for renewing the war. But Pontius refused to accept the surrender and, upbraiding the Romans for their breach of faith, prepared to continue the struggle.

The Roman Recovery, 321–311 B.C.   The disaster of the Caudine Forks produced a great effect and the Romans had the worst of matters till 314 B.C. Luceria fell at once and Fregellae soon after, while Capua showed signs of going over to the Samnites and even inside Latium there were risings which kept the Romans occupied for several years. It was not till 315 B.C. that they were able to invade Samnium again. In that year Q. Fabius Rullianus penetrated into the hill-country but on his way back suffered a severe reverse at Lautulae near Ánxur (Tarracina), and Capua seized the opportunity of openly revolting from Rome. But with 314 B.C. matters improved and a great victory was won near Capua, which secured Campania. In 313 Fregellae and Luceria submitted ; in 312 the Via Appia was built as far as Capua, and, with Campania in Roman hands and a strong Roman colony at Luceria, the Samnites were hemmed in on all sides.

The Etruscan Rising. In 311 B.C. the war entered on a new stage. In that year a forty years' truce with Northern Etruria came to an end, and the Etruscans, alarmed at the successes of the Romans, rose in arms and besieged Sutrium. One consul Q. Fabius Rullianus was sent against them but failing to raise the siege forced his way north through the Ciminian forest, where no Roman army had been seen before, and for some weeks no news of him reached the city. His colleague meanwhile was defeated in Samnium and there was great consternation in Rome. However Fabius reappeared after a successful march and in 310 B.C. crushed the Etruscans at Lake Vadimo, while in the south the Dictator Papirius Cursor defeated the whole Samnite army, annihilating a special corps of their men and carrying off their gold and silver shields. The Etruscans now made peace ; but a fresh danger arose in 308, when the Umbrians and Marsi joined in the war. Fabius again marched north and scattered their forces ; and the Hernici and Aequi who ventured to take up arms in 306 were easily routed. The Samnites were now fighting single-handed once more. Two Roman armies were in the field against them, which penetrated Samnium from two sides and captured Bovianum the capital in 305. Peace was made in 304, the Samnites still retaining their independence, not entirely crushed but shut in by the power of Rome on every side.

The Third Samnite War, 298–290 B.C. Peace lasted only for six years. In 298, while the Romans were occupied in Etruria, the Samnites raided the Lucanians and refused to withdraw when ordered to do so by Rome. War broke out and for three years the Samnites kept to the hills where the Romans could not get at them. In 295 a new Samnite general came on the scene, Gellius Egnatius, who grasped the fact that the Samnites needed allies and that the ineffectiveness of the Etruscan and

Umbrian risings in the previous war had been due to the fact that they were made too late and without any combination. He now organized a league of Samnites, Etruscans and Umbrians, with the assistance even of the Gauls in the north, and arranged that the various contingents should meet in Umbria and there make ready to fight out once and for all the battle of Italian freedom. It was a great crisis for Rome. Eight legions were enrolled and Fabius and Decius sent out against the combined forces of the Italians. There at Sentinum in Umbria, where the Apennines slope down to the Tiber valley, the battle which decided the fate of the Italians was fought in 295 B.C. The Etruscans and Umbrians went off before the battle to protect their own lands, but the Samnites and Gauls fought desperately. Not till Decius, in imitation of his father's action at the battle of Veseris, had devoted himself to destruction, did the Romans win the day. For five years more the Samnites under Pontius continued the war and even defeated Fabius's son ; but their day was over, and in 290 B.C. M'. Curius Dentatus brought the struggle to a close. The Samnites were allowed to retain their independence but were made to serve in the Roman armies. For two hundred years they remained the one disaffected spot in Italy, till Sulla put an end to the danger by their annihilation.

There was still something to be done before Rome secured North and Central Italy. The Etruscans and Umbrians came to terms with the Romans in 295 and for some years were kept busy by the Gauls, either suffering from their raids or buying Gallic help against Rome. In 285 they called in the Senones to besiege Arretium, but the Senones were defeated and a colony was placed at Sena their capital in 283. The Boii about the same time joined the disaffected Etruscans but were routed at the second battle of Lake Vadimo in 284, and with this

the trouble in N. Italy ceased for a time.   Rome was mistress of Italy from the Apennines to the south of Samnium,
and colonies and roads secured what she had won.
Crowds of Roman settlers were let loose on the conquered
territory, especially the land of the Sabini east of Rome,
while Hadria and Sena in the north-east, Luceria and
Venusia on the southern frontier were among the strong
military colonies which first overawed and then Latinized
the districts in which they stood.   The south of Italy with
its Greek cities was still outside Roman control.   The
story of its conquest and the first conflict of Rome with
a foe from across the sea will be told in the next chapter.

DATES

343–341.   1st Samnite War.
    343.   B. of Mt Gaurus.
    342.   Mutiny of the Army in Campania.
    340.   Latin revolt.   B. of Veseris.
    338.   Dissolution of Latin League.
327–304.   2nd Samnite War.
  (i)   327–322.   Roman successes.
  (ii) 321–315.   Roman disasters.
    321.   Caudine Forks.   Luceria and Fregellae.
    315.   Lautulae.
  (iii) 314–311.   Roman recovery.
  (iv) 311.   Etruscan rising.
    310.   1st B. of L. Vadimo.
    308.   Umbrian rising.
    305.   Capture of Bovianum.
    304.   Peace.
298–290.   3rd Samnite War.
    295.   League of Samnites, Etruscans and Umbrians de-
       feated at Sentinum.
    290.   Samnites subdued.
    284.   Boii subdued.   2nd B. of L. Vadimo.
    283.   Conquest of Senones.

CHAPTER VII

THE WAR WITH PYRRHUS

The Greek cities of South Italy. When the Romans had conquered the Samnites, they came into direct contact with the great cities of the south, of which Tarentum was the chief. The southern shore of Italy by its position had from early times attracted Greek settlers, and in the palmy days of Greek colonization Rhegium, Locri, Croton, Thurii and Tarentum had been flourishing towns. The name of Magna Graecia still remained, but luxury and dissension had done their work, and Tarentum alone retained something of its former greatness. Founded by Sparta before 700 B.C. this town had kept up friendly relations with its mother-city and by its position had secured a good share of the trade between Italy and the East. It now regarded itself as champion of the other Greek cities of Italy against the attacks of Samnites and Lucanians ; though as a matter of fact it was only with the help of Greek mercenaries and adventurers such as Alexander and Archidamus, of whom we read in the last chapter, that it could secure its own position. Tarentum had viewed with alarm the growth of Rome and, wishing to play off Rome and Samnium against one another, had offered to arbitrate between them in the Samnite wars. On the conclusion of these wars she was not only face to face with a strong military state but also found that Rome, by her policy of isolating her allies from one another, was herself becoming more and more the commercial centre of Italy and therefore touching the pockets of the Tarentines. War was inevitable sooner or later, and as Tarentum would have to rely on help from over the sea, we must look for a moment at the outside world, into which the new state of Rome was pushing its way.

The Mediterranean World. Alexander the Great by means of the army which his father Philip of Macedon had left him had conquered the East as far as India. On his death in 323 B.C. his vast empire broke up into three main divisions. (*a*) *Asia Minor and Syria* became the kingdom of one of his generals, Seleucus, most of whose successors were called Antiochus. With one of them the Romans came into collision a century later. (*b*) *Egypt* passed to another general, Ptolemaeus, whose descendants the Ptolemies, some of them patrons of art and literature, were still ruling in the days of Julius Caesar. (*c*) *Macedonia and Greece* were the scene of a long struggle and maintained the Greek character for division and disunion. Among the claimants for supremacy in this district was Pyrrhus of Epirus, the Red King, a cousin of Alexander the Great and nephew of the Molossian Alexander, who had come to Tarentum during the Samnite wars. Pyrrhus, though insecure enough on his own throne, had great ambitions and thought he might conquer the West, as his cousin had conquered the East.

The western half of the Mediterranean was the sphere of Carthaginian influence. We shall have to speak of this people later ; at present it is enough to remember that Carthage was a colony of Tyre and the Carthaginians had taken in the West the place of their Phoenician ancestors as the traders and over-sea carriers of the world. Besides their territory in Africa and ' factories ' on various parts of the coast of the western Mediterranean, they had overrun most of Sicily with the exception of the strip of land on the east coast in which stood Syracuse.

War between Pyrrhus and Rome. In 283 B.C. some of the cities of Magna Graecia suffering from the attacks of the Lucanians appealed not to Tarentum but to Rome, and the Romans to the great indignation of the Tarentines put garrisons in Rhegium, Locri, Croton and Thurii. While relations between Rome and Tarentum were in this strained state, ten Roman ships on a coasting voyage sailed into the harbour of Tarentum in 282, blundering in contrary to an old treaty between the two towns.

Rome and Pyrrhus

This was too much for the Tarentines; they attacked the squadron, killed the admiral, sank some ships and drove off the rest. When ambassadors came from Rome to protest, the populace laughed at their bad Greek and threw mud on Postumius's white toga. Postumius bade them laugh while they could, for the toga would be washed white in their blood; and the war, which had really begun

already with an attack of the Tarentines on the Romans in
Thurii, was now formally declared.

Tarentum applied at once to Pyrrhus for help but was
already getting the worst of the encounter, and the
aristocratic party was inclined for peace, when the help
from Greece arrived. Milo, Pyrrhus's general, and three
thousand men were sent in 281 B.C. to garrison the citadel
of Tarentum and with them Cineas, the chief counsellor and
orator of Pyrrhus, while Pyrrhus himself followed soon after
with twenty-five thousand men and twenty elephants, the
' Lucanian Oxen ' as the Roman soldiers nicknamed them.
The Tarentines soon found that they had a hard master,

Coin of Tarentum [Taras] 4th cent. B.C.
Obv. Philip. *Rev.* Taras on dolphin

as Pyrrhus stopped all the amusements of the town and
made every citizen drill for service with the army. But
he was no less disappointed himself. There was no sign
of a general rising of the Italians, which he had been led
to expect ; and instead he found himself face to face with
a well-disciplined Roman army. The Roman legion, with
its maniples of 200 men arranged *quincunx* fashion (i.e.
like the pips on the Five in a pack of cards) in three
ranks of Hastati, Principes and Triarii, was to meet the
Macedonian Phalanx, a compact body with long spears
projecting far in front and the spears of the rear ranks
passing between the men of the front rank. The legion

was a handy force in which one rank could support and relieve another ; the phalanx was irresistible in a direct charge but incapable of meeting a flank attack or getting successfully over rough ground.

The consul Laevinus was sent out in 280 to bring on an engagement before Pyrrhus could raise troops from the Italians. He met Pyrrhus at Heraclea near the R. Siris, and though the Romans were a match for the Greek cavalry, they found themselves unable with their short swords to get through the bristling spears of the phalanx ; and when the elephants charged at the end of the battle, the legions broke and fled leaving 7000 dead on the field. It was an obstinately fought battle and Pyrrhus could ill afford to lose many men. But as a result of the engagement he found that the Greek cities began to come over to his side ; though Thurii with the help of Campanian freebooters took advantage of the disordered state of affairs to declare itself independent of both sides, as Messana in Sicily had done.

At the end of the year 280 Pyrrhus advanced as far north as Anagnia in Latium and sent Cineas with proposals of peace to Rome. The Senate was inclined to waver under the eloquence of Cineas ; but Appius Claudius, now blind in his old age, kept the Romans steady, and Cineas returned unsuccessful telling Pyrrhus that the task of conquering Rome would be a hard one, as the Senate was an assembly of kings. At this time the Carthaginians, who recognized that Pyrrhus as champion of the Greeks would dispute their supremacy in Sicily, made an alliance with Rome against him. Pyrrhus meanwhile, unable to subdue the fortified towns of Capua and Neapolis in Campania, returned for the winter to the neighbourhood of Tarentum.

Next year, 279 B.C., he advanced into Apulia hoping that the Samnites would join him. He met the Romans in a two-days' encounter at Asculum, and though the Romans were again beaten, they inflicted such heavy loss on Pyrrhus that a Pyrrhic victory has become proverbial for a success which is in effect a defeat. In the spring of the following year, 278, a servant of Pyrrhus made his way to the consul Fabricius offering to poison the king. But Fabricius sent him back as a prisoner to Pyrrhus saying that the Romans did not make war on their foes in that fashion, and Pyrrhus in gratitude liberated all his Roman prisoners without ransom.

Pyrrhus's dream of a western empire was fading away as far as Italy was concerned, and he now crossed to Sicily, hoping that the conquest of that island would be easy with the help of the Greek cities there. At first he drove the Carthaginians before him and at one time had cleared them out of the island with the exception of the one fortress of Lilybaeum. But he was in the situation in which Hannibal found himself sixty years later in Italy. He could get no reinforcements, while war and disease were thinning his ranks ; and the Sicilian Greeks after his first successes began to quarrel with him and among themselves. After three years in Sicily, 278–275 B.C., he returned to Italy, and the Carthaginians at once re-conquered most of the island, destroying also the fleet which had covered his crossing to Italy.

On his return to the mainland Pyrrhus found that Milo, whom he had left in Italy to hold the southern cities, had been gradually forced back till Tarentum alone remained in his power. There were no signs of an Italian rising, the Romans had learnt to cope with the elephants and to break up a phalanx, and Pyrrhus felt that his schemes of conquest had failed. He did succeed in recapturing Locri and forcing his way north into Samnium. But at Beneventum, 275 B.C., he met M'. Curius Dentatus who fifteen years before had finished off the Samnite War.

In the battle of Beneventum the elephants, goaded by the missiles of Roman light-armed troops, trampled on the phalanx and left Pyrrhus's army a prey to the legions. Pyrrhus sailed back to Epirus, leaving Milo to hold Tarentum, and three years later came to an inglorious end, being killed during an attack on Argos by a woman who threw a tile on his head from the top of a house.

In the same year 272 Tarentum surrendered, and the Bruttii in the toe of Italy and the Sallentini and Messapii in its heel were subdued a few years later. Measures were now taken by Rome to secure her hold on the peninsula. Colonies were placed at Paestum, Beneventum and Aesernia to watch Samnium and the south, while the Via Appia was extended from Capua to Beneventum and Venusia and twenty years after to Brundisium, the gateway to Greece and the East. In the north Ariminum secured the frontier between the Adriatic and the Apennines against the Gauls ; and the restlessness of Northern Etruria led to the destruction of the old town of Volsinii and the transference of the inhabitants to a new town on the Volsinian Lake. Rome was now undisputed mistress in Italy, the newest and the strongest of the Mediterranean Powers, no longer concerned with the affairs of the peninsula alone, but by strength of character and central position driven, whether she would or not, to play the chief part among the nations of the old world.

United Italy. What was the Italy which Rome had welded into one state ? In modern times we talk of countries not of towns as our states, of England, France or Germany not of London, Paris or Berlin. By the device of representation in Parliament we are able to give a man in Cumberland an equal share in the government of the country with a Londoner. But the ancient world knew very little of representation ; a state in the Greek world meant a town with a few square miles of land round its walls, in which every qualified citizen voted in person on political questions. Rome had to deal with a new situation, to try to adapt the ideals and principles of a city-state to a country; and we must not be surprised that her methods were not the same as ours. Roughly speaking

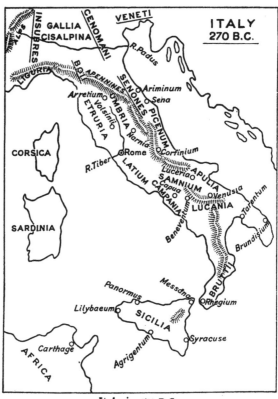

Italy in 270 B.C.

the principle on which she had gone was to incorporate as citizens the nearest and earliest of her subjects and to join to herself as allies all the other Italians, isolated from each other and bound only to the central city. We must get some notion of how this worked out in practice.

(i) In 241 B.C. the number of the tribes was raised to thirty-five, at which it remained fixed. They were local tribes originally but afterwards lost their connection with a particular district. To them belonged the *full Roman citizens* who were drawn principally from Rome itself, ' Roman ' colonies and parts of Latium. There was also a class of *inferior citizens* without right of voting or holding office, among whom were the Sabines, Hernici, Aequi, Volsci and Campanians. Thus a great part of central Italy had the citizenship in some form and the citizen communities were classed together as *municipia*, some managing their own local affairs with their own magistrates, senate and assembly on the Roman model and serving in the Roman legions, and others like Caere (see p. 46) being governed by magistrates sent from Rome.

(ii) The other Italians were ranked together as allies but in two grades. The *Nomen Latinum* consisted of those Latin towns which had not been given citizenship, and the ' Latin ' colonies throughout Italy, i.e. colonies of the second rank formed of Latins or of poor citizens who for the sake of a grant of land had been willing to surrender their citizenship. They had local independence, and the local magistrates, if they migrated to Rome, could become citizens. The rest of the *Socii* were also independent in local matters but had no direct relations with any other place except Rome and their exact position depended on the terms of the treaty made with Rome at the time of their submission. Both classes of allies were excluded from the Roman legions but supplied contingents of their own to the army or the fleet.

DATES

323. Death of Alexander the Great.
282. Attack on Roman ships at Tarentum.
281. Pyrrhus and Milo at Tarentum.
280. Battle of Heraclea.

CHAPTER VIII

THE FIRST PUNIC WAR

Carthage. On the coast of Africa in the bay which faces the western end of Sicily a colony of Phoenicians had settled before the eighth century B.C. The 'New Town,' as its name of Carthage means, became as early as 500 B.C. a great commercial centre, and its ships plied over the waters of the western Mediterranean and through the Pillars of Hercules to the Atlantic coasts, as the Phoenician ships of an earlier age had done. With the decay of the Etruscans and of the Greek cities in Sicily and S. Italy Carthage had scarcely a commercial rival in the fourth century B.C. and regarded the north coast of Africa from Cyrene to the Ocean, the mines of Spain and the islands of Corsica and Sardinia, as its own preserve. The chief block of Carthaginian territory was however round the city itself, and here the population was of three grades, the Libyans, the Liby-Phoenicians and the Phoenicians or Carthaginians. The Libyans were the natives of the country, not unlike the Arabs of to-day, to whom Carthage in its early days paid rent for its site and whom afterwards it made serfs or used as the mainstay of its army. The Liby-Phoenicians were half-breeds, ground down by oppression and taxation. The Carthaginians or Poeni were descendants of the Phoenician settlers, and they alone had any share in the government.

Constitution and character. At the head of the state were two *suffetes* or Judges like those of early Jewish history ; but they had lost their old power, which had passed first to a committee of thirty including the two judges, similar to the *Gerousia* or council of elders at Sparta, and from them to a body of One Hundred, which was nominally elected but through influence and bribery practically confined to a few great trading families. Beyond this body, in whom all real power centred, there was a general assembly, which met only when disaster or popular feeling led to an appeal to the mass of the citizens.

It was an admirable form of government to secure the aims which Carthage had in view, not unlike the directorate of a big company and with less conscience. For Carthage with all its growth could not and did not greatly wish to build up an empire. Her aim was frankly money, and her extension was marked not by the organization of new provinces but by the establishment of ' factories,' at which the wealth of the district could be stored to await shipment. The world was in her eyes a vast treasure-house which could be ransacked. No development of conquered lands, no care for conquered peoples appealed to her. So long as the streams of money poured into her treasury, so long as the money-chests of her great merchants were filled, Carthage was content. But she paid the penalty. Her government was unblushingly corrupt ; her soldiers were mercenaries ; her contribution to literature was a treatise on farming ; and her art was the cheap reproduction of the art of other countries for sale to unsophisticated barbarians. While in the Roman state every subject community was the stronger and safer through union with Rome, the subjects of Carthage stood to gain by her overthrow. The Romans fought their own battles and their allies were eager to fight by their side; Carthage relied on mercenaries who would turn against her if they had

the chance. Carthage might be dangerous under a great
general; Rome was great in spite of her generals. The
strength of Carthage lay in money; the strength of
Rome was character.

Outbreak of War. During the war between Rome
and Pyrrhus a body of Campanian mercenaries had seized
Rhegium, and Hiero king of Syracuse had afterwards
helped Rome to subdue them. In 265 B.C. Hiero himself
had similar trouble with Campanian mercenaries of
Agathocles, who on the death of their leader had esta-

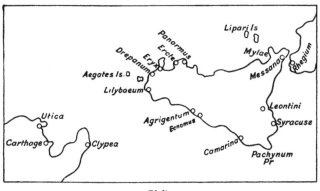

Sicily

blished themselves in Messana under the name of the
Mamertini or men of Mars. The Mamertini, being hard
pressed by Hiero, were divided between appealing to Rome
or to Carthage; but as they were of Italian descent, the
majority turned first to Rome and by so doing put the
Senate in an awkward dilemma. It would be base in-
gratitude to help the Mamertines against Hiero after the
affair at Rhegium; but on the other hand it would be
intolerable to have the Carthaginians in Messana and the
newly-won supremacy of Rome in S. Italy endangered.
Carthage and Rome had been in alliance, when the

Etruscans and Greeks had been rivals to both ; but those days were past. The Senate referred the matter to the Assembly, which voted for helping the Mamertines, and Appius Claudius, brother of the Censor, was sent out. But in the meantime the Mamertines had admitted a Carthaginian garrison under Hanno, who boasted that no Roman should so much as wash his hands in the sea. Claudius however sending on an advance-party induced the Mamertines to change sides once more. Hanno was compelled by treachery to surrender the citadel and for this was crucified on his return to Carthage. Thus the Romans came into collision with the Carthaginians and the First Punic War began in 264 B.C.

First stage. Sicily, 264–256 B.C. Appius Claudius crossed the straits with two legions and at once drove off the Syracusans, who with Carthaginian help were besieging Messana, and in the course of the year made himself master of the north-east of Sicily and even laid siege to Syracuse. In the next year, 263, both consuls were sent to Sicily and conducted operations so successfully that they drove the Carthaginians out of the east of the island and overran Hiero's territory. Hiero, recollecting that the Carthaginians were his hereditary foes and that alliance with them was costing him dear, pocketed the affront which the Romans had offered him in occupying Messana, and concluded an alliance with Rome to which he remained loyal for the rest of his life.

In 262 the Romans laid siege to Agrigentum, the second city of the island, which the Carthaginians had made their head-quarters and had occupied with a strong force under Hannibal, Gisgo's son. Famine and disease played havoc with the Roman troops, but they held on and repelled a relieving force ; and at last in the seventh month of the siege the garrison cut its way out leaving the town to the Romans.

The Roman Navy. Agrigentum was situated a short distance from the sea, and this fact helped the Romans not a little in the siege. For while they had made themselves masters of most of the inland parts of the island, they could not keep the Carthaginians out of the coast towns of the west, where their fleet could be of use. Carthaginian squadrons from the Lipari Islands backed up Carthaginian garrisons in these towns and even swooped down on the coasts of Italy, till the Romans realized that the war called upon them to become a sea-power. The story goes that they took a stranded Carthaginian boat as a model, built a fleet in 60 days, and trained their men to row on a staging built on shore. As a matter of fact the men of S. Italy were very fair sailors and had already furnished contingents to a Roman navy, though their old-fashioned triremes may have been no match for the Carthaginian quinquiremes. The first engagement off the Lipari Islands proved a victory for the Carthaginians, who were more familiar with the handling of war-ships. But C. Duilius in 260 B.C. overcame the skill of the Carthaginians by a device which made a sea-fight very much like one on land. On the prow of each ship he set up a drawbridge attached to a mast in such a way that it could be swung round to either side of the boat and let down upon the enemy's boat. Underneath the further end was a spike, which would be driven by the weight of the falling bridge into the deck of the hostile ship and hold it fast. This *corvus*, as the whole contrivance was called, grappled the two ships together and gave the Romans a means of scrambling over and fighting the enemy hand to hand.

At Mylae near Messana 260 B.C. Duilius met the Carthaginians and captured 50 of their ships before they could realize the meaning of the *corvus*, destroying at once their absolute naval supremacy. In honour of this victory Duilius for the rest of his life was escorted at night in the streets of Rome by a flute-player and torches, while a Columna Rostrata, adorned with the rams of the captured ships, was set up in the Forum.

For the next few years Rome was making successful attacks upon the Carthaginian possessions in Corsica and Sardinia and gradually winning Sicily, though Panormus and Lilybaeum still held out for the enemy and Drepanum, 20 miles from Lilybaeum, was founded as a new naval arsenal by the Carthaginians. It seemed that the best way to finish the war was to make an attack upon Carthage itself rather than to waste time on the reduction of their strongholds in Sicily.

Second stage. Invasion of Africa, 256–255 B.C. After preparing a huge fleet of 350 ships the Romans under Volso and Regulus sailed along the south of Sicily in 256 with 40,000 troops on board for the invasion of Africa. Off the promontory of Ecnomus they met an equal force of Carthaginians and with the help of the *corvus* accounted for 84 of the enemy's ships, while they lost but 24 of their own, and going on they landed at Clypea and ravaged the country up to the walls of Carthage. They were welcomed by the oppressed native tribes, took Tunis, and from the rich but badly defended country captured prisoners and booty without end. Carthage, with its bad system of oppressive government and mercenary troops, seemed to have collapsed like a house of cards, and Volso sailed home with half the army thinking the work was done.

The Carthaginians indeed offered terms of peace, which Regulus rejected. But they had among their mercenaries a Spartan, Xanthippus by name, who was not only a good soldier but capable of inspiring enthusiasm. Pointing out the mistake of the Carthaginians in not selecting ground for their fighting in which they could use their cavalry and elephants with effect, he attracted the notice of the authorities and was at last put in command of the whole army.   In the beginning of 255 with a force largely composed of cavalry he offered battle to Regulus, who came down on to level ground expecting little resistance. The Romans were overwhelmed, Regulus was taken prisoner and a small remnant only escaped to Clypea. A second disaster followed ; for the fleet which came to take the survivors home was wrecked near Camarina.

Third stage.   Sicily, 254–243 B.C.   The invasion of Africa had failed ; but the Carthaginians were for some time busy in conquering their revolted African subjects, and the Romans made use of their opportunity to capture Panormus in 254 B.C.   Encouraged by their success, they raided the coast of Africa; but on its return their fleet was wrecked off Cape Palinurus, and this last disaster so much impressed them that for ten years they abandoned naval warfare as far as they could.   The war now centred round the west of Sicily.   In 251 the Carthaginians having settled their troubles in Africa sent a large army with 140 elephants to recover Panormus.   Metellus the consul keeping his legions inside the gates filled the ditch round the town with light-armed troops, while others enticed the Carthaginians up to the ditch.   There a cloud of javelins and fire-darts so frightened the elephants that they charged back on their own troops ; and Metellus issuing from the gates with the legions routed the enemy and captured 100 elephants.   The Carthaginians for the rest of the war avoided meeting the Roman legions in open battle, and the story of the war becomes the story of the Roman attempts to reduce the strongholds in the west of Sicily.

The Romans blockaded Lilybaeum and Drepanum by land, but as the sea was open, the Carthaginians were able to send in provisions and even to throw fresh troops into Lilybaeum, which in a sortie destroyed the Roman siege-works.   To put a stop to this the Romans were forced to send out a fleet in 249 under the consul P. Claudius Pulcher. On the voyage he was told by the augurs that the omens were against him, for the sacred chickens would not eat. " Let them drink then," he said, as with Claudian disregard for propriety he dropped the chickens into the sea. But the omens worked. On his arrival he was enticed by the Carthaginians into the harbour of Drepanum and lost all but 30 out of 210 ships. Later on in the same year the other consul Junius with a second fleet was wrecked off Cape Pachynum, and the reinforcements and supplies for the troops at Lilybaeum were entirely lost.

About this time the Carthaginians, not understanding the dogged perseverance of the Romans, thought that their naval disasters might have inclined them to peace ; and they sent Regulus, still a captive, to Rome to negotiate a peace or at least an exchange of prisoners, under promise to return to Carthage if he did not effect their purpose. The story goes that he refused at first to enter the Senate House, as being disgraced by his captivity, and then strongly urged the Romans to refuse the proposals which he brought. Afterwards he returned to Carthage knowing that torture and death awaited him, and the war dragged slowly on.

In 247 the one great Carthaginian general of the war Hamilcar Barca (the same word as Barak of the Book of Judges, meaning ' Lightning ') was sent to Sicily, great general himself and father of a greater son Hannibal. He seized the strong hill of Ercte, close to Panormus and with an anchorage at its foot, and from there he raided Sicily and the Italian shores for three years, paralyzing the Romans with the rapidity of his movements. At the end of that time he established himself at Eryx which overlooks Drepanum, surprising the Roman garrison there, though a small body of Roman troops held the Temple of Venus at the top of the mountain.

Fourth Stage.   The Romans recover command of the sea.   For two years Hamilcar continued his devastations, but both sides were by now exhausted.   The Carthaginians, content with holding Lilybaeum and Drepanum, gave no support to Hamilcar and neglected their fleet.   The Romans had lost 50,000 men out of their whole number of 300,000 citizens, and their treasury was exhausted.   But they still had their resolute determination and with a despairing effort raised a new fleet which they put under the command of C. Lutatius Catulus. He, in the absence of the Carthaginian fleet, occupied the harbour of Drepanum after some fighting with the garrison in 242 B.C. and trained his sailors there while he waited for the Carthaginians.   At length in 241 a hastily raised fleet, encumbered with transports, put out from Carthage. Catulus, disabled by a wound, sent his praetor to intercept the enemy's ships and off the Aegates Insulae inflicted on them a complete defeat.

This was the last effort of the Carthaginians, and they now sent orders to Hamilcar to make peace.   After some haggling it was agreed that Carthage should give up Sicily and the neighbouring islands and pay an indemnity of 3200 talents (£800,000) within ten years.   Thus the First Punic War was ended, and Sicily became a new department or *Provincia* of the Roman administration.

The whole of the island, with the exception of Hiero's dominions, which fell to Rome on the death of that king, was placed in charge of a Praetor, and taxes were collected in the shape of tithes (*decumae*) and customs dues (*portoria*), while much of the land was made Ager Publicus to be exploited by Roman occupiers.   It was a misfortune for Rome that her first province was a conquest from the Carthaginians.   For she took over with it the bad principle that provinces were to be a source of income to the state and of plunder to individual governors.   It was bad

for the provinces and bad for the Romans, who lost in
time their simple strength under the tide of wealth which
their successive conquests brought to them.

DATES

264–241.	First Punic War.
264.	Mamertines of Messana appeal to Rome.
264–256.	First stage. War in Sicily. Roman Navy.
262.	Capture of Agrigentum.
260.	Battle of Mylae. (The Corvus.)
256–255.	Second stage. Invasion of Africa.
256.	Battle of Ecnomus.
255.	Defeat of Regulus by Xanthippus.
254–243.	Third stage. Panormus, Lilybaeum and Drepanum.
254.	Romans capture Panormus.
251.	Battle of Panormus.
249.	Defeat of Claudius at Drepanum.
247–242.	Hamilcar Barca. Ercte and Eryx.
242–241.	Fourth stage. Romans recover control of the sea.
241.	Battle of Aegates Insulae.
241.	Peace concluded.

CHAPTER IX

PREPARATIONS FOR A NEW STRUGGLE

THE First Punic War was fought in and around Sicily
and victory rested with the nation which controlled the
sea. The slackness of the home government, which
allowed the Romans to win this control, was galling to
the war party in Carthage and especially to Hamilcar
Barca, whose long successful efforts at Eryx and Ercte
had been rendered fruitless. He had in his mind plans
for a new war with Rome, which should be independent

of the home government and the accidents of naval warfare; but circumstances delayed the accomplishment of his designs.

The Truceless War, 241–238 B.C. The failure of the war and the payment of the indemnity left Carthage without funds to satisfy her mercenaries, who rose in revolt and were joined by the Libyans and Numidians. Hanno, the political opponent of Hamilcar, was defeated by the rebels, and in a few months only the towns of Carthage, Utica and Hippo held out against them. In these straits Carthage appealed to Hamilcar, who in the course of three years succeeded in crushing the revolt, but only after such ruthless cruelty on both sides that the struggle was known as the Truceless War. Meanwhile the Romans, taking advantage of the weakness of their rival, seized Sardinia and Corsica and made a second province out of them under another Praetor after the model of Sicily.

War between Rome and Illyria. Hamilcar was now free to begin his preparations for another war with Rome; and with this in view he crossed into Spain in 238, while the Romans were busy with affairs nearer home. The conquest of the mountainous interiors of Sardinia and Corsica took Rome several years and further fighting was soon afterwards necessary on the other side of Italy. The Illyrians had long made use of their broken coastline on the east of the Adriatic for purposes of piracy, screening their privateers among its creeks and islands and becoming under their Queen Teuta a perfect scourge to all traders. The murder of two Roman envoys, who had been sent to Scodra (Scutari) to protest, brought matters to a head. Two small wars, one in 230–228 B.C. against Teuta, the other in 221–219 B.C. against her lieutenant, Demetrius of Pharos, crushed the Illyrians and earned for Rome the gratitude of the Greeks; Rome was thus secure from real danger on that side in her coming struggle with Carthage.

Gallic Wars. The Romans were no less busy inside the peninsula. A rising of the Boii in 238 came to nothing, but five years later a tribune C. Flaminius, to relieve the distress which the First Punic War had left behind it, proposed to distribute in allotments to poor citizens the *Ager Gallicus* formerly occupied by the Senones. The wealthy nobles, who had occupied some of the land, in vain tried to defeat his proposal. But the law had unexpected results. The Boii, living nearest to the land in question, scared the Insubres who lived north of the Po with news of the arrival of Roman settlers and tales of the designs of Rome on all the land south of the Alps. Engaging hordes of Transalpine Gauls to aid them they prepared for war. But the Gauls were slow to rise and it was not till 225 that the storm broke. The Romans had made their preparations and 200,000 men were under arms. One army lay at Ariminum to bar the Adriatic coast-road, another at Arretium to block the western route, while other troops were posted further south to protect Rome. The Gauls slipped in between the two northern armies and then turning back from Clusium defeated the western force at Faesulae. But the eastern army from Ariminum was now close behind them, and the consul Atilius had landed near Pisa with another army from Sardinia. Hemmed in between two forces the Gauls were almost exterminated at Telamon near the coast. Three more years of fighting followed before the Insubres finally submitted, Marcellus winning the Spolia Opima in 222 by slaying their chief in single combat. The safety of the district was then secured by the planting of colonies at Placentia and Cremona, and in 220 Flaminius as Censor built the Via Flaminia through the Apennines and on to Ariminum.

The Barcine Empire in Spain. The Romans had set their house in order before the great struggle. Meanwhile in Spain Hamilcar Barca and his successors had achieved wonders. The east coast of Spain had long been known to Carthaginian traders, but of the interior little was known beyond the fact that it was rich in minerals, fertile and inhabited by warlike tribes. Hamilcar in 238 crossed into the peninsula taking with him his nine-year-old son Hannibal, whom he had made to lay his hand on the altar and swear undying hatred against Rome. Though it was left to his son to strike the blow, Hamilcar had his own purpose of crushing Rome clear from the start; and he saw in Spain the means he needed for his purpose. Its wealth would give him the resources required for war and enable him to keep the home government in a good temper by subsidies of money. From the native tribes he looked for the best of raw material for his army. Above all he knew that from Spain he had an overland route into Italy, full of difficulties but possible to a good general, and that in Spain no inconvenient orders from Carthage were likely to hamper his designs. So for nine years he laboured, fighting and negotiating, winning by his charm of manner and just dealing the friendship of the native princes, till by 228 he had founded an empire in southern Spain and gathered the material of an excellent army.

In that year he fell in battle ; but his work went on under his son-in-law Hasdrubal, who consolidated the work of Hamilcar, building Nova Carthago (Carthagena) as a capital for the new state and by alliances and treaties extending Carthaginian influence through the peninsula. In his time the Romans noticed the danger which threatened them ; but they were busy with the Gauls in Italy and were content to make a treaty with Hasdrubal that the Ebro should be the boundary between Carthaginian and Roman in Spain.

In 220 Hasdrubal was assassinated and Hannibal, 26 years old, was appointed as successor to his brother-in-law. The time had now come for action and Hannibal took the step which must lead to war with Rome. Saguntum, a coast-town well to the south of the Ebro, was independent still and vaguely under Roman protection. It could not be left as a source of danger in his rear, when Hannibal began his march on Italy, and he determined to attack it without delay. The Saguntines appealed to Rome which sent an embassy to protest, but Hannibal denied the right of the Romans to interfere south of the Ebro, and the embassy, going on to Carthage, received a similar answer there. After a siege of eight months Saguntum fell ; and the Romans, surprised and indignant, sent Q. Fabius Maximus with other ambassadors to Carthage to demand the surrender of Hannibal. After futile arguments Fabius held up the fold of his toga, saying, " I bring you here peace and war. Choose which you will." The Carthaginian senators answered, " Give us which you will." When Fabius said, " We give you war," they cried out, " And we accept it."

Thus began the Second Punic War, the Hannibalian War, a war of one House against Rome. It proved the greatest war of Greek or Roman times, a struggle to the death between two opposing types of civilization, a struggle of perhaps the ablest of all generals against the most resolute of all nations. The great battles in Italy catch the eye, but the enduring strength and cohesion of the Roman state and the little noticed work of the Scipios in Spain were the deciding factors in the struggle.

DATES
241–238. The Truceless War.
230–228. First Illyrian War.
    225. Gallic War. Battle of Telamon.
    220. Via Flaminia.

DATES

221–219.	Second Illyrian War.
238–228.	Spain. Hamilcar.
228–220.	„ Hasdrubal.
220.	„ Hannibal.
219.	„ Siege of Saguntum.
218.	Second Punic War begins.

CHAPTER X

THE SECOND PUNIC WAR TILL CANNAE

SAGUNTUM fell about the close of the year 219, and in the spring of 218 Hannibal crossed the Ebro with a force of 90,000 African and Spanish infantry, 12,000 Spanish and Numidian cavalry, a contingent of Balearic slingers and about 30 elephants, leaving his brother Hasdrubal in command in Spain. The conquest of north-east Spain and the passage of the Pyrenees delayed him till summer and cost him the lives of many men, while a force was left behind to hold the newly-won district. But in the middle of summer he came into Gaul with an army of about 60,000 men in all. The Romans, feeling secure against an invasion by sea, had laid plans for invading Africa and for meeting Hannibal in Spain. With this in view they sent one consul, Sempronius, to Sicily to prepare for the invasion of Africa, and the other, P. Scipio, was commissioned to enroll an army for Spain, while a small force was to keep the Cisalpine Gauls in check, as it was known that Hannibal had been intriguing with their kinsmen north of the Alps. But a rising of the Boii delayed the departure of Scipio, and before he could set sail for Spain he learnt that Hannibal was already in Gaul.

Hastening to Massilia, Scipio was too late to hinder

Hannibal's passage of the Rhone. The latter, anxious
to cross the Alps before the snows set in, had crossed the
river near Avignon 50 miles from its mouth, turning the

Hannibal

flank of the Gauls who were drawn up to oppose him by
sending a detachment over the Rhone some miles higher
up. He had then moved up the east bank of the river

and was out of reach of Scipio's force. Scipio acted promptly. Sending on his army under his brother Gnaeus to Spain with orders to prevent at all costs reinforcements from following Hannibal, he himself sailed for N. Italy to raise what troops he could and unite them with the small force already there. Orders were sent to Sempronius, as soon as Hannibal's movements were known, to leave Sicily and hasten with his troops to Cisalpine Gaul. The uncertain loyalty of the Gauls made it impossible to hold the Alpine passes and it was decided that the Po should be the line of defence.

Hannibal's March

Hannibal crosses the Alps, 218 B.C. Meanwhile Hannibal, moving up the east bank of the Rhone, came on the fourth day to the ' Island,' the land enclosed between the Rhone and the Isara. Here by settling a dispute between rival chieftains of the Allobroges he secured the friendship of the Gauls in his rear and turning eastwards began the ascent of the lower slopes of the Alps. It is uncertain by what pass he made his way over the mountain barrier. Livy and Polybius, from whom we draw the account of his march, give no means of identifying the pass exactly. But the latter seems to make him follow

the Isara to its source and thence cross by the Little
St Bernard Pass into the land of the Salassii.   Livy on
the other hand represents him as coming down among
the Taurini, in which case he must have left the Isara
and struck south to the upper course of the Druentia
and thence have crossed the Cottian Alps probably by
the Pass of Mont Genèvre.

In either case it was a marvellous piece of work.   It
was late autumn, the rivers were swollen with snow and
rain, and the mountain tribes harassed him incessantly.
At the ' White Rock ' he found himself surrounded, the
enemy rolling boulders down upon his men, and it meant
a night in the open and hard fighting before he could
continue his march.   At length, after toiling upwards for
nine days, he reached the summit of the pass, and pointing
out to his men the fertile plains of Italy below them, he
allowed them a rest of two days before he began the
descent.   But the new snow lying on top of the old
made the descent more dangerous than the ascent.   Men
and horses rolled over precipices; and at one point a land-
slip had carried away the path, and a new way had to be
cut and the rocks splintered by heating them white-hot
and pouring vinegar upon them, if Livy's account may
be believed.   Seven days of terrible labour brought Hannibal's army out on to the plains, where he was welcomed
by the Gauls.   It was five months since he had crossed
the Ebro, and of his whole force only about half, some
30,000 men, reached Italy.   The march had cost him
dearer than he expected, but he hoped by a few crushing
blows to shake the allegiance of the Italians to Rome.
He did inflict on Rome the most crushing defeats, but
the Italians for the most part only drew closer to their
centre.   The war proved abundantly Hannibal's military
skill and the enduring strength of Rome's work in Italy.

Battle of the Trebia, 218 B.C.   Scipio was waiting

near Placentia and his position was difficult. Sempronius had not yet arrived from Sicily and the Gauls on either side of the Po were restless. On the Ticinus, a northern tributary of the Po, his cavalry came into collision with Hannibal's Numidian and Spanish horse. The Romans were driven back, and the consul, himself severely wounded, was only saved by his son, who was destined afterwards to be the conqueror of Hannibal. As he fell back, Scipio broke down the bridges over the Ticinus and Po in face of Hannibal's vanguard and took up a position behind the Trebia, a stream which flows from the Apennines into the Po.

Here he was joined by Sempronius, who wished, contrary to Scipio's advice, to fight a decisive action before his year of office was over. It was playing into the hands of the enemy. Hiding his brother Mago and 2000 men in a hollow west of the Trebia, Hannibal sent his Numidian cavalry across the river on a rough snowy morning to entice the Romans back over the swollen stream, while his main body, well fed and warmed, were in readiness for the fight. Elated by a small success on the previous day, Sempronius advanced his army of 40,000 men across the river in pursuit of the Numidians. Wet and hungry and cold they found Hannibal ready for them. The Carthaginian cavalry put the Roman horse to flight and fell on the flank of the legions, while Mago's ambush attacking in the rear completed the disorder. Ten thousand Romans cut their way through to Placentia; of the rest only stragglers made their way back to the camp. But under cover of the storm Scipio was able to retreat east to Cremona, picking up the remnants of the army at Placentia on the way. At the end of the year he followed his brother to Spain.

Battle of Lake Trasimene, 217 B.C. For the year 217 Flaminius was consul with Servilius as his colleague.

Flaminius won the hatred of the Roman nobles by his
democratic politics and his neglect of the due ceremonies
on taking office, but he was a good soldier of the blind
and impetuous type, no match for his great opponent.
He took post at Arretium in Etruria, Servilius at Ariminum.   Hannibal, wishing to get to closer grips with
Rome without delay, crossed the Apennines early in the
year well to the west and came down into the valley of
the Arno, which was in flood owing to the severe winter.
Here for four days the army floundered through swamps

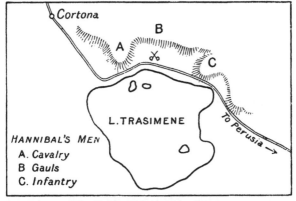

The Battle of Lake Trasimene

exposed to rain and sleet, and Hannibal, riding on the
sole surviving elephant, lost the sight of an eye from the
exposure.   Resting for a few days at Faesulae, he slipped
past Flaminius's left and followed the road towards Rome
past Cortona.   Flaminius, as Hannibal hoped, left his
fortified position at Arretium and followed the enemy.
Between Cortona and Perusia the road ran along the
northern edge of Lake Trasimene.   At the N.W. corner
of the lake hills come down almost to the water, then
receding they leave a fairly wide plain along the northern
shore, coming down once more to the N.E. end of the lake.

Here Hannibal laid his trap. The eastern exit he blocked with the main body of his infantry, the Gauls he stationed along the hills to the north of the plain, the cavalry placed in hiding were to close the western entrance as soon as Flaminius had passed through it.

Flaminius with no attempt at scouting walked into the snare. It was an April morning with fog lying on the low ground, and above the fog Hannibal's men could signal across to one another in the sunshine and hear the tramp of the Roman army coming up through the white mist below. The cavalry closed the entrance at the right moment and from all sides the Carthaginians rushed down on their bewildered foe. The Romans fought but they had no chance. Flaminius and many of his men were cut down as they stood ; others fell in the shallow waters of the lake into which the horsemen pursued them. More than 20,000 prisoners were taken, of whom Hannibal released the Italians, as he had done at the Trebia, that they might win over their kinsmen to his side. A few days later 4000 horsemen sent by Servilius to the assistance of Flaminius were destroyed, and Hannibal advanced along the road towards Rome. But at Spoletium he was foiled in an attempt to surprise the town, and seeing no signs of a revolt of Italians, he moved eastward to the Adriatic coast and thence south to Apulia, ravaging the country as he went.

Q. Fabius Maximus Cunctator, 217 B.C. At Rome the news of Trasimene caused a panic. The Senate met forthwith, and at evening the praetor coming out announced to the excited crowd, " We have lost a great battle." The walls of the city were repaired, bridges broken down, and new troops enrolled, while Q. Fabius Maximus was appointed Dictator with M. Minucius Rufus Master of the Horse. Fabius grasped the situation. Hannibal's losses might be small, but he had a small army to

begin with   So long as no reinforcements reached him from
Spain, the wastage of a long campaign would inevitably
tell on his army.   On the other hand the Romans had no
general to compare with Hannibal and must not play
into his hands by risking another great battle, though
they might hamper his movements and cut off stragglers.
The presence of Hannibal and the ruin of their farms
would be a severe test of the loyalty of the Italians.
But the only chance was to put that loyalty to the test
and to gain time.   Ennius wrote of Fabius:

> Unus homo nobis cunctando restituit rem.
> One man by his delaying restored our fortunes.

From putting these tactics into practice the general won
the name of Cunctator.

Following Hannibal into Apulia Fabius ran no risks,
and Hannibal seeing the danger of delay marched into
Campania with the hope that Capua would join him.   But
Capua as yet closed her gates against him, and while
Hannibal ravaged Campania, Fabius seized the passes
near Cales by which Hannibal must return to Apulia.
Hannibal was not to be caught.   Binding faggots on the
horns of two thousand oxen, he sent them off at midnight
with light-armed troops to drive them up the pass.   The
oxen, infuriated by the flames on their heads, rushed up
the sides of the hills, and the Romans in the pass, thinking
the Carthaginians were escaping over the hills, rushed up
after them leaving the pass unguarded.   Hannibal then
passed safely through, since Fabius, who could not understand the meaning of the lights, kept his main body within
the camp.

Fabian tactics were sound but not exciting, and the
Romans were impatient and incensed at the impunity
with which Hannibal pillaged the peninsula.   While
Fabius was away at Rome on religious duties, Minucius

won a small success, and the people made him Co-Dictator. But Hannibal enticed him into a conflict in which he was only rescued from disaster by Fabius, and in gratitude he resumed his lower position as Master of the Horse.

Battle of Cannae, 216 B.C. At the end of 217 the popular party, forgetting former disasters, thought something ought to be done. As colleague to the experienced L. Aemilius Paullus they appointed a pushing demagogue, M. Terentius Varro, a loud-voiced ex-butcher-boy, as his opponents said, and in 216 they sent out both consuls with 90,000 men to overwhelm Hannibal in Apulia. The anxiety of the Romans for decisive action was natural enough. They had seen the sky red at night with the flames from Italian homesteads and they did not know how long the Italians would remain loyal. But they did not understand that they had to face a military genius and that no chance must be given him of showing his skill. Hannibal had seized the town of Cannae with the corn supplies of the Roman army; and the consuls came upon him here, Paullus seeing the danger of fighting in a level plain where Hannibal's superiority in cavalry would tell, Varro anxious to fight anywhere. The Carthaginian camp was on the right bank of the Aufidus; the Romans made two camps, the larger one on the left bank, the smaller on the right not far from Hannibal's camp, that it might protect the Roman watering parties and annoy those of the Carthaginians. Hannibal now moved his camp across the river within striking distance of the larger Roman camp and waited events.

The consuls still adhered to the antiquated custom of taking command on alternate days, of which Hannibal did not fail to take advantage. For the day of Paullus's command Hannibal contented himself with chasing the Roman watering parties back to their camp. On the

next day, Aug. 2nd, 216, he gave Varro his chance of
battle. The Romans drew up their forces on the right
bank of the Aufidus in deeper and closer order than usual
with Paullus in command of the cavalry on the right and
Varro with the Italian cavalry on the left. Hannibal

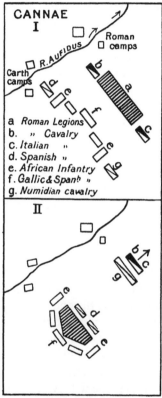

a *Roman Legions*
b. *„   Cavalry*
c. *Italian   „*
d. *Spanish „*
e. *African Infantry*
f. *Gallic & Spanh „*
g. *Numidian cavalry*

The Battle of Cannae

drew up his Gallic and Spanish infantry in a thin arc in
his centre with African infantry massed at either end,
the heavy Spanish cavalry opposite to Paullus and the
Numidians facing Varro, while the wind from the S.E.
blew the dust in the eyes of the Romans.

The Roman centre by sheer weight drove in the centre of the enemy. But after a desperate encounter Paullus's cavalry gave way before the Spaniards and fled over the river. Not wasting time in pursuit, the Spanish horse fell on the rear of Varro who was holding the Numidians in check and scattered his men. Then turning again they fell on the rear of the legions who were busy with the infantry. The legions had fought well but being closely drawn up to begin with had gradually become wedged tight as they pushed forward. Now with African infantry and Spanish cavalry pressing on flank and rear they became a solid mass incapable even of raising their arms to defend themselves. 70,000 men were cut down, Paullus and Minucius among them, 80 Senators and countless Equites, whose golden rings were sent as a token of victory to Carthage. Varro escaped to Venusia and a few thousand stragglers made their way to Canusium.

Hannibal lost about 6000 men, but his cavalry was almost untouched, and Maharbal their leader begged his general to march at once on Rome. " In five days you shall sup with me on the Capitol." But Hannibal could not afford the loss of his 6000, still less the possibility of a check before Rome. Failing reinforcements from Spain, a rising of the Italians was his one hope of lasting success. Three sledge-hammer blows he had dealt the Roman state ; surely some signs of disintegration would show themselves. He was right. Samnium, Apulia, Lucania and most of S. Italy now declared for him, except the Greek cities and such towns as were held to their loyalty by Roman garrisons. Worst of all, Capua, the second city of Italy, forgetful of its past fair treatment by Rome threw in its lot with the victor of Cannae. But Rome had no thought of submission. Q. Fabius Maximus took the lead in steadying the city in its hour of panic ; the envoy of Hannibal was forbidden to enter Rome. New legions were enrolled from boys and freedmen and slaves ; the survivors of Cannae were formed into two legions and bidden to retrieve their disgrace. Varro was thanked for not having despaired of the state, and Rome set herself once more to face her danger.

DATES

218. Hannibal crosses the Alps.
218. Battles of the Ticinus and Trebia.
217. Battle of Lake Trasimene.
217. Q. Fabius Maximus Cunctator.
216. Battle of Cannae.

CHAPTER XI

THE SECOND PUNIC WAR. CANNAE TO ZAMA

THE battle of Cannae was the low-water mark for the Romans in the war. They learnt now at last that genius counts and that it was no good meeting Hannibal in pitched battles, until they had a general fit to compare with him. On the other hand they had a network of colonies, which even with his recruits from S. Italy Hannibal could not capture ; and by dividing their forces into several small armies, which acted from these colonies as their bases, they wore out their foe. The day of great battles was over for the present, and the chief incidents of the next six years, during which Q. Fabius the ' Shield ' of Rome and M. Claudius Marcellus her ' Sword ' were the upholders of Rome, gather round the towns of Capua and Tarentum in Italy and Syracuse in Sicily.

Capua, 216–211 B.C. Capua had revolted after Cannae, and Marcellus, though he won the first Roman success against Hannibal at Nola, was unable to hinder his movements. The Carthaginians wintered at Capua at the end

of 216, and the luxury of the city is said to have destroyed
their morale; but it is nearer the truth that the Romans
had become veteran soldiers by this time and found their
enemy less formidable. For two years Hannibal made
Mt Tifata near Capua his base, withdrawing at will into
Apulia, when his presence was needed there or hopes of
help from Macedon or of the surrender of Tarentum called

South Italy

him. But the Romans kept eight legions in Campania,
and when in 212 Tarentum at last went over to Hannibal,
it meant that they were free for a while from his presence
in Campania. Gradually they closed in on Capua, and
though they could not prevent Hannibal throwing a
force of cavalry into the city at the end of the year, in
211 the two consuls with the praetor Nero shut in the city
with a double line of fortifications. Hannibal hurried
back to his old quarters at Mt Tifata, cutting up a slave
army under Gracchus, which had done the state good

service, but still the Romans did not stir from their entrenchments. Famine was doing its work in Capua, and Hannibal, as a last chance of drawing off the Romans, marched on Rome. He pitched his camp three miles from the city, but there was no danger with reserve legions at hand, and the Romans knew it. The army at Capua did not stir; and Hannibal after riding slowly round the walls of Rome—a wolf round the full sheepfold—recognized that he could do no more and retiring to S. Italy. left Capua to its fate. The city soon after surrendered. The ringleaders slew themselves or were executed, and all concerned in the revolt were sold as slaves. Capua, deprived of its constitution and despoiled of its land, was reduced to the status of a village.

Syracuse, 214–212 B.C. In 216 Hiero, the old ally of Rome, died and the bad government of his son Hieronymus caused a revolt. The Syracusans murdered him and his family and set up a republic. While they were wavering between Rome and Carthage, Sicily in general became restless; and as a disloyal Sicily would offer an easy way to reinforcements for Hannibal, Marcellus was sent to the island in 215. By his severity in dealing with rebels he drove Syracuse into the arms of the Carthaginians and a siege of two years followed.

For a time the Carthaginians had free access to the Great Harbour, and afterwards the devices of the great engineer Archimedes kept the Romans at bay. Gigantic catapults hurled stones which smashed the Roman ships, huge cranes gripped their prows and capsized them, and a great mirror—if one may believe the story—concentrated the sun's rays and set fire to them at a distance. At last in 212 Marcellus took the plateau of Epipolae above the city, defeated the Carthaginian relieving force and gradually drove the defenders back into the ' Island ' of Ortygia, which before long surrendered. Marcellus had wished to spare the lives of the citizens; but giving up the city to plunder he was unable to keep his men in hand. Among the killed was Archimedes. Marcellus had given strict orders that he should not be harmed; but being fatally engrossed in some mathematical calculations Archimedes did not tell his name, when a soldier enquired who he was. Two more years passed before Sicily was quiet, but in 210 the Carthaginians finally left the island and Syracuse was at last incorporated in the Roman province.

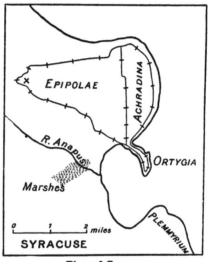

Plan of Syracuse

Tarentum, 212–209 B.C. Tarentum's loyalty had been suspected since 216. The nearness of Hannibal's headquarters in Apulia was a constant temptation, and in 212 the city went over to him. M. Livius was able to save the citadel for the Romans and with it the command of the harbour; but Tarentum's example was followed by the other Greek cities, and Hannibal gained thereby ports at which reinforcements could land. But with the citadel still in Roman hands and all his attacks upon it failing,

Hannibal gained little from Tarentum. In 209 while Hannibal was forced to move into Bruttium to meet some Roman troops who had crossed from Sicily, Q. Fabius laid siege to Tarentum. With the help of the garrison of the citadel and through the treachery of the Bruttians, whom Hannibal had left to hold the place for him, the town was taken and its inhabitants massacred or sold into slavery.

General course of the war, 216–209 B.C. So much for the three great cities and their fortunes. But besides this there were marches and counter-marches and battles innumerable—comparatively small affairs, for the Romans had learnt wisdom. Hannibal could now draw men and supplies from S. Italy. But the Romans strained every nerve, enrolled slaves and freedmen, distributed 20 legions over S. Italy, and though Hannibal scarcely once suffered defeat himself, he could not be everywhere. The fact too that he had now Italian towns to defend destroyed his power of rapid and unexpected movement which in earlier years had paralysed the Romans. Northern Italy was undisturbed, and no chance was given him of welding the south together—as he hoped at first—into one united state capable of standing up against Rome. With the exception of a small force sent from Carthage in 215 he had to depend on what he could do for himself, and the fighting value of his army was growing less each year.

He had hoped for help from Philip V of Macedon whom he induced to declare war on Rome in 215. But the Romans availed themselves of the hostility of the Aetolian League against Philip, and their fleet operating off the coast of Epirus easily kept him in check. Philip eventually came to terms with Rome in 205.

But the length of the war was exhausting the Romans. The drain of men and money was unbearable and the loss of S. Italy diminished the district on which they could draw. Special contributions were made by the rich, and soldiers agreed to serve without pay. But in 209 twelve Latin colonies declared that they were simply unable to supply any more men or money, and it was clear that the resources of Rome were running low. It was in these desperate straits that the long deferred crisis of the war came, and the new army from Spain which Hannibal had long expected arrived in Italy.

Spain

Spain, 218–208 B.C. It must not be forgotten that the Romans had the command of the sea throughout the war and that Hannibal looked for substantial reinforcements only by the overland route from Spain. At the beginning of the war P. Scipio failing to intercept Hannibal on his way to Italy, sent on his troops under his brother Gnaeus to keep Hasdrubal busy Cn. Scipio succeeded in clearing the Carthaginians out of the land between the Pyrenees and the Ebro, and when after the battle of the

Trebia he was joined in 217 by P. Scipio, the two brothers
set themselves to work, in the first place to prevent Hasdrubal leaving for Italy with a new army and then to
undermine the Carthaginian power in Spain. Welcomed
by the Spaniards as deliverers from the oppressive Carthaginian yoke, they secured their hold on the land north
of the Ebro; and when in 216 Hasdrubal was ready to
start with his army, they inflicted a crushing defeat on
him and were able at last to advance south of the river.
The Spaniards in the south and west rose at their coming,
and even across the straits in Mauretania Syphax raised
the standard of rebellion. Saguntum fell to the Romans
and Cn. Scipio advanced as far as the valley of the Baetis
(Guadalquivir). So far from starting for Italy, Hasdrubal had to cross to Mauretania, and troops from Carthage
under Mago intended for Italy were diverted to Spain.
But the Spaniards found that in supporting the Romans
they had only changed their masters, and on the return
of Hasdrubal in 212 they deserted the Scipios. The
brothers were defeated and killed in two battles in 211.
But they had done their work. For six years Hannibal
had waited in vain for Hasdrubal and Rome had survived
the shock of her early disasters.

Nero, set free for new work by the fall of Capua, held
Hasdrubal at bay for some months. But in 210 the Senate
decided to create an exceptional proconsular command for
the war in Spain. Young P. Scipio, though he had held
none of the offices which would qualify him for the post
and was only 24 years old, offered himself as a candidate.
He had shown the qualities of a good soldier at the Ticinus
and after Cannae, and it was fitting that he should avenge
his father and uncle. He was a Roman of a new type,
of high family but popular with the lower classes, acquainted with the Greek culture which was beginning to
make way in Rome, one whose brilliant genius startled

the dull and solid Roman world, but at the same time not free from an un-Roman love of splendour and display. Against all precedents the people took the matter into its own hands and appointed him to the command in Spain.

Taking a new legion and auxiliaries he landed at Tarraco, raised a large native force and in the spring of 209 advanced on New Carthage which he knew to be weakly garrisoned. The town was on a tongue of land, strongly walled on the land side and protected for the rest by the waters of the harbour and a lagoon. Scipio learnt that at low tide the lagoon could just be crossed on foot, and making a feint of attacking at the wall he sent a picked body through the shallow water and entered the city almost without resistance. The fleet, stores and treasure of the Carthaginians with all their Spanish hostages fell into his hands. In 208 however Hasdrubal at last gave the Romans the slip, making his way unexpectedly round the western end of the Pyrenees. Scipio stayed on in Spain for two years, during which time he drove out the Carthaginians and by his tact reconciled the Spaniards to Roman rule.

Battle of the Metaurus, 207 B.C. Hasdrubal wintered among the Arverni and in the spring of 207 crossed the Alps. Many Cisalpine Gauls and Ligurians joined him, and with them his army numbered over 50,000 men. Hannibal had waited eleven years. The fateful day had come at last. The two brothers were at last to join their forces for the destruction of Rome.

The consuls were C. Claudius Nero and his personal enemy M. Livius Salinator, who had conquered the Illyrians twelve years before and had been in disgrace ever since for misappropriating the spoils. But it was no time for private enmities. Every available soldier was put into the field, and while Nero watched Hannibal in the south, Livius was to meet Hasdrubal in the north.

Hasdrubal sent off news of his arrival to his brother ; but
the horsemen, who carried the message together with his
plans for a united attack upon Rome itself, were captured
and the despatches fell into Nero's hands. Feeling sure
that Hannibal would not move far without news of
Hasdrubal, Nero with a touch of genius rose to the occasion.
Leaving the bulk of his army in the south he hastened
north with 7000 men to help his colleague. It was a
memorable march. The fate of Italy hung in the balance.
At each village of the 250 miles the people were ready
with transport and provisions for his men, and their
words of prayer and encouragement went along with his
travel-stained column. In seven days he joined Livius
who was confronting Hasdrubal south of the Metaurus
in Umbria.

He entered the camp by night but the double trumpet-
calls in the morning betrayed his presence to Hasdrubal,
who, fearing that his brother had met with a reverse, retreated next night towards Ariminum. But being misled
he could not find the ford and was compelled to accept
battle next morning with the Metaurus at his back.
The Gauls, whom he could not trust, were on his left
behind broken ground, and Nero not being able to get
at them led most of his men round behind Livius's legions
and fell on the rear of the Spaniards and Ligurians who
were fighting stubbornly. This decided the day. Hasdrubal met a soldier's death and his army was cut to
pieces. Hannibal knew nothing of his brother's fortunes
till Nero on his return brutally acquainted him with the
facts by throwing Hasdrubal's head into the Carthaginian
camp. Hannibal saw in this ghastly token the end of all
his hopes. He retired to Bruttium and for four years
more maintained himself among its hills and forests.

Africa. Conclusion of the War. When Scipio drove
the Carthaginians out of Spain, Mago took his troops

across the Gulf of Genoa to Liguria in 205. But it was too late now that Hannibal was shut up in Bruttium; and Mago with difficulty maintained his footing in the peninsula for two years. Scipio meanwhile got into touch with the Numidian Prince Masinissa who offered his assistance if Scipio would invade Africa. Q. Fabius and the old-fashioned Romans were aghast at such a project, while Hannibal was still in Italy. But other tactics than those of Fabius were needed now. The people welcomed the scheme. Scipio was elected consul for 205, and though the Senate would allow him only the two legions of Cannae, still serving under a cloud in Sicily, he was allowed to collect what volunteers he could. At last in 204 he landed near Utica but found that Masinissa could give him little help, since Syphax his rival had gone over to the Carthaginians and with their aid driven him from his kingdom. Scipio found himself in difficulties, but pretending during the winter to negotiate he seized an opportunity in the spring of 203 for a sudden attack upon Syphax's camp. He set fire to the huts of dry boughs and straw, in which the Africans were sheltered, and in the panic killed 40,000 of Syphax's men. By this time Masinissa had gathered an army from his own adherents and returning to the help of Scipio captured Syphax in his capital of Cirta. Under these circumstances the Carthaginians proposed peace, and terms were arranged with Scipio subject to the approval of the Senate. But the war-party once more got the upper hand in Carthage, and Hannibal and Mago were recalled from Italy to renew the struggle in Africa. Hannibal had for 15 years been the terror of Rome, and the prize had once been almost within his grasp. Now he obeyed his country's summons and sailed for Carthage to help her at her need.

In 202 after a fruitless interview between the two great generals the final battle was fought at Zama. Scipio had arranged his maniples directly behind one another, so that the Carthaginian elephants charged harmlessly through the gaps in his line. In the battle Hannibal's veterans turned on the raw African troops of Carthage and Masinissa's cavalry completed the rout.

Further resistance was hopeless and Carthage submitted, surrendering Spain and all dependencies outside Africa. She gave up all her ships of war but ten and promised to pay an indemnity of 10,000 talents (£2,500,000) within 50 years and to make no war without the consent of Rome. Numidia and part of Syphax's dominions were given to Masinissa that he might be a thorn in the side of Rome's prostrate foe. Thus in 201 the long duel was ended by the utter humiliation of Carthage. Scipio received the title of Africanus, and the people were ready to grant him almost royal honours. But the price of victory, which Rome had paid in loss of life and the ruin of her lands, was enormous, and those whom she had lost were the best of her sons.

DATES

216–211.	Capua lost and retaken.
214–212.	Syracuse lost and retaken.
212–209.	Tarentum lost and retaken.
215–205.	Macedon in alliance with Hannibal.
218–211.	Spain. The brothers Scipio in Spain.
210.	„ Young P. Scipio appointed.
209.	„ Capture of New Carthage.
208.	„ Hasdrubal starts for Italy
207.	Battle of the Metaurus.
204.	P. Scipio invades Africa.
203.	Hannibal leaves Italy.
202.	Battle of Zama.
201.	Peace concluded.

CHAPTER XII

MACEDON, ANTIOCHUS AND GREECE

THE war with Hannibal was over, but the Romans without any interval for recovery found themselves involved in new fighting. We must leave the consideration of the great political and economic results of the struggle with Hannibal, till we have seen the first expansion of Rome eastwards which followed the start of her western empire. Force of circumstances rather than deliberate choice brought about the extension to the East; but we must remember that the Second Punic War had practically, though not in name, given Rome a new class of professional soldiers, who were out of employment when there was no war. The series of wars which brought Rome to the Aegean and the coasts of Asia has not the interest of the great war with Hannibal. Greece was a shadow of her former self, and words rather than deeds her forte. What strength she had was hopelessly divided, and the hosts of Antiochus were fitter for parade than real fighting.

The Eastern World. We have seen in the account of Pyrrhus how the Eastern world had been partitioned after the death of Alexander. Greece itself was fallen on evil days. Athens and Sparta were nominally independent, but the former was fast becoming a university town and nothing more, the latter was disgraced by the government of a brigand called Nabis. The rest of Greece proper was for the most part divided between two leagues, the Aetolian league comprising the states to the north and west of the Corinthian Gulf, the Achaean those to the south. Philip V of Macedon, whose interference in the Second Punic War has been dignified by the name of

the First Macedonian War, was the northern neighbour
of Greece, and compared with the disunited states his
power was formidable. He held Thessaly and kept the
Greeks in check by three great fortresses, Demetrias on
the Gulf of Pagasae, Chalcis in Euboea, and Corinth, the
Fetters of Greece as they were called. But he too lived
largely on the past reputation of his country and could not
realize that a war with Rome would have but one result.

Of other Greek or half-Greek states mention must
be made of Rhodes, which by its position had become the
commercial centre of the Eastern Mediterranean, and Per-

Coin of Philip V of Macedon (220—178 B.C.).
Obv. Philip. *Rev.* Athene

gamum on the coast of Asia Minor, which by trade and
attention to its fleet held an important position and as a
patron of literature vied with Athens and Alexandria.

In 205 the King of Egypt died and was succeeded by
Ptolemy Epiphanes, a boy of five. Philip and Antiochus
of Syria, thinking their chance had come, arranged to
partition the dominions of Egypt, Antiochus taking Egypt
itself with Phoenicia and Palestine, while Philip was to
have the Egyptian possessions in Thrace and the Aegean.
But Rome had an interest in Egypt from which she was
already drawing supplies of corn, and Philip in his attempt

to seize the Aegean islands made no scruple of attacking
the possessions of Pergamum and Rhodes.   Appeals from
these two countries reached Rome; and the Senate, not
wishing to have a war with Philip and Antiochus combined,
detached the latter from his ally by consenting to his
occupation of Phoenicia and Palestine, declared that the
young king of Egypt was under Roman protection and
then sent an ultimatum to Philip bidding him keep his

Northern Greece

hands off all Greek cities, restore his conquests to Ptolemy
and settle his differences with Pergamum and Rhodes by
arbitration.   He refused to obey and war broke out.

Second Macedonian War, 200–196 B.C.   Philip had
the support of the Achaean league; but the Aetolians
who were at first inclined to help him, as they had got
nothing by their assistance of Rome in the earlier war,
threw in their lot with the Romans after the first year.

The Roman populace weary of fighting had no liking for the war, and none but volunteers were enrolled in the legions. In the first year nothing was done, as the Roman general could not penetrate the passes into Macedonia. In 198 Flamininus starting from Apollonia, opposite Brundisium, moved up the Aous valley and found Philip holding the passes. Learning from a shepherd of a path across the hills he dislodged the Macedonians, who fell back on the Pass of Tempe, where the river Peneus flows out from Thessaly between Mts Olympus and Ossa. But they ravaged the country as they went, and Flamininus on his descent into Thessaly was forced to fall back to the Corinthian Gulf for food.

Anxious to end the war himself he obtained an extension of his command and in the next year, 197, met Philip in Thessaly at a range of hills called Cynoscephalae. The armies were in close proximity for two days, and on the third, a thick misty morning, both commanders had directed their advanced guards to occupy a certain height. The unexpected meeting of these troops brought on a general engagement. Philip, elated at driving in the small Roman force, advanced his phalanx over the hill to where Flamininus was waiting near the foot. The right wing of the phalanx drove the Romans down the slope, but the left wing was broken by the Roman elephants, and the right wing being then attacked from the rear fled in confusion. Philip hurried off to Macedonia abandoning even the Pass of Tempe.

Peace was made in 196. Philip had to pay 1000 talents and become the subject ally of Rome. He had to give up all his conquests outside Macedon, making over Phocis and Locris to the Aetolian League and his possessions in the Peloponnese to the Achaeans. Thessaly was split up into four independent states to the disappointment of the Aetolians, who looked to get it in return for their help at Cynoscephalae. Rome took nothing but the indemnity, and at the Isthmian games the same year Flamininus announced to the astonished crowd that the *Greek cities were henceforth to be free*. The herald had to repeat the proclamation before the multitude could take it in. Then with the wildest delight they rushed on Flamininus almost smothering their 'Liberator' with garlands and embraces. A new era seemed to have dawned for Greece. But there were no leaders, no ideals, nothing but deceit and jealousies among the Greeks. Flamininus bade them make good use of their freedom and withdrew to Italy.

War with Antiochus, 192–190 B.C. Antiochus had stood on one side, while Philip was getting the worst of it. But his ambition to figure as the true successor of Alexander the Great led him to interfere with the Greek cities of Asia Minor, which brought on him the warning of Flamininus in 195 that the Romans would not permit him to meddle with them. The Romans were very reluctant to come into conflict with him, for they had as yet no idea how hollow the power of an Eastern despot could be. But continual protests from Rhodes and Pergamum reached them; and when Hannibal, denounced by his political opponents on a charge of plotting against Rome, had fled for refuge to Antiochus, they began to be seriously alarmed. Hannibal indeed had plans for uniting the whole of Greece with Antiochus, for calling on Spaniards and Gauls to make another effort, for inducing Carthage herself to make trial of war again. Such an attack on Rome from all sides at once was too great an undertaking for the mind of Antiochus to grasp, and while keeping Hannibal with him he steadily rejected his advice. Meanwhile in Greece war had broken out between the Achaean league and Sparta, and the Aetolians joining with Sparta had appealed to all the Greeks, to Philip and to Antiochus

to stand up for the rights of Greece against Roman interference. They resented the fact that Thessaly had not
been given to them and they styled themselves the true
victors of Cynoscephalae.

Philip had had his lesson and kept out of the trouble.
But in 192 Antiochus landed in Greece with a small force,
declared war on the Achaeans and captured a few towns
in Thessaly. The Romans were bound to interfere.
Glabrio was sent to Greece in 191 and found Philip ready
to co-operate with him. On the other hand the Aetolians
and Antiochus were disappointed with the weakness of
each other. With little confidence the king tried to hold
the Pass of Thermopylae, while the Aetolians guarded the
path by which in 480 the Persians had got round to the
rear of Leonidas. M. Porcius Cato easily dispersed the
Aetolians, and Antiochus escaped with no more than 500
men to Ephesus. On sea the fleets of Rhodes and Pergamum acting in conjunction with a Roman squadron
defeated Antiochus's fleet, and further danger to Europe
from that king was at an end.

In 190 the consul L. Scipio, with his brother Africanus
as his Legatus to share with him the management of the
war, was sent to crush Antiochus in Asia. Hannibal had
collected a Phoenician fleet, and for safety the Romans
took the overland route through Thrace. But Hannibal's
fleet was defeated at the R. Eurymedon near the S.W. of
Asia Minor, and Antiochus in alarm tried to negotiate
with the Romans on their arrival. Receiving the answer
that he must surrender all land west of the Taurus Mts,
he prepared for his last effort at Magnesia west of Sardis.
Antiochus had a phalanx of 16,000 men and a host of
camels, elephants, chariots and archers so vast that the
Romans and their allies could not see the whole of his
line. But their 30,000 men had scarcely any fighting.
Eumenes of Pergamum drove in Antiochus's right on to

the phalanx, which fell into disorder, and the whole closely packed array of the Asiatic army became hopelessly entangled. 50,000 men were killed and the Romans lost only some 400. Antiochus submitted, surrendering his lands west of the Taurus, his elephants and all his ships of war but ten, and these ten were never to come west of Cilicia. Moreover he had to pay 10,000 talents and surrender all enemies of Rome. But Hannibal, at whom the last clause was aimed, escaped for the moment.

Rome still aimed at no extension of her own territory. The coast of Asia Minor was divided between Pergamum and Rhodes. Philip, Rome's ally in the war, received practically nothing. The Aetolians had to acknowledge vaguely the supremacy of Rome, to pay an indemnity and to promise to supply her with troops, while the Achaean League was allowed to swallow up the whole of the Peloponnese. Thus Rome had broken the power of the Near East, and without assuming the responsibility of government where she had conquered she left the Greeks to look after themselves. Her foreign policy aimed at no Eastern conquest for the present. But her treatment of the Greeks was perhaps guided not a little by the feeling that they were the intellectual superiors of the Romans, who were as mere barbarians in the presence of Hellenic art and literature.

Hannibal and Scipio, 183 B.C. The fate of two great men remains to be told. Hannibal at the conclusion of peace took refuge with Prusias king of Bithynia. But the Romans demanded his surrender, and the son of Hamilcar true to his early oath of hatred to Rome foiled his enemies by taking poison, which he had long carried concealed in a ring. The same year, 183, saw the death of his conqueror Africanus. He, as well as his brother, who had taken the name of Asiaticus, was prosecuted for misappropriating money received from Antiochus.

Proudly reminding the people that the day was the anniversary of Zama he scorned to plead in his defence, and the prosecution was vetoed by a tribune, Gracchus, to whom afterwards he gave his daughter Cornelia in marriage. Africanus withdrew from Rome and would not again enter the city.

Third Macedonian War, 171–167 B.C. Philip had good reason to be dissatisfied after the war with Antiochus; for his help to Rome had balanced the hostility of the Aetolians, and he had not even been allowed to retain a part of Thessaly. However, knowing that complaints

Coin of Perseus of Macedon (179—168 B.C.).
Obv. Perseus. *Rev.* Eagle on thunderbolt

would be ineffective, he set himself to re-organize his kingdom and to ally himself with his neighbours. The Romans were alarmed at his progress, and continual quarrels between the Achaean League and its new member, Sparta, kept the attention of the Senate directed towards Greece. Philip died before the trouble came to a head. Demetrius, a son of Philip, was accused by his half-brother Perseus of being a better friend to Rome than to Macedon, and Philip put him to death. Later the old king found that he had been deceived and died broken down with grief in 179.

Perseus, who now became king, was a clear-headed man and continued his father's policy of building up his country. His weakness was that he was too timid to use effectively, when the time for action came, the power which he had already prepared. By alliance with Syria, Rhodes and Illyria he was in a strong position, and in every state of Greece he encouraged the formation of a Macedonian party. He aroused the fears of Eumenes of Pergamum, who came to Rome and exposed all the intrigues of the Macedonians, and Rome in 171 declared war on Perseus.

The Macedonians were strong enough to put up a good fight against Rome, but Perseus wasted time and allowed the Romans to detach from him the support of all his allies with the exception of Illyria. However the Romans made little headway under incompetent leaders, and disorder and pillaging disgraced their armies. Crassus in 171 and Mancinus in 170 were unable to dislodge Perseus from Tempe. Philippus in 169 forced his way over the slopes of Mt Olympus and found himself in an awkward position between Perseus's main army at Dium to the north and the garrison of Tempe to the south. But the king's nerve failed him. He fled in panic from Dium. Tempe now surrendered to the Romans, who however met with no further success in this year.

The ill-success of the Romans had greatly lowered their prestige. Epirus joined with Macedon; Eumenes, who was availing himself of the war to extend his own territory, could not be trusted. Perseus, thinking he had a chance of obtaining favourable terms of peace, was prepared to negotiate, and the Rhodians ventured to declare that they would attack whichever side refused to submit to arbitration. Perhaps this threat opened the eyes of the conquerors of Hannibal to the scandalous mismanagement of the war. In 168 they sent out L. Aemilius Paullus,

son of the general who fell at Cannae, to end the war.
He found Perseus at Dium where Macedon meets Thessaly,
and sending a detachment over the hills forced him to
fall back northwards to Pydna. At Pydna in 168 the
Phalanx and Legion met for the last time. The phalanx
crashed through the line immediately in front of it, but
falling into disorder on broken ground and assailed on the
flank it was helpless. Perseus surrendered soon after the
battle, and with him the power of Macedon came to an end.

In the settlement which followed the war Rome still
refused to reconstruct where she had destroyed. Macedon
was not made into a province but the monarchy was

Coin of Rhodes, about 200 B.C.   *Obv.* Head of Sun god.   *Rev.* Rose

abolished and the country divided into four peasant states,
forbidden to hold intercourse with one another and condemned to pay tribute to Rome.   Illyria was divided into
three similar districts.   Upon Epirus all the Roman troops
in Greece were turned loose with the result that the
inhabitants were driven off as slaves and the country never
recovered.   From the cities of Greece, in which anti-Roman
parties had not unnaturally come to the front, hostages
were taken.   From the Achaean League in particular
1000 leading men were deported to Italy, among them
the historian Polybius, who by his friendship with the
Scipios obtained most valuable information for the history

of the times which he wrote. Rhodes was punished for its interference in the war by the loss of its mainland possessions, and its trade was hard hit by the establishment of the island of Delos as a free port. Eumenes of Pergamum fell under Roman displeasure, and a commission was sent out to enquire into his conduct during the war.

Conquest of Greece, 146 B.C. It is all a sordid story. Greece on its last legs is a pitiable spectacle, and the Roman interference, while it shows the decline of Roman methods since the Second Punic War, destroyed also what little power of managing their own affairs the Greeks still possessed. After the war with Perseus was over and the friends of Rome were left supreme in the Greek cities, they found life intolerable. Children cried " Traitor " after them in the streets, no one would be seen at the public baths in their company, and they were hooted at the public games. One application for the return of the exiles was refused by the Senate, but in 150 Polybius by his influence among the leading men of Rome obtained permission for the survivors, now some 300, to return. At once the intrigues against Rome began again. Diaeus, one of the exiles, was elected general of the Achaean League and through a quarrel with Sparta brought about a rupture with Rome.

A rebellion in Macedon led by a pretended son of Perseus was suppressed by Metellus in 148, and Macedon was in 146 formed into a Roman province including the south of Illyria and Epirus. About the same time the strip of coast from the head of the Adriatic to the borders of Macedon was formed into a province under the name of Illyricum. In 147 at a congress held in Corinth Roman commissioners announced that henceforth non-Achaean towns, such as Sparta, Argos and Corinth, should cease to belong to the Achaean League. An outburst of fury followed. Critolaus, the new leader of the League, urged his followers to take advantage of the pre-occupation of the Romans in Spain and Africa, where they were involved in fresh wars, as we shall see, and war was declared.

Critolaus was defeated and killed at Thermopylae, Diaeus at the Isthmus; and the consul Mummius in 146 by command of the Senate, which resented the commercial greatness of the city, utterly destroyed Corinth. The inhabitants were killed or enslaved, the statues and pictures removed to Rome, the unappreciative consul stipulating in his contract for their removal that in the event of damage they must be replaced by others of equal value, and the city was then burnt to the ground. Greece was at first put under the general supervision of the governor of Macedon but soon became the Roman province of Achaea. Its history becomes part of the history of the Roman Empire.

Greek influence on Rome. In another sense the captive took prisoner the conqueror,

> Graecia capta ferum victorem cepit,

as Horace writes a century or more afterwards. The treasures of Greek literature, her philosophy and history and drama, the treasures of Greek art, her sculpture and architecture and painting, products of mind and skill which no country or age can excel, opened up a new world to the uncultured Roman. Scipio Africanus was one of the first Romans to learn Greek, but after his day the new knowledge quickly gained adherents. It was in vain for Cato, a typical Roman of the old school, to oppose. He drove from Rome Carneades, who came on an embassy from Athens in 155 and used the opportunity to give displays of his eloquence, on the ground that his arguments upset the plain notions of right and wrong. But in the end he had to learn Greek himself that he might teach his son.

Nearly all Latin literature which has survived is Greek in origin. The Romans were not slavish imitators ; there was too much vigour in them for that. But they were untaught, a hard fighting and ruling race, till wealth gave them leisure and expansion brought them the knowledge of Greece. Then on Greek models and under Greek inspiration they struck out a literature and a style of their own, of which Plautus and Terence were the greatest first-fruits. Later the prose of Cicero and Caesar, the poetry of Lucretius and Catullus, and the glories of the Augustan Age showed that the pupil of Greece could equal and in some ways surpass its master.

The growth of Greek influence had its bad side, especially as it came at a time when Rome had suddenly emerged from poverty to wealth. The ingenious but non-moral Greek mind had made pleasure an art, almost the chief end of life, and the rough strong coarse Roman nature was a ready prey to such an influence. In religion too the simple practical Roman gods with their homely but useful virtues were identified with the more questionable Greek divinities ; the splendour of their worship grew, while belief in them weakened. The way was opened to the admission of Eastern gods and their orgiastic worship with the introduction of the Eastern Cybele, the Magna Mater, by Africanus. The frenzied worship of Bacchus with his Greek rites gave rise to such hideous orgies that the Senate in 186 appointed a commission to enquire into it and suppressed the worship when it was found that 7000 men of all ranks of society were contaminated by it.

DATES

215–205. First Macedonian War.
200–196. Second Macedonian War.
    197. Battle of Cynoscephalae.
    196. Flamininus declares Greece free.
192–190. War with Antiochus.

DATES

191.	Battle of Thermopylae
190.	Battle of Magnesia.
183.	Death of Hannibal and of Scipio Africanus.
171–167.	Third Macedonian War.
168.	Battle of Pydna.
150.	Return of exiles.
148.	Macedonia and Illyricum provinces.
146.	Destruction of Corinth. Achaea a province.

CHAPTER XIII

THE DESTRUCTION OF CARTHAGE AND THE SPANISH WARS

WE have seen that the attempt of Rome to shield herself on the east with a screen of weak states and to decline the responsibility of government failed. Macedonia and Achaea became Roman provinces. During the period of the Macedonian and Greek wars something of the same sort was happening in the south and west also at the expense of Carthage and Spain.

Carthage. After Zama Carthage under Hannibal's leadership and with its natural genius for trade recovered very quickly its commercial prosperity; and the expulsion of its great leader within ten years after the conclusion of peace goes to show that the Carthaginians realized the danger of too great prosperity and were anxious to prove to Rome that they aimed at no other greatness than that of commerce. But Roman jealousy was aroused, and Masinissa was encouraged to hamper Carthage and encroach upon its territory whenever occasion offered, while Carthage by the terms of the peace was forbidden to protect itself by force of arms. Disputes with Masinissa had to be referred to the Senate, and that body took care never to settle any question decisively but to leave open every source of irritation. In particular the king's occupation of Tripoli to the east of Carthage and with it the seizure of the whole *hinterland* of Carthage was winked at, and Carthage was thus cut off from trade with the interior.

In 157 M. Porcius Cato was sent out with a Senatorial commission to make enquiries. Amazed at the signs of wealth on every side, means of a new war against Rome as he regarded them, he came back with the conviction that Carthage must be destroyed. His continual harping on the words *Delenda est Carthago* suited the Romans. The old fear of the power of Carthage was supplemented now by jealousy of her wealth, and the same spirit, which led the Romans to destroy their commercial rival in Greece, brought about the destruction of Carthage in the same year as that of Corinth.

Third Punic War, 149–146 B.C. In 151 Carthage, annoyed past endurance by Masinissa, declared war upon him. The Senate stopped the war, and the Carthaginians repenting of their breach of the treaty of 201 sent humble apologies to Rome. It was too late. They surrendered three hundred hostages at the bidding of Rome, but the consuls Manilius and Censorinus were sent from Sicily to Africa with 80,000 men in 149. They landed near Utica and demanded from Carthage the surrender of all materials of war. The Carthaginians obeyed. Two hundred thousand suits of armour and two thousand catapults were handed over to the invaders. Then at last with the city at his mercy, as it seemed, Censorinus made known the final orders. *Carthage was to be destroyed and a new city built at least ten miles from the sea.* The treachery of the Romans in using each surrender as the basis of further demands is past excuse, but they forgot that a Semitic nation could be roused by despair. Indignation and fury possessed the Carthaginians when they knew the fate in store for them.   Frantic efforts were made to provide for the defence of the city, iron and lead were stripped from the buildings, women gave their hair for catapult strings, factories were set going to turn out shields and swords. Behind their strong walls the Carthaginians under the leadership of one Hasdrubal made ready for a siege, while outside the city another Hasdrubal gathered a field force of 20,000 men.

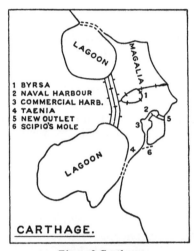

1 BYRSA
2 NAVAL HARBOUR
3 COMMERCIAL HARB.
4 TAENIA
5 NEW OUTLET
6 SCIPIO'S MOLE

CARTHAGE.

Plan of Carthage

Siege of Carthage.   The city stood on a headland with a lagoon on either side of the isthmus which connects it with the mainland, and across the isthmus a huge wall 40 ft. high protected the town on the land side.   In the centre of the headland was the citadel Byrsa, to the north of which lay the suburb Magalia.   On the south side was the town with two harbours; the inner naval harbour circular and the commercial harbour oblong with an out- let to the N.E. of the *Taenia* or land spit which extended as a barrier of sand across the mouth of the southern lagoon.

The consuls allowed a month to pass before they moved towards the city, and they were surprised to find it fortified against them. Manilius encamped on the isthmus before the great wall, Censorinus approached by the Taenia. But no success attended them. Their siege engines were destroyed by the defenders, and Hasdrubal's field force more than once brought them into great danger, from which they were only rescued by Scipio Aemilianus, son of Aemilius Paullus and grandson by adoption of Africanus. Masinissa too died, dissatisfied with the interference of Rome, and by the dead king's will Scipio was given the task of dividing his kingdom between his three sons. Thus two years passed and the Romans were no nearer success than they were at the commencement of the war. Disease was spreading among their troops, encamped as they were on low ground, and the host of traders and camp-followers who had followed the army to Africa caused disorder and demoralization throughout the camp.

At the end of 148 Scipio returned to Rome to stand for the Aedileship. But the people, hearing of his services in the war and placing their confidence on one who bore the name of Scipio, made him Consul, though he was only thirty-seven, six years below the legal age for the office. His first task in 147 was to clear out the camp-followers and restore discipline in the army before Carthage. He then managed to get possession of the suburb Magalia, as the Carthaginians were unable to defend a long line of wall with their hastily contrived means of defence. But supplies still reached the enemy by sea, and Scipio was obliged to undertake the difficult task of constructing a mole from the Taenia to the shore below the town that he might prevent all access to the commercial harbour.

After long and exhausting labour he completed the mole, only to find that the Carthaginians had cut a canal through from the naval harbour to the sea beyond the point at which his mole reached the shore. However a few days later the Carthaginian ships returning from an indecisive fight were fallen upon by the Roman squadron, as they crowded together to pass in at the narrow entrance, and so severely handled that they could not put to sea again.

By this time Hasdrubal's field force had been broken up by Laelius, Scipio's colleague, and disunion and factions within the walls were weakening the city. In the spring of 146 Scipio captured the commercial harbour, while Laelius surprised the naval harbour, and the whole of the lower part of the town fell into the hands of the besiegers. The Byrsa and the streets leading up to it alone held out. Incessant fighting followed for six days and nights along each street and from house to house amid the grimmest scenes of slaughter. To prepare for the final attack on the citadel Scipio ordered the whole of the buildings already captured to be burnt to the ground, and thousands of poor wretches who had concealed themselves in the cellars perished miserably. Then at last the citadel and the 50,000 survivors surrendered, among them Hasdrubal, whose wife scorning submission threw herself and her children into the flames.

When all was over, the plough was drawn over the site of Carthage and a curse laid on the man who should rebuild it. The land of Carthage was made the Province of Africa with Utica for its capital. Rome's great rival was gone; but the Rome which destroyed Carthage was not the Rome of the First Punic War. Conquest and the wealth which conquest brought had weakened the strong simple Roman character, and the money-loving spirit which had been the curse of Carthage was taking a firm hold on the conqueror.

Spain. In the West the Second Punic War was followed by a series of small wars. The Cisalpine Gauls and the Ligurians in turn kept the Romans busy ; and Corsica and Sardinia gave considerable trouble, until Tiberius Gracchus defeated the Sardinians decisively in 177 and brought so many slaves to Rome that *Sardi venales*, ' Sardinians for sale,' became a proverb for a low-priced article. But it was in Spain that the Romans had most to do. Nearly seventy years passed before order was established here, and the mountain tribes of the North-West were not finally subdued till the days of Augustus. The story of these seventy years is a disgrace to Rome, for military incapacity and treacherous dealing went hand in hand. Moreover Rome with her taste for exacting indemnities expected wars to be profitable. Tribute must be paid by the province and supplies requisitioned from the provincials. The generals caught the same spirit and, being freed by distance from the control of the government, used the opportunity to fill their own purses at the expense of the province.

At the close of the Second Punic War Spain was divided into two provinces, Hither Spain on the east coast and Further Spain to the south and west. But the interior was still unconquered, and the Celtiberi and the Lusitani in the centre and west of the peninsula were by no means ready to submit to Rome. In 195 Cato defeated the Celtiberi and pulled down the walls of many of the native towns and, by arranging a fixed amount of tribute to be paid by each community, freed the inhabitants for a time from the extortion of the tax-collectors. Fifteen years of comparative quiet followed, and Gracchus in 179 after suppressing a revolt won the confidence of the Celtiberi by firm and honest government. By founding towns and encouraging the leading natives to enlist in the Roman army he gave the Spaniards a prospect of orderly development under Roman influence. The memory of his work kept Spain quiet under twenty-five years of misgovernment. But in 153 the Lusitani and Celtiberi took up arms and twenty years fighting followed, in which the incompetence of the Roman generals and the lack of discipline among their men were only matched by the treachery which they used towards the natives.

Lusitanian War, 153–136 B.C. After three years of unsuccessful warfare the Romans in 150 managed to make their way into the lands of the Lusitani on the west of the peninsula. Thereupon Sulpicius Galba, the Praetor of Further Spain, by offering them better lands than their own, induced some thousands to surrender their arms and then massacred them; and although he was prosecuted by Cato for this act on his return to Rome, his wealth procured his acquittal. Viriathus however, a young Lusitanian chief, escaped from the massacre and for ten years by his skill in guerilla warfare he inflicted repeated defeats upon the Romans. In 141 he even entrapped the Roman army under Fabius in a rocky valley and compelled them to buy their lives by a treaty which recognized Viriathus as king of the Lusitani. The next year however the Romans repudiated the treaty, and Caepio who was sent out to Spain bribed some Lusitanian officers to murder Viriathus in his sleep. With the loss of their leader the power of the Lusitani was broken, and D. Junius Brutus by 136 reduced Further Spain to order.

Celtiberian War, 153–133 B.C. Disputes with different tribes of the Celtiberi kept Hither Spain in a ferment during the whole of the Lusitanian War, and Viriathus in 143 induced the strong town of Numantia to take up arms. Defeats of the Romans were followed by treaties which the Senate repudiated, but neither force nor treachery could subdue the town. In 137 the Consul Mancinus was surrounded and forced to surrender with his army, the Celtiberi sparing the lives of the Romans only at the intercession of young Gracchus whom they trusted for his father's sake. But the Senate, just as at the Caudine Forks, repudiated the bargain now made and thought that honour was saved by handing over Mancinus himself to the enemy. At last in 134 Scipio Aemilianus the conqueror of Carthage was sent out to end the war. He took with him a staff of personal friends, the Praetorian cohort of later days, and as at Carthage by rigorous discipline restored the character of the army and then set himself to stamp out all opposition in the open country. After this had been done, he surrounded Numantia with a double line of walls five miles in extent and began the siege. For fifteen months the city held out, and with its fall in 133 the resistance of Spain except for the tribes of the North West was at an end.

The story of the seventy years which followed Zama does not reflect credit on Rome, whether we look at the course of events in Greece, Africa, or Spain. But it must be remembered that the period is a time of reaction from the strain of the struggle against Hannibal, and that Rome was face to face with the problems of ' Empire ' for the first time. We shall have to consider in the next chapter the effects of war and expansion upon Rome, and we shall find that they changed her character. But there was in her still the genius for government. Spain in particular prospered in after years under her rule and assimilated much of the Roman spirit, producing Latin writers of a high order such as Lucan and Martial, and in Trajan one of the greatest of the Emperors.

DATES
195.   Cato in Spain.
179.   Tiberius Gracchus in Spain.
153–136.   Lusitanian War.
140.   Murder of Viriathus.

DATES
153–133.   Celtiberian War.
    133.   Numantia taken by Scipio Aemilianus.
149–146.   Third Punic War.
    146.   Destruction of Carthage by Scipio Aemilianus.

CHAPTER XIV

ROME, ITALY AND THE PROVINCES

IN the course of the 150 years of continuous fighting
which had made Rome the head of an Empire, changes
had taken place in the city itself which were the result
of the new set of circumstances with which Rome had to
deal.   The city had passed through a tremendous crisis,
which had called for every steadying influence which she
possessed and for the continuous services of her best men.
Emerging from the struggle with Hannibal to find her
population diminished, her treasury exhausted, Italy devastated and the Italian yeomen ruined or killed, she was
none the less the dominant power of the Mediterranean.
From conquest and trade wealth soon poured in upon her
and with it a desire to keep for herself the advantages for
which she had paid so dearly.   The old idea of ' incorporation ' which had made Italy one body and Rome its heart
was forgotten, and exclusiveness—the claim that the
Romans alone should profit by expansion—became the
prevailing spirit of Rome.

The Senate and Magistrates. We have seen (Chap. III)
that, while the Senate was in theory nothing more than
a body which the magistrates might consult, it became
in practice the supreme power in Rome, since no magistrates would act contrary to its wishes.   It was in reality

a collection of magistrates and ex-magistrates appointed for
life ; for election to the Quaestorship (the lowest Curule
office) was the qualification for a seat, and though a man
might be excluded by the Censors at the revision of the lists
every five years, such exclusions were rare and good reasons
for them had to be given. It was thus a tremendous power
in the state, an "Assembly of Kings" as Cineas had termed
it, containing all those Romans who had experience of
government and independent of the changing breeze of
popular favour. During the long wars and especially during
the struggle with Hannibal the Romans wisely left the
conduct of affairs in the hands of such a body, and its
steadying influence and wise, determined administration
pulled Rome through the crisis. Year after year the best
available men were put in command of the Roman armies,
Fabius or one of the Scipios, Marcellus, Aemilius Paullus,
Gracchus or Flamininus, and these men neither shirked
their responsibilities nor grudged their lives, if need arose,
in the service of the state.

Little by little the circle of families which supplied
men for the great offices narrowed. Naturally the Romans
looked to those families, in which there was a great tradition and where father had handed down to son the experience he had gained, and a narrow ring of official
families came into being. This development could not
fail to be bad in the end. Beginning with the selection
of certain families because they were specially capable,
it ended in the exclusion of all other families whether they
had ability or not. The tendency of the governing aristocracy to harden into an exclusive caste had been already
seen in the adoption of certain marks of officialdom, the
right to carry masks (*imagines*) of dead ancestors in funeral
processions and afterwards to range them in the halls of
their houses, the senatorial ring, the special seats at public
festivals, and the stripe of purple on the toga ; and the

practical abolition of the Dictatorship after the Second
Punic War aimed at preventing the intrusion of an outsider
into the official class under the influence of a great crisis.
With the narrowing of this caste a danger arose of the
oligarchy overreaching itself and ending in despotism.
Scipio Africanus, through the merits of his father and uncle
and his own successes, found the people willing to give
him almost royal honours.   By his influence his mediocre
brother L. Scipio Asiaticus rose to high position, and for
many years the family of the Scipios was not unlike a
ruling dynasty. To meet this danger the *Lex Villia Annalis*
of 180 was passed fixing a definite order in which offices
should be held and an age-qualification for each.   This
with the revival of the rule suspended during the war with
Hannibal, that no man should hold the same office twice
within ten years, kept excessive power out of the hands
of one family and made safe the position of the oligarchy.

The *Nobiles* or official families stood in sharp contrast
to the unofficial and resented the intrusion of a *novus
homo* as much as in the old days the Patricians had resented the rise of a Plebeian.   There was opposition, no
doubt, to the official clique. A Flaminius or a Varro
owes his unpopularity in history as much to the fact that
he opposed the ruling caste as to the disaster at Trasimene
or Cannae; and Cato, from the point of view of an old
Roman, could not endure the changes in Roman ways
which years had brought with them.   But oligarchy stood
firm, even when oligarchs were degenerate. The brother
of Africanus was accused of misappropriating money
received from Antiochus; the brother of Flamininus was
guilty of murder ; and the generals who showed ability or
honesty between 200 and 130 B.C. were few and far between.
But apart from other considerations office was a costly
matter, and few could afford to give the shows and presents
which were expected ; it was also a profitable matter,

and the fewer families to share in the plunder of a conquered enemy or the pickings from a province, the better
for those few. In the next century the government of
the war-period was looked upon as a golden age, but from
the first it contained the seed which produced the fruits
of exclusiveness and corruption.

The Comitia and the People. With the real business
of government left to the Senate the Comitia rarely did
more than elect the magistrates and pass the formal
declarations of war. The *Comitia Centuriata* was reor-
ganized about the year 241 to accommodate the divisions
by classes and centuries to the division of the citizens
by tribes; this had the effect of making the centuries
subdivisions of the tribes and reducing the predominance
of wealth. But the Comitia was unsuited to take any
prominent part in affairs. The body of Roman citizens
was not confined to the city of Rome but distributed
through the western part of Central Italy as well as in the
colonies throughout the peninsula. Those who remained
in Rome were not likely to be the most capable, and the
hard-headed farmers of Latium were not likely to come up
to Rome to vote, if they could help it. Moreover while
the wars with Hannibal, Macedon, Carthage and Spain,
were in progress, many of those who might have voted
were unable to exercise their vote owing to their military
duties. Thus the regular voters did not represent the
whole body of citizens, and at best they could in time
of danger do no more than follow the wishes of the
well-informed Senators. Once and again the Comitia
took matters in its own hands, appointing Africanus to
command in Spain and Scipio Aemilianus to finish the
siege of Carthage. But such action only served to remind
the people that the power was ultimately in its own hands
and emphasized the general supremacy of the Senate.

In the course of the wars the loss of Roman life was

enormous. The number of citizens sank from 270,000 before the Second Punic War to 214,000 at its close, and the loss would fall on the best class, the strong and able-bodied who could do something for their country. With the decay of the relationship of Client and Patron (p. 10), which was inevitable in the life of a large city, and with the poverty which long wars cause, the clients had become a rabble of beggars and swelled the ranks of the ineffectives. At the close of a war the long-service soldiers would volunteer for a new war or go to a Roman colony or try their hands at farming. Many of them sank down into the ruck of the Roman mob and with their acquired taste for violence and plundering increased the number of criminals. Besides this, Rome as the head of an Empire and the centre of Mediterranean commerce began to attract foreigners of all sorts, and these brought with them the vices and not the virtues of foreign countries. On this miscellaneous crowd was turned some part of the stream of wealth which conquest brought with it. Distributions of corn had begun in times of severest stress, and games and shows innumerable were given to keep the populace in a good temper. The noble anxious for office bribed ; the wealthy trader, who feared prosecution if an enemy were elected, bribed also. The result was that the populace of Rome degenerated in the course of a century to a very low level. It became a weak and clamorous mob, eager for bread and the games, *Panem et Circenses*, eager for any novelty except work. Public spirit was at a discount. The duty of filling the legions was shirked more and more, and an increasing proportion of the Roman army was drawn from Italians and allies, while in the matter of distribution of rewards and booty the claims of the Romans grew as their services decreased.

Italy. The effect of the sound policy of Rome in early days towards Italy was seen in the Second Punic

War. No general rising in support of Hannibal took place, and little real help reached him from those districts which did join him. But the war ruined Italy. For fifteen years the struggle went on over the face of the peninsula ; farms were ruined, buildings destroyed, stocks exhausted, and the land so devastated that throughout the south the work of cultivation must be undertaken from the beginning once more. Unfortunately the men who should have gone back to their farms were dead. We do not know the loss of life among the Italians which was caused by the war, but it must have been heavier than among the Romans, since the former supplied half the troops and the war was in their midst. At any rate from large districts of Italy the farming class disappeared entirely. In its place veteran soldiers were planted on Italian soil ; but at best they could not have been fitted to settle down at once into steady and successful farmers, while in fact they were faced with an unexpected difficulty. Expansion had brought Rome into touch with the great corn-producing countries of the ancient world, Sicily and Egypt and Africa. Italy was never a great corn-producing country, but the Italian farmers had found a ready market for what corn they grew. Now the corn imported from those places undersold in Rome the produce of Italian cornfields. No doubt the amount imported at first was small, but it had its effect ; and with the increased cost of living which the spread of luxury brings with it, the farmer could make no profit and gave up his land. Roman capitalists had already turned their attention to Italian land, and they had snapped up large slices of Ager Publicus, when conquests had brought fresh lands to the state[1]. The punishment of those districts which had helped Hannibal took the shape of confiscation of territory,

---

[1] Cp. Flaminius's law of 232 dealing with the land of the Senones (p. 81).

and now the capitalists, with no one else able to make a living out of the land, had their chance. Land which would not support free farmers might be made to pay by slave-labour, when the supply of slaves was plentiful and cheap. No scruples of humanity interfered. Cato himself advocated the working of slaves to death and disapproved of caring for them in any way, as being less profitable than grinding the life out of them and then buying a new lot. So with vineyards, olive-gardens and pasture-land some profit was made out of the soil of Italy. But over wide areas runaway slaves who had turned brigands were the terror of the country, and hardly a free labourer was to be found. The vigorous farming class, once the backbone of Italy, had almost passed away.

Meanwhile the attitude of Rome to the Italians had undergone a change. Perhaps the help given to Hannibal alienated Roman sympathies, but the wealth which followed expansion and the desire of keeping all the good things in Roman hands were mainly responsible. Once Rome had opened her gates to all the best Italians and in one grade or another of citizenship had welcomed them as members of herself. Now the policy was changed. Of colonies sent out after 200 B.C. only four were Latin colonies in which non-Romans might share, and Aquileia, the latest of them, was founded in 181. Between the years 200 and 150 decrees were passed expelling Latins from Rome, and laws enacted which limited strictly their old right of migration to Rome. In the distributions of land or money, which followed conquest, the Italians received a smaller share than the Romans. The Romans seem to have drawn between themselves and the Italians the same distinction which once existed within their own ranks between Patrician and Plebeian. They were now keeping to themselves not office only or political power, but money and the material advantages of conquest.

The Provinces. Rome by 140 B.C. had conquered a great part of the lands round the Mediterranean. Along the northern shore from the Aegean on the east to Spain in the west all the coast was in her possession except the south of Gaul; and the province of Africa gave her a footing in the southern continent. From 241 B.C., when Sicily became the first Roman province, no attempt was made to bind up the overseas dominions with Rome as Italy had been bound. They were to be dependencies

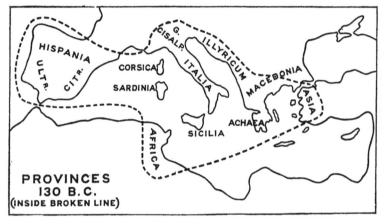

The Provinces of Rome in 130 B.C.

governed from Rome for the profit of Rome, and the fact that no *tributum* was collected from Italy after 167 proves that the provinces fulfilled their function in this respect.

The guiding principle in the treatment of these dominions was to break up all leagues and confederacies, but to leave untouched all local institutions and customs which were not dangerous. The government of the province was in accordance with the *lex provinciae* or conditions imposed at the time of its conquest; and the administration of affairs was under a Roman governor or

Praetor, with a Quaestor as financial officer to assist him, Legati or deputy governors, and as large a force as was necessary to keep the province in order. The distance from Rome and the length of office—for a governor often had his tenure prolonged under the title of Propraetor— coupled with the absence of any right of appeal (*provocatio*) for the provincials from his decision, gave the governor an almost royal position, and it is not surprising that he often misused it. Even if he meant to be honest, he had no experience to help him, and presents from natives or tax-collectors were rarely to be distinguished from bribes ; and since the state intended to make a profit, the governor, who had not obtained his post without heavy expenses, followed the state's example by filling his own purse. This plundering of provincials led in 149 to the establish- ment of a special court in Rome to try cases of extortion (*quaestio de rebus repetundis*). But the time had not yet come when the remark was justified that a governor must make three fortunes, one to pay the expenses of obtaining office, one to bribe the jury which tried him on his return, and one for himself.

The taxes of the provinces were generally collected in the way which had been usual before the Roman occupa- tion, as *decumae* (tithes) in Sicily, *stipendia* (fixed sums) in Spain ; and the amount exacted by the Senate was fre- quently less than had been previously demanded. But the method of collection was bad. Big capitalists or Publicani farmed the taxes, i.e. paid to the treasury the amount required from the province and then recouped themselves by squeezing what they could out of the provincials by extortion. However, with all its faults Roman provincial government was a good thing. Security for life and pro- perty was on the whole assured, and with good order trade and general prosperity increased. Roads and har- bours were built, the frontiers protected from the raids of barbarians, and the natural resources of the province developed. The Romans had a genius for government, and they did govern. That they fell short of the standard which the modern world would require, does not discount the good work which they did achieve.

CHAPTER XV

THE GRACCHI

The coming revolution. Selfish exclusiveness was the characteristic of the Rome which we have described in the last chapter. Wealth had poured in and luxury in its train, and each class was bent upon keeping for itself the good things which it could lay hands on. The *Nobiles* formed a narrow clique and resented the intrusion of a *novus homo* into the circle which shared the profits of office. The ordinary citizens held the Italians at arm's length and denied them the vote or their fair share in the rewards of victory. But neither the official class nor the common people had preserved its old character, which might have justified them in arrogating to themselves any special privileges. A state in which a portion of the community enjoys a position, which neither its superiority in character and ability nor its effective strength will justify, is on the way to a revolution. In the story of the next hundred years we have to trace the steps of that revolution in Rome. It begins with the discovery of the Gracchi that one man with the mob of Rome behind him could shake the citadel of Senatorial government. Next Marius showed that an army was a more effective force than a mob ; but he was no statesman and could not use the power which he had. Sulla combined the qualities of a general and a statesman

and for a year or more was an Emperor in all but name;
but he used his power to bolster up the tottering government of the Senate. Pompeius wavered between loyalty
to the old order of things and the wish for his own
aggrandisement, till his rival Caesar, strong alike in
the support of an army and his own unmatched abilities,
became the master of Rome. Just as the revolution
overthrew the government of the nobles without giving
the ordinary citizen any less powerful a master, so the
Italians won by degrees admission to Roman citizenship
only to find that the power of the vote had passed away
and that everything was under the control of the master
of the legions.

The Land Question. The Land Question first brought
into play the forces of revolution. Of land confiscated
after war the Romans had commonly given or sold
the part which was already in cultivation in allotments to
any citizen who applied. Rough uncultivated land any
citizen might ' occupy ' (*possidere*) and bring into cultivation, as a tenant paying a nominal rent but fairly sure
of never being disturbed. On land unsuited for the
plough cattle might be pastured on payment of a tax
called *Scriptura*. From the start it was not likely that
men with little capital could take up rough land and wait
till it became productive, and the larger part of the Ager
Publicus had inevitably got into the hands of rich men.
As years went on, the nominal rent was often not collected;
and not unnaturally the occupiers began to regard themselves as owners, not tenants, and sold or bought Ager
Publicus as though it were private property. A difficult
situation arose. On the one hand if the state asserted its
legal claim to such land, it would in many cases be de-
priving men of property for which they had paid or which
they had at any rate improved in value ; while if no
change were made, the land would benefit none but a few.

We have seen that the war with Hannibal brought ruin to Italian farms and almost wiped out the farming class, and that new economic conditions, such as the competition of foreign corn and the increase of slave-labour, accentuated the difficulty. Not only one class of state-land but every class had in great measure fallen into the hands of big capitalists; and their slave-gangs had taken the place of the free labourers and small farmers of earlier days. This system of *Latifundia* or large estates worked by slaves was bad in itself; and the inequality between the landed and the landless classes was now keenly felt. So long as Rome was still conquering Italy and Italian land was still being distributed, the grievance did not press heavily. But after the war with Pyrrhus, which marked the completion of the conquest, distributions of Italian land naturally ceased, except where small portions remained undivided or rebellion gave an excuse for further confiscation. Then came the pinch. Roman citizens were anxious for land but could get none, since the state-land which should have been available was in the hands of a few great landlords.

Tiberius Gracchus. Tiberius Gracchus, whose father had done much for the re-organizing of Spain, was brought up by his mother Cornelia, a daughter of Scipio Africanus and the most cultured woman of her time; and his sister married Scipio Aemilianus. He was thus in touch with the most distinguished and at the same time the most liberal-minded family in Rome and had himself gained credit at the siege of Carthage and in the recent Spanish war. He had been struck on his return from the west by the desolation of Etruria, through which he passed; and in standing for the Tribuneship for 133 B.C. he was determined to make an effort to get the free labourers and small farmers back on to the soil of Italy.

He was duly elected Tribune and introduced a *Lex*

Agraria on the lines of the obsolete Licinian law of 367. Dealing only with the land held in ' occupation ' he proposed :

(i)   That no one should hold more than 500 *iugera* (300 acres) with a further allowance of 250 for each son, provided that the total amount did not exceed 1000 *iugera*. Compensation was to be paid for any improvements effected on the land which was surrendered.

(ii)   That the land thus recovered for the state should be let in small lots on perpetual leases to poor citizens.

(iii)   That a Commission of three should be appointed to carry out the redistribution of land.

The proposals were certainly an honest attempt to deal with the question ; but though they were welcomed by the mass of the citizens, there was vigorous opposition from the rich occupiers. Octavius, another Tribune, interposed his veto and forbade the submitting of the measure to the votes of the people. Tiberius was apparently checkmated; but he was an enthusiast, convinced of the justice of his cause and impatient of opposition. He tried the effect of his own veto in stopping all business ; but his adversaries would not yield, and he then introduced his proposals once more, but this time without the compensation clause. Octavius renewed his veto and stood firm against all entreaties and against the suggestion that a vote should be taken as to whether he or Tiberius should resign. Then Gracchus made his first unconstitutional step. He proposed in the Assembly that Octavius should be deposed. Seventeen out of the thirty-five tribes had voted for the deposition, when Gracchus made a last appeal to his colleague to withdraw the veto before the eighteenth tribe should decide the day. But it was in vain. Octavius was obstinate; the next vote went against him, and he was deposed. Soon afterwards the Agrarian Law was passed, and Tiberius with his brother Gaius and his father-in-law Appius Claudius were elected as the commissioners to carry it out.

Tiberius had done something more important than pass a law. He had broken the constitution. It was a wise principle in the Roman state which made a magistrate secure during his term of office and postponed the calling of him to account till the year was ended. For independent and honest government was at an end, if a magistrate was at the mercy of a momentary wave of popular feeling. Tiberius had set the example of disregarding the law and appealing to the force of the People who supported him; an example which others who had an army instead of a mob at their backs would copy with far-reaching results.

For the present the distribution of land went on, and the new settlers were helped to stock their farms by grants of money from the treasures of Attalus, who had just died and left his wealth and the lands of Pergamum to Rome. But it was known that Gracchus would be prosecuted at the conclusion of his year of office. To secure immunity for a further period he offered himself for re-election for the year 132 contrary to the established rule, if not the actual law of the constitution. But his popularity was on the wane. The disturbance caused by the redistribution of land had alienated many supporters, and the country voters who would have backed him up were busy with their harvest-work at the time. The veto was again employed by his opponents, and at an adjourned meeting on the Capitol rioting broke out between the two parties. The Senate was sitting near at hand in the Temple of Fides, and wild rumours reached it that Gracchus was demanding the crown. The consul refused to interfere; but the younger Senators led by Scipio Nasica broke up the benches of the Senate House, and arming themselves with the fragments and calling on their adherents to join with them, sallied forth upon the friends of Gracchus. Gracchus and 300 of his party were beaten to death and their bodies thrown into the Tiber. The first blood had been shed in the civil strife which lasted for the next hundred years.

Scipio Aemilianus. The Agrarian Law remained in force, and the vacancy on the Commission caused by Tiberius's death was filled up. But the disturbance of the old occupiers of the land caused much discontent, especially in the case of those Italian occupiers who were deprived. Scipio Aemilianus, the conqueror of Numantia, had not returned from Spain before Tiberius's death and had maintained a cautious attitude when informed of it, saying that his brother-in-law deserved his fate, if he had aimed at royal power. Now on his return men looked to see what line he would take; for his military successes made him the leading man in Rome and he was known to have sympathy with the Italians. He succeeded in transferring the powers of the Land Commission to the Consuls, probably in the hope that they would consider Italian interests. He may even have had the aim of admitting the Italians to the franchise and by their votes diminishing the power of the degenerate city populace. But his wise policy aroused the jealousy of all parties. In 129 Scipio was found dead in his bed, under circumstances which suggested murder, on the day on which he was to have set forth his views in a public meeting.

The question of the status of the Italians however continued to engage attention. In a reactionary spirit a Tribune carried a law in 126 expelling all Italians from Rome. In the following year Fulvius Flaccus, one of the Land Commissioners, proposed the extension of the franchise to the Italians. This proposal caused great excitement throughout Italy. When it was rejected and Flaccus sent off in haste out of the way to a war in Liguria, Fregellae, which had been one of the most loyal of Latin towns during the war with Hannibal, revolted from Rome. But it was taken by treachery and utterly destroyed together with its inhabitants.

C. Gracchus. Tiberius Gracchus had been a single-minded enthusiast without much practical knowledge of politics, led by his impetuosity into revolutionary methods. His younger brother Gaius shared his liberal views but was at the same time an abler and less scrupulous man. Setting out with the definite purpose of avenging his brother, he saw the need of organizing a party which would enable him to carry through his policy. For this end he tried to combine every element which would help him to break down the Senatorial monopoly of government; he appealed alike to the mob of Rome and to the Italians, to honest-minded reformers as well as to capitalists who wished to share in the spoils of office. He had served in Sardinia as Quaestor; and the Senate recognizing that he was a dangerous man kept him out of Rome for two years by prolonging his office. But in 124 he returned and was elected Tribune for 123.

During that year by his extraordinary personal influence and the baits, which he held out to each class in turn, he ruled like a king and passed a series of laws almost without opposition. We can group them to some extent according to their subjects without going into all their details. But it must be remembered that Gracchus acted from mixed motives, revenge for his brother's death and a desire to get the power of government out of the hands of a narrow clique; while for his purpose he was forced to be unscrupulous in holding out every bait to win the support of this class or of that.

(i) **Revenge.** After securing his position by a law allowing a tribune to be re-elected he re-enacted the old law of appeal, dating from the first year of the Republic, that no citizen should be put to death without the right of appeal to the Comitia. Popilius, who had acted on the commission which after 133 hunted out and punished Tiberius's friends, went into exile to avoid condemnation.

(ii) **Bidding for support of the Populace.** New laws were passed to improve the conditions of military service and to lighten punishments in the army; and the Agrarian Law of Tiberius was again put in force. But most of the land inside Italy had already been distributed, and Gaius arranged for the foundation of colonies, especially of one on the site of Carthage to be called Junonia and to be open to citizens and Italians. This wise proposal was however more than balanced by the introduction of a *Lex Frument-aria* or corn-law to provide corn for the populace below market-price. Each citizen was to have the right to buy each month a sufficient amount of corn to feed him at just half the current price. This law won the support of all the idlers of Rome, who were set free by it from the need of doing regular work; and it attracted to the city men who preferred idleness and food in Rome to work and slender fare on their farms. Gracchus had begun on a path on which it was hard to stop. Gradually under later agitators the number of the recipients of corn grew, and the price was lowered, till at last the Roman mob became convinced that it was entitled to free corn, free amusements, and above all freedom from work.

(iii) **Bidding for the support of the Equites.** When we speak of the Equites at this period of Roman history, we are speaking not of the cavalry—that was mainly supplied by the allies—but of a social class in Rome. While the Nobiles had hardened into a clique or caste, there had grown up in opposition to the official order a sort of unofficial aristocracy of wealth. A *Lex Claudia* of 218 had forbidden Senators to engage in commerce. This had left the exploitation of Rome's new position as the commercial centre of the Mediterranean to non-Senators, who made enormous profits and became something like the commercial magnates, bankers and financiers of a modern capital. They were called Equites, because they possessed the amount of property which would qualify them for admission to the old centuries of Knights, but apart from this they had no connection with the army. Gracchus, honestly seeing the advantage of opening up an official career to men of this class, saw at the same time the opportunity of using their influence to overthrow the government of the Senate which had killed his brother. His object was to make them feel that he was their friend and that they were capable of acting together as an organized political party. He began by passing a law that the taxes of the new province of Asia, which had been formed out of Attalus's dominions, should be put up to auction at Rome, and thus practically prevented any provincial *publicanus* from competing with the financiers of Rome. He then went on to enact that the juries which sat in the *Quaestiones Perpetuae* or standing courts should be composed no longer of Senators but of Equites. These were courts, each for the trial of one special class of offence; we have heard already (p. 135) of the court which dealt with cases of extortion in the provinces. It was good, no doubt, that the jury which tried a Senatorial governor on his return should not be composed of Senators. But the Equites were no more honest than the Senate and would be prejudiced against an honest governor who had protected the province against extortionate *publicani*; and the purity of the law-courts was in no way improved. From Gracchus's point of view however the Equites, by having a special duty assigned to them, were led to feel their unity, and the two classes of Senators and Equites were brought into conflict.

(iv) **Italian Citizenship and the fall of Gracchus.** This legislative programme took up the whole of one year;

but C. Gracchus was re-elected without protest as Tribune for 122 B.C. With the co-operation of Fulvius Flaccus, now returned from Liguria, he proposed a law for giving citizenship to the Italians. But the Roman mob, which had welcomed the worst of his proposals, turned against the best of them in its jealous exclusiveness, and Gracchus with all his eloquence could get no support for his measure. Moreover the foundation of the new colonies had to be seen to, and Gracchus was forced to cross to Africa to superintend the building of Junonia. With the spell of his personality removed the Senate had its chance. A tribune, Livius Drusus, was put up to outbid Gracchus with the promise of twelve colonies to be founded and the abolition of corporal punishment in the army. Stories were spread abroad that, in fulfilment of Scipio's curse on the rebuilding of Carthage, hyaenas had torn up the boundary stones of the new colony; and Gracchus on his return to Rome found his popularity gone. He was not re-elected Tribune, and a proposal was made to rescind the law for the founding of Junonia. On the day of voting there was great excitement. Antullius, a servant of the consul Opimius, by his insolence provoked Gracchus's supporters and was killed. The meeting broke up, and the Senate passed the Ultimum Decretum—*videant consules ne quid detrimenti respublica capiat*—a declaration of martial law corresponding to the appointment of a dictator in earlier times. Next morning Opimius summoned all his party to meet him with armed attendants in the Forum, sent orders to Gracchus and Flaccus, who had taken refuge on the Aventine, to appear before him, and on their refusal advanced against them. Two hundred of Gracchus's friends were killed. Flaccus was discovered in hiding and put to death. Gracchus, saved for the moment by the devotion of two friends who gave their lives for his, fled across the Tiber with a slave and was found dead with the slave at his side in the Grove of the Furies. Three thousand of his adherents were subsequently tried and put to death by Opimius, who then dedicated a Temple of Concord to mark the occasion.

The agrarian reforms of the Gracchi had no permanent effect. The allotments of land were left in the hands of the new tenants; but within a year the prohibition on their sale was withdrawn, and gradually their occupiers drifted back into the city. In 118 all further distribution was stopped; and in 111 all Ager Publicus held in ' occupation ' was made definitely the property of its occupiers to be dealt with as they pleased. But the influence of the political work of the Gracchi remained. They had given voice to the discontent of the masses with Senatorial government and had shown that one man could resist it for a time; and the younger brother had organized the Equites as a class which was not likely to submit tamely to the Senatorial monopoly of power.

DATES

133–132. Ti. Gracchus.
129. Death of Scipio Aemilianus.
125. Flaccus proposes citizenship of Italians.
125. Revolt of Fregellae.
123–121. C. Gracchus.

CHAPTER XVI

JUGURTHINE AND CIMBRIAN WARS

Sicily, Asia and Gaul. During the period of the Gracchi things were not at a standstill outside Italy, but important events were happening in various quarters. The evil of large estates worked by gangs of slaves, which Ti. Gracchus had aimed at checking, was rampant in

Sicily. The hold, which an overseer could exercise over his gang, was precarious, and the hills of the island at all times gave a refuge to runaways. Outbreaks of the slaves were put down without great trouble in 139 and the following years. But matters came to a head in 134, when a Syrian slave, named Eunus, by his pretension to magical power inspired a body of four hundred of his fellows with enough confidence to seize Enna and massacre the inhabitants. This gave the signal for a general rising of the slaves in the island, and free labourers, brigands and gladiators joined in. Eunus assumed the style of a Roman governor, drilled his bands into an organized army, and for three years held his own against consular armies. At length in 132 the Consul Rupilius stormed Enna; and within a year Eunus was taken and the revolt stamped out by wholesale crucifixion of the rebels.

In the East, when Greece became part of the Roman dominions, the king of Pergamum had been left independent. But expansion was in the air; and when in 133 Attalus III died, the Senate gladly accepted the kingdom and treasures which he bequeathed to Rome. We have seen how the money was used to further the ends of the Gracchi. The organization of the country into the Province of Asia was not carried out wisely. The right to collect the tribute became a bribe which C. Gracchus used to attract the Roman financiers to his side; and of the land itself considerable parts were given over to neighbouring kings, one of whom, Mithradates of Pontus, proved a dangerous foe later on; while the suppression of the fleet which the kings of Pergamum had kept up gave a free hand to the pirates of the Eastern Mediterranean.

In South Gaul Massilia had retained its independence and prospered greatly. But the Romans were gradually extending their dominions along the coast of the Gulf of Genoa, and a series of small wars brought Rome into

contact with the tribes of Gaul itself.   While C. Gracchus
was busy with his schemes in Rome, hard fighting was
going on against the Arverni, who were the leading tribe
of South Gaul, and their allies the Allobroges.   Rome
was victorious with the help of the Aedui, the chief rivals
of the Arverni.   Entering into a lasting friendship with
this tribe she formed in 121 along the coast from the Alps
to the Pyrenees a new province, Gallia Narbonensis, named
after its capital Narbo, but known in Gaul as the Province.
The name still survives in the modern Provence.

Numidia.   More serious fighting followed a few years
later in Africa.   On the death of Masinissa in 149
Scipio Aemilianus had divided Numidia between three
sons of the late king, of whom two died and the third
Micipsa ruled as sole king till his death in 118.   Micipsa
left his dominions between his two sons, Hiempsal and
Adherbal, and his nephew Jugurtha.   The nephew was
older and much more able than his cousins.   Handsome
and with a charm of manner and a soldierly bearing which
won the hearts of the Berber race he led, he had learned
at once the arts of war and the degeneracy of the Roman
army by serving with a Numidian corps under Scipio at
Numantia.   He had unlimited ambition and no scruples
in employing treachery and cruelty to win his objects.
Jugurtha murdered Hiempsal; and provoking a war with
Adherbal in 116 he drove him eastwards into the Roman
province of Africa.   Adherbal was forced to appeal for help
to Rome.   But Jugurtha was not behindhand.   Bribes
were freely distributed, and a commission, which was sent
to Africa under Scaurus, divided Numidia between the
cousins, Adherbal receiving the more civilized eastern
half with its capital Cirta and Jugurtha the fertile and more
warlike west.   After four years Jugurtha began again.
Invading Adherbal's country he shut him up in Cirta and
with the help of bribes deluded the Roman embassies

which Adherbal's entreaties brought on the scene. At
last in 112 Cirta fell. Adherbal and his supporters were
put to death and with them some Italian traders.

War with Jugurtha, 111–105 B.C. Even now Jugurtha
might have gone on unmolested, had it not been that a
tribune Memmius saw a chance of making the matter
a party question in Rome. Accusing the Senate and
its leader Scaurus of dishonesty and mismanagement he
forced on a declaration of war. The consul Bestia was
sent out with a force and made some pretence of fighting
Jugurtha. But the king, finding that Bestia could be
bribed, went through the farce of surrendering on condition that he should give up a few elephants, pay a small
indemnity and be allowed to keep the whole of Numidia.

All this mockery of war and surrender was bringing
discredit on Rome; and Memmius saw in the popular
indignation a means of pressing home his attack on the
government. He proposed that an enquiry should be
held as to the conduct of Bestia and that Jugurtha should
be summoned as a witness to Rome. The prince came
willingly enough, hoping to further his ends by bribes;
and when Memmius questioned him, another tribune
forbade him to reply from fear that the shady actions
of the Senators might come to light. The populace was
furious; but even then nothing might have come of it
all, had not Jugurtha overstepped all bounds by murdering in Rome his cousin Massiva, whom he regarded as
a possible rival for the throne. Then at last the Senate
was shamed into ordering him out of Italy, and he left
Rome with the words, 'A city for sale and soon to perish,
if it can but find a purchaser.'

War began again in 110, and the consul Sp. Albinus
could effect nothing. After he had come home to hold
the elections, his brother Aulus, who was left in charge,
was enticed out into the desert to attack a fort called

Suthul and there was surprised by Jugurtha, who spared the lives of the soldiers only on condition that the Romans should evacuate Numidia after passing under the yoke.

Metellus. The Romans were thoroughly ashamed. An inquiry was held into the whole scandal of the dealings of Rome with Jugurtha, and Sp. Albinus and others were exiled. The peace was repudiated, A. Albinus given up to Jugurtha, and an honest and fairly able general appointed in the person of Q. Metellus. He took out on his staff not the leaders of Roman fashion, but experienced soldiers. Among them was C. Marius, who, serving with distinction at Numantia, had risen from the ranks and, becoming tribune and later praetor, had married into the family of the Caesars. Metellus set to work in 109 by restoring the discipline of the army. He then advanced into the deserts of Numidia, steadily refusing Jugurtha's bribes and himself bribing the ambassadors to betray Jugurtha. His command was prolonged for 108, and in this year he fought the one big battle of the war. On the road to Cirta, as he drew near to the River Muthul, swarms of Numidian horse swept down on him, cut him off from the river, got between his advanced guard and the main body, and then turned upon the flanks of the army. Discipline however and the able support of Marius saved the day, and the Romans fought their way forward to the river. But the battle did nothing to settle the war. Jugurtha formed an alliance with Bocchus, king of Mauretania, and aided by the nature of the country adopted guerilla tactics; and the year drew to a close without any real success.

Marius. Marius had increased his reputation by his service to Metellus, and he was ambitious. Hoping to profit by the ill-success of his commander and the general distrust of the populace towards the Senate, he applied for leave to go home and stand for the Consulship. Metellus ridiculed the idea but at last gave leave; and Marius, though he had but a few days in which to canvass before the elections came on, found such support among all classes that he was elected Consul and appointed by the Assembly to supersede Metellus. His popularity and military reputation induced many veterans to join his army, and he enrolled many of the lowest class, who had not hitherto been eligible for service. He arrived in Africa in 107, having under him as quaestor his future rival L. Cornelius Sulla. He soon got Eastern Numidia into his hands and marched throughout the country. But it was Jugurtha's plan to avoid a pitched battle, and the efforts of the legions to round up hordes of Numidian horsemen in the desert were futile. Marius was succeeding no better than Metellus, and seeing that other means must be tried he entered into negotiations with Bocchus for the betrayal of Jugurtha. The Mauretanian king in the course of the negotiations formed a strong liking for Sulla and agreed to hand Jugurtha over to that officer. Sulla, with the cool courage which in after life stood him in good stead, ventured into Bocchus's camp, not knowing whether Bocchus would betray Jugurtha to him or him to Jugurtha. However Jugurtha was invited to a conference, his guards were cut down and he was handed over a prisoner to the Romans in 105. With his surrender the war came to an end. Numidia was not made a province but divided between Bocchus and Gauda, a half-brother of Jugurtha. The ex-king, after being led in Marius's triumph, perished miserably in the Tullianum, the dungeon at the foot of the Capitol.

The Teutones and Cimbri. No sooner was the war in Numidia at an end than Marius was called upon for further work. In 113 the Roman world was startled to hear that vast hordes of barbarians were approaching the eastern end of the Alps. They were German tribes, the

Teutones and Cimbri, moving southwards in search of new homes, perhaps only with the natural restless instincts of barbarians, or it may be that they were seeking for the fabled home of the Gods. At any rate they came in their hundreds of thousands with wives and children and their belongings stored in waggons, leaving a track of devastation where they passed. They awoke in the Romans the memory of the Gauls and the Allia nearly three centuries before, and the consul Carbo, who was fighting in Illyricum, received orders to march against them. He made a treacherous attack on them, while pretending to negotiate, and was only saved from destruction by a storm which stopped the fighting.

However the barbarians moved off westward into Gaul and did not come into conflict with the Romans for four years. In 109 they were on the frontiers of Gallia Narbonensis and defeated the consul Silanus. Two years later in 107 the Tigurini, a Helvetian tribe, roused by the example of the German invaders, began to move and utterly defeated L. Cassius Longinus. It was fortunate for the Romans that the invaders had no fixed aim in their wanderings and made no attempt to invade Italy during the Numidian war. But in 105 they joined with the Tigurini in a direct invasion of Gallia Narbonensis; and at Arausio on the Rhone they cut to pieces Caepio's army of more than 60,000 men. The panic in Rome was complete. The days of Cannae and the Allia came vividly before men's minds. These German giants with their fair hair and light eyes, their suits of mail and copper helmets, their huge whirling swords, their women as brave and more cruel than their men, were going at last to swoop down irresistibly upon Italy.

Marius was the only hope. He was elected consul for 104, while still in Africa, and on his return set to work to raise an army for the new war. But once more the danger rolled by. The barbarians turned west again and for two years satisfied themselves with the easy plunder of Spain. Marius, who was re-elected consul for the whole interval, spent the time in consolidating Southern Gaul and training his men.

The Teutones. Aquae Sextiae, 102 B.C. At last in 102 the barbarians re-appeared. The Cimbri and Tigurini moved along the northern side of the Alps and made their way through the Eastern passes to where Catulus was holding the line of the River Athesis. The Teutones were to advance along the coast road of the Riviera, which would bring them into conflict with Marius. The Roman general did not oppose their passage of the Rhone but for three days kept his men within the camp in spite of the repeated attacks of the enemy. Then for six days he watched the long line of the Teutones, as they slowly moved past him towards Italy with shouts of insult and offers to carry the last messages of the Romans to their friends at home. When they had passed, he followed slowly and caught them up at Aquae Sextiae. He posted his legions on high ground, ordering them to wait till the barbarians had come up the hill to close quarters and then to hurl their *pila* and rush down on the exhausted foe. At the same time three thousand men were sent round beyond the enemy to take them in the rear when the battle should have begun. Marius's tactics were completely successful. The Teutones were caught between two forces and the whole tribe, men, women and children, annihilated.

The Cimbri. Campi Raudii, 101 B.C. Marius learnt on the day of Aquae Sextiae that he had been appointed to his fifth consulship for the year 101, and turned his attention to the Cimbri who were now in Cisalpine Gaul. Catulus had withdrawn behind the Padus, and the Cimbri had moved westwards in expectation of the arrival of the

Teutones. In the summer of 101 Marius had joined forces with Catulus and accepted the challenge of the Cimbrian leader to fix the time and place for the battle. At the end of August the armies met on the Raudine Plain near Vercellae. Catulus's men were near turning to flight, but the well-disciplined veterans of Marius won the day. The Cimbri were exterminated, the survivors of the Tigurini fled beyond the Alps, and Marius returned to Rome in a blaze of glory to celebrate a twofold triumph.

Army reforms and their political effect. With the name of Marius are coupled various reforms in the Army which took place about this time, whether they were entirely his work or not. He abolished the old distinction of Hastati, Principes and Triarii and the separate tribal ensigns, making the legion a homogeneous body of nominally 6000 men with the Eagle as its standard. The men, armed with *pilum* and short sword, were divided into ten cohorts, which were themselves subdivided each into six centuries under their centurions. The cavalry was henceforth to be furnished by the allies; and auxiliary cohorts of light-armed men, enrolled from the allies, took the place of the old *velites* or skirmishers. The legionaries were now enlisted voluntarily from the *Capite Censi* or poorest class as well as from other citizens; making the army their profession they served for twenty years and underwent a vigorous course of drill and training. From the military point of view all these changes were clear gain. The Roman army retrieved its name, which a century of inefficiency had tarnished, and for many years was an almost irresistible fighting force, well-disciplined and practised in every kind of warfare.

But the military reforms had a far-reaching political result. The soldiers were no longer a citizen force mustered for a summer campaign, but a standing army of professional soldiers, who swore allegiance to their general rather than to the state; and in their long absence from home they learnt to look to him rather than to the home government as the source of authority. Meanwhile the long wars had led to the extension of commands. Marius

Roman Standard-bearer

had been at the head of the Roman army without a break from 107 to 101, and the precedent was followed later in the case of Sulla, Pompey, Caesar and others. Such men had a force behind them, which would conquer Rome

or Rome's enemies without making much distinction;
and the continual opposition and fighting between the
Optimates, or government-party, and the Populares, or
opposition, made it easier for them to forget that in
overthrowing one party they were overthrowing the
constitution. Marius, as we shall see, had not the political
ability to use the force which he had at his disposal. His
successors had the ability, and they used it.

CHAPTER XVII

MARIUS, THE SOCIAL WAR AND SULLA

Marius. The end of the Cimbrian War left Marius
undoubtedly the most prominent man in Rome. He had
saved the country and year after year had commanded
armies, which knew that his skill had made their success
possible and that his military reforms had opened an
honourable career to the poorer citizens. Two courses
lay open to him, if he was to retain the reputation which

he had won. He might have stood aloof from all political parties, the great man above party-strife, but ready to serve the state if need should arise ; or he might have used the power behind him to rule the state, as a despot in fact, if not in name. For the latter course he had none of the necessary statesmanlike qualities ; for the former he had not the nobility of mind. He was a soldier and little more. Gaunt, big-featured and unpolished, he was a force in the camp but a failure in the city, where the young nobles sneered at his rough manners and his humble origin. Sensitive to insult and ambitious for power, the chance of which had been long in coming, he went down into the sordid battlefield of politics with no qualification for success beyond his military reputation.

The wars against Jugurtha and the Northern invaders had widened the breach between the Optimates and the Populares, or the party of the Senate and the Opposition. The incapacity and dishonesty of the Senatorial leaders had been shown in Africa ; and the appointment of Marius, first to supersede Metellus and afterwards to his long and unconstitutional series of consulships against the barbarians, was a triumph for the Populares, who had seen in him a likely champion for their cause as well as the preserver of the country. Force of circumstances as well as his own origin inclined Marius to the side of the Populares. He formed an alliance with L. Appuleius Saturninus and C. Servilius Glaucia in opposition to the Optimates, who acknowledged his old rival Metellus as their leader.

Saturninus and Glaucia, 100 B.C. Marius was elected to his sixth consulship for the year 100 and Glaucia to the praetorship, while Saturninus, by the murder of one of the successful candidates, obtained the last place on the list of tribunes. Saturninus and Glaucia were ne'er-do-wells turned politicians, fishers in troubled waters for what they could get, though in opposing the Senate they were taking a side which an honest man might well take. Saturninus, with Marius supporting him, now proposed an Agrarian law for giving allotments to Marius's veterans and for founding over-sea citizen-colonies, to which Italians might be admitted and so gain access to citizenship; and also a law reducing the price of the corn doles. The laws were passed, and Marius was to have the superintendence of the colonies. But Saturninus went on to add a clause that every Senator should on pain of exile within five days take an oath to observe the new law. Metellus stubbornly refused to take the oath and withdrew to Rhodes; and Marius himself, feeling that he was following in the train of his new allies rather than leading them, found the position humiliating to his sense of his own importance and turned against Saturninus and Glaucia. He would only take the oath so far as 'the law was legally binding.' The Optimates saw their chance in the cleavage between their opponents. In the elections at the close of the year, when Saturninus stood again for the Tribuneship and Glaucia for the Consulship, rioting took place. The Senate declared the state in danger. Marius wobbled hopelessly between both parties. His efforts to arrange a compromise were laughed at. Saturninus and Glaucia were driven on to the Capitol where they surrendered to Marius. He did his best to save their lives by placing them in the Curia Hostilia or Senate House. But the mob of young nobles unroofed the building and pelted them to death with tiles. So ended Marius's first political adventure—in the destruction of his own party through his own failure to support them. Hated now by both sides, he was politically ruined and withdrew for some years to the East on the excuse of a vow, still nursing the hope of a seventh consulship which an old fortune-teller had promised him in days gone by.

Meanwhile there were questions pressing for settlement which needed a strong hand. A second Slave War had broken out in Sicily in 103. A Syrian slave Tryphon and a Cilician brigand Athenion posed as kings and overran the island, the towns alone holding out against them. For three years fighting went on, till the consul Aquillius put down the rising and carried the ringleaders to Rome, where they slew one another rather than fight wild beasts in the arena.

In the East Sulla was praetor of Cilicia in 92 B.C. on the borders of the kingdom which Mithradates of Pontus had been able to build up after the death of Attalus of Pergamum. Mithradates, trained by exile in his youth to live a hard life and fortified, it is said, by antidotes against every possible poison, combined great physical strength and determination of character with all the vices of Greek and Eastern civilization. He had taken possession of the Crimea and now seizing Cappadocia came into collision with Sulla, whose province lay along the south side of that district. Sulla acted with promptness and tact. A small victory over Tigranes of Armenia was enough to keep his ally Mithradates within bounds; and Sulla then went eastwards to the Euphrates to confer with the Parthians, whose friendship to Rome might be a means of keeping Pontus and Armenia quiet. For the moment order was restored in Asia Minor, but trouble was to come there in a few years.

Italian Citizenship. The great problem which faced Rome was the question of the admission of the Italians to the franchise. The Romans found it hard to look at the question on its merits. Apart from selfish considerations they had at the back of their minds the notion that a state was not a country but a city with a certain extent of subject territory round it. So the claims of the Italians, recognized by C. Gracchus in 122 and Saturninus in 100, were still unsatisfied, and the rules limiting the right of the allies to settle in Rome had lately been made more strict. At the same time the exclusive attitude of the citizens towards men who formed half the army was not justified either by the efficiency or integrity of Roman rule. The Samnites and the Marsi, those mountain tribes of Central Italy whom Rome had reduced with great difficulty, specially resented their inferior position. But for the present they kept quiet watching the efforts of a champion of their cause in Rome, Livius Drusus, son of the rival of C. Gracchus.

Drusus. C. Gracchus had achieved one at least of the purposes at which he aimed. He had set the Equites in strong opposition to the Senate by giving them the right of filling the Judicia or juries in criminal cases. So long as there was this feud, it was difficult to unite the best men of both classes for the settlement of the more serious franchise question. Drusus therefore proposed as a compromise to give back the juries to a Senate strengthened by the admission of 300 of the best Equites, while he aimed at conciliating the common people by new colonies in Italy and Sicily and by fresh doles of corn. These laws he carried in 91, after riots had taken place, but only by putting them to the vote as one measure contrary to a law lately passed against ' tacking.' Then he turned to his main object and brought forward his proposal for giving citizenship to the allies. At once all parties turned against him. Charges of conspiring with the Italians, of having 10,000 Marsi in readiness to march on Rome, were levelled at his head. Civil war seemed close at hand, when one evening Drusus was struck down at his own doorway by the hand of an assassin, 91 B.C.

The Social or Marsian War, 90–88 B.C. The murder of Drusus convinced the Italians that they would not obtain citizenship except by rebellion; and the insolence

of a Roman praetor at Asculum in Picenum kindled the
conflagration. All the Romans in the town were slain.
The men of Picenum and the Marsi took up arms, and their
example was followed by the other hill-tribes of the Centre
and South. An embassy was sent to Rome to demand
citizenship. When this was refused, the Italians proclaimed their independence as a federal state with
Corfinium, almost in the centre of the peninsula, as their
capital under the name of Italica, and consuls and Senate
on the Roman model. The Latins and some of the
Campanians supported Rome ; Etruria and Umbria
wavered but had too small a free population to be
dangerous ; the strength of the rebels lay in the hard
fighting stock of the Marsi and Samnites. Rome was
unprepared but in her colonies had a series of fortresses,
whose loyal resistance gained her a breathing space.

The war is variously known as the Social war from the
Socii or Italian allies, against whom it was waged, or Marsian war from the Marsi, one of the leading tribes engaged ;
but of the struggle, desperate as it was for Rome, the records
are scanty and confused. There was plenty of fighting
but no real genius on the Italian side to organize a plan
of campaign; and the efforts of the insurgents were directed
towards reducing the colonies and defeating the Roman
forces which marched to their relief. Aesernia in the
south resisted for a while the Samnites under C. Papius
Mutilus. But when the consul L. Julius Caesar, with Sulla
under him, was defeated in an attempt to raise the siege,
Aesernia fell, and Mutilus, pressing home his advantage,
overran most of Campania and took the town of Nola.
Further north on the Marsian frontier the colony of Alba
Fucentia was hard pressed, and the other consul Rutilius
with Marius under him was defeated and slain as he
marched to its assistance. This gave Marius the chief
command in the north ; but beyond inflicting a small

defeat on the Marsi he could do little, and it is uncertain whether he even saved Alba Fucentia.

The ill-success of the first year's fighting and the knowledge that Mithradates was on the move in Asia Minor, ready to take advantage of Rome's difficulties, caused the Romans to reconsider their position. At the end of the year 90 the consul Julius carried a law granting *citizenship to all those Italians who had remained loyal*. This law granted the very thing for which the Italians had taken up arms and naturally prevented the extension of the revolt among those who had been wavering during the year of Rome's failure. A second law passed in the beginning of 89 gave *citizenship to any Italian, rebel or loyal, who applied for it within sixty days*. The new citizens both in this and the former law were confined to eight out of the thirty-five tribes lest they should swamp the votes of the old citizens.

These concessions induced all the Italians to make their peace within a short time with the exception of the Marsi and Samnites, whose old enmity to Rome had revived from its sleep of two centuries. But they were less dangerous alone, and the course of the war in 89 was entirely favourable to Rome. In the north Pompeius Strabo defeated the Marsi and took the rebel stronghold of Asculum. Italica became once more the country-town of Corfinium, and the revolt died down as far as this district was concerned. Further south Sulla, who unlike his rival Marius had been continued in command, recovered Campania with the exception of Nola and penetrated into Samnium. By his success he won the consulship for the year 88 and with the aid of Pompeius Strabo had nearly ended the war, when affairs in Rome called for his attention before the Samnites had been forced to lay down their arms.

Sulpicius and the Mithradatic Command. The war had not only cost the peninsula considerably more than one hundred thousand of its best fighting men, but had also caused a financial crisis. The treasury was empty, the currency debased, and the load of debt pressed heavily not only on the poorer citizens, but on the leading men of the state as well. Then again the Italians were dissatisfied with the restriction imposed on their citizenship and called out for admission to all the tribes. And lastly Mithradates, who had kept himself well-informed about Italian affairs, was busy with a project of driving the Romans out of Asia Minor. The last danger was the most pressing; and the Senate turned to the man, whose coolness had put the finishing touch to the Jugurthine war, who alone had emerged with credit from the Social war, and whose sympathies were with Senatorial government. It was arranged that Sulla should complete the conquest of the Samnites and then start at once to fight Mithradates.

But the other two questions—the financial crisis and the restriction on Italian citizenship—called for settlement also. P. Sulpicius Rufus, who had been a friend of Drusus, came forward in 88 B.C. with proposals that the Italians should be distributed through all the tribes and that any Senator who owed more than two thousand *denarii*[1] should be expelled from the Senate. Marius undertook to support these measures, if a third proposal were added that he and not Sulla should have the command against Mithradates. Sulpicius, whose sympathies were with the Populares and who welcomed the support which Marius's name seemed able to give him, joined the third proposal to the other two. Rioting followed, and Sulpicius, as the declared leader of the Populares, carried his laws by force. Sulla left Rome for his camp before Nola, explained the situation to his army and then marched on Rome. Two military tribunes sent by Marius to take over the command of Sulla's army were stoned,

---

[1] A denarius contained about as much silver as a franc.

and Sulla's six legions entered Rome. They easily put an end to the street-fighting which was all the resistance they met with. Marius and his son and ten others were declared outlaws. Sulpicius was caught and put to death, and Sulla was left as master of Rome.

Sulla. He had done for the first time in 88 a thing to which the whole course of events from the time of the Gracchi had been leading. The Gracchi had shown that force was politically effective in the hands of a man who did not fear to break up the constitution. Marius had shown that an army—organized force—could become attached to its general rather than to the state. Sulla had used that organized force to overthrow the constitution. Henceforward the dominating factor in the Roman state is the army, and he who commands the army is really the master of Rome.

For the present men hardly realized this truth, and Sulla himself used his power with moderation. Rescinding Sulpicius's laws, he added three hundred new members to the Senate in the hope of strengthening its authority and decreed that no legislation should come before the Comitia, for which consent had not been previously given by the Senate. He then held the consular elections for the following year, at which an honest but stupid aristocrat Cn. Octavius and an able but unscrupulous democrat L. Cornelius Cinna were elected. Sulla exacted an oath from the new consuls that they would make no change in the constitution and then set out for the war in the East on which his heart was set, trusting that his legates, who were left with the duty of subduing Nola and Samnium, would be able to keep things quiet during his absence.

Some results. The war had given citizenship to the Italians. But how were they to use it ? The city-state of Rome had changed into the country of Italy. But there was no practical means, short of representation, which would make a vote worth having to any one who lived fifty miles from Rome. At the same time the power of the vote had gone. The real ruler of Rome is henceforward not the Comitia nor even the Senate but the master of the legions. There is an accidental fitness in this. The legions were drawn from all Italy, and the general was the man who knew his soldiers' needs and was the object of their affection and loyalty. The leader of the army was the one person, in whom all soldiers, Roman and Italian alike, saw the idea of authority visible and expressed. He was to all what the Comitia or Senate could never be to the Italians—the one centre on which all thoughts of loyalty could be focussed. The establishment of the general as Imperator or Emperor some sixty years later was the recognition of something more than his mere force.

Since Sulla had been fighting the Samnites at the time when he came definitely into conflict with the popular party, it followed not unnaturally that a kind of friendship grew up between the two classes of his enemies. During Sulla's absence in the East the Samnites were largely left to their own devices, and on his return we shall find that they threw in their lot with the revolutionary party in Rome; so that the Social war interrupted by Sulla's departure is caught up in the civil war to which his return gave rise and only ended with the massacres which ended the civil struggle.

DATES

103–99. Slave war in Sicily.
100. Saturninus, Glaucia, and Marius.
92. Sulla in the East.
91. M. Livius Drusus.
90–88 (82). Social War.
90. Lex Iulia, Italian Franchise.
89. Lex Plautia Papiria, Italian Franchise.
88. Sulpicius.

CHAPTER XVIII

FIRST MITHRADATIC WAR

Mithradates. Leaving for a moment the story of home events we must follow Sulla to the East, where Mithradates of Pontus had built up a powerful kingdom and made war on the Roman dominions. His father Mithradates V had taken advantage of the dissolution of the kingdom of Pergamum to lay the foundations of a strong kingdom of his own ; and the son Mithradates VI ascending the throne in 114, had in the course of twenty-five years gone far beyond the limits of Pontus proper, the small strip of territory on the south coast of the Black Sea. The Crimea with the control of the Scythian corn-supply had passed into his hands and most of the northern sea-coast from the mouth of the Danube to the Caucasus. Giving his daughter in marriage to Tigranes of Armenia, he had secured a strong ally on his eastern frontier, and by continual aggressions on neighbouring princes he was gradually getting possession of most of Asia Minor. We have seen that Sulla in 92 checked his designs on Cappadocia ; but on Sulla's return home Mithradates had continued his career. On the death of Nicomedes of Bithynia in 91 he tried to set up a nominee of his own as king but apologized when M'. Aquillius, who had been sent out from Rome to stop his encroachments, ordered him to withdraw. However he felt that the time for action had come ; and when the new king of Bithynia in turn attacked him and the avarice and meddling of Aquillius had alienated all sympathy from Rome, he declared war in 89, posing as the champion of all the East, Greeks and Orientals alike, against Rome.

Massacre of Italians and invasion of Greece. For the moment he swept Asia Minor. Having caught the avaricious Aquillius he carried him about on a donkey and at last killed him by pouring molten gold down his throat. There was no considerable Roman force in Asia; and as he was at first on his best behaviour, the provincials welcomed him as an improvement on the rapacious Roman tax-collectors. He established himself at Pergamum, while his fleet from the Black Sea in co-operation with the pirate fleet of Cilicia commanded the Aegean. But in 88 the true barbarian came out in him. He ordered a massacre of all the Italians in the province, and the decree was carried out faithfully. One hundred thousand or more victims fell, and Mithradates, who till then might perhaps have hoped for some Italian support against Rome, had now made it plain that he was no better than any other Oriental despot. In the spring of 87 he invaded Greece, his main army marching slowly overland through Thrace, while his best general, Archelaus, crossed the Aegean, massacring the Italian traders in Delos, occupying Athens which welcomed him readily enough, and advancing from there into Boeotia.

Chaeronea and Orchomenus. Such was the position when in the summer of 87 Sulla crossed from Brundisium into Epirus. He had only five legions and no money, while he knew that his enemies at Rome would supersede him if they could. Seeing that everything turned on securing Athens and defeating Archelaus before the main army arrived, he marched straight on Athens. Archelaus fell back, and the Greeks, alarmed at the tales of Mithradates's savagery, came back to their allegiance to Rome. Sulla, who looked to them for supplies, took no notice of their late disloyalty. Raising what troops he could from the Aetolians and Thessalians he blockaded Athens and turned his attention to the siege of the Piraeus, to which Archelaus

had retired that he might keep in touch with his fleet. In
the spring of 86 Athens was taken by storm and given up
to the soldiers to plunder ; for Sulla knew how to make his
men serve him well. Soon afterwards the Piraeus fell with
the exception of the hill of Munychia within it, to which
Archelaus had retreated as a citadel, and Sulla hastened
north to meet the main Pontic army which was by this

Boeotia and Attica

time coming down into Thessaly. He had about thirty
thousand men ; the enemy, one hundred thousand strong
with many scythe-chariots, were under the command of
Archelaus, who had left Munychia to join the invading
army, when Sulla went north. The armies met in Boeotia
at Chaeronea, 86 B.C., where Philip of Macedon had conquered Greece in 338. But trenches and a palisade protected the Romans against the Pontic cavalry and chariots,

and the unwieldy barbarian force fell into confusion from its very numbers. Archelaus with ten thousand men escaped to Euboea. Sulla gave out that the Romans had lost no more than fifteen men.

One danger was gone, and Sulla could now turn against Flaccus, whom, as we shall see later, the Populares in Rome had sent out to supersede him. But Flaccus, finding his men were deserting to Sulla, moved off towards the Hellespont in the hope of getting the credit of arranging peace with Mithradates. Sulla could not follow him ; for news reached him that a second Pontic army was on its way to Greece. This force crossed the Aegean and landing in Euboea put itself under the command of Archelaus. The second great battle of the war took place at Orchomenus, 85 B.C., not far from Chaeronea. Archelaus's cavalry broke the Roman line, and the issue of the battle was in doubt, till Sulla, dashing into the fray, bade his veterans go home and tell how they deserted their general at Orchomenus. The victory was won, and only a few barbarians escaped with Archelaus. Mithradates now opened negotiations with Sulla ; for his hope of winning Greece was shattered, and his oppression of the Greek cities of Asia had turned that district against him. But he would not agree to the terms which were offered him, and Sulla, after passing the winter in Thessaly, moved north to the Hellespont in the beginning of 84.

Flaccus and Fimbria. The two legions, which Flaccus had brought with him, were in this neighbourhood but no longer under his command. At Byzantium he had quarrelled with Fimbria, one of his officers, and the men rising in mutiny had killed Flaccus and put Fimbria in his place. Fimbria was no bad general. He advanced into Asia and might have caught Mithradates at Pergamum, if Lucullus, Sulla's admiral, had been willing to co-operate. But the situation was impossible. Fimbria's men did not know whether Mithradates or Sulla was the real enemy against whom they had been sent, and a long spell of plundering and aimless marching had made them little better than a horde of mercenaries ready to join any one who would lead and pay them. At Sulla's approach they went over to him in a body, and Fimbria in despair slew himself.

Peace concluded. In the meantime Sulla had concluded peace with Mithradates. Affairs in Rome needed his attention, and he had not the leisure to crush the enemy once and for all. He forced Mithradates to give up all his conquests and to confine himself to his original kingdom of Pontus, to pay an indemnity and to provide him with ships for the transport of his legions to Italy. He then re-arranged the affairs of the Province of Asia, exacting arrears of tribute for the last five years and a fine of twenty thousand talents (£5,000,000) in addition, subdividing the province into forty-four districts for the assessment of the amount due and fixing the dates at which the instalments must be paid. The provincials could only pay by borrowing, and the country fell more than ever into the clutches of the money-lenders.

Sulla. Sulla left the two Fimbrian legions to garrison the Province of Asia and wintered in Greece before returning to Italy in the spring of 83. He had shown consummate ability in the war. Generals before him had conquered Eastern armies, but they had an undivided Rome behind them. Sulla with a small force had not only conquered Mithradates but won over without a struggle the legions which had been sent against himself as much as against the king. He was admittedly one of the ablest of all Roman generals, never losing a campaign and seldom defeated in battle, cool in the face of danger, taking his risk wisely and never erring in his estimate of the chances. As a man he was a strange mixture. For his appearance, his face was of the colour of a mulberry sprinkled with flour and his eyes a light blue. In private life he was a man who entered to the full into all the pleasures which a luxurious and unscrupulous Roman society had to offer. Probably the only real ambition he had by nature was for military renown, and the part which he played as a statesman was forced upon him by the interference of Sulpicius with his proposed command against Mithradates. When he did come back to take charge of Rome, he came with an army absolutely devoted to him not only from the licence to plunder which he gave them after a victory but from the strong confidence and loyalty which he inspired. Conservative in the extreme but without any deep political insight, he was content to bolster up the power of the Senate for the time and to leave the next generation to settle questions which might arise after his own death. Contemptuous of human life and with no care for the absolute power which was in his grasp, he deluged Rome in blood to set up the Senate once more and then quietly withdrew to his own private pleasures. Yet he provided Rome with a sound means of administering justice in criminal cases and organized a satisfactory system of provincial government. He was a strong, clear-headed man, capable of ruling but with a cynical contempt for the government he was called upon to support ; able to put life into whatever he touched, but in great matters short-sighted from deliberate choice.

DATES

89. Mithradates declares war.
88. Massacre of Italians in Asia.
87. Invasion of Greece by Archelaus.
87. Sulla lands in Greece.
86. Sulla takes Athens and Piraeus.
86. Flaccus lands in Greece.

DATES

86. 1st Pontic Army defeated at Chaeronea.
85. 2nd Pontic Army defeated at Orchomenus.
85. Fimbria succeeds Flaccus.
84. Death of Fimbria.
84. Peace concluded.
83. Sulla returns to Italy.

CHAPTER XIX

ANARCHY AND SULLA'S REFORMS

Marius. We must now go back and see what had
been happening in the West during Sulla's absence.
Marius claims attention first, and we have to trace his
fortunes since he fled as an outlaw on the fall of Sulpicius
in 88. He had had an exciting time. The ship he sailed
in was driven back on to the coast of Latium, and he only
avoided capture by wading out to a little coasting vessel
which lay close to the shore. The skipper would not
surrender him but did not welcome his dangerous pas-
senger and put him ashore at the first opportunity near
Minturnae. Here he lay hid in the marshes up to his
neck in mud and water, while Sulla's men scoured the
country for him. Caught at last he was handed over by
the soldiers to the magistrates of Minturnae, who sent
the executioner, a Cimbrian slave, into the prison to kill
him. But the grim old man with glowing eyes and a
terrible voice called out through the darkness, ' Man,
darest thou slay Gaius Marius ? ' and the slave in terror
dropped his weapon and fled. The magistrates now re-
considered matters and sent Marius away by sea. At
length he got to Carthage and, when warned off by the
Roman governor, told the messenger to tell his master

that he had seen ' Marius sitting amid the ruins of Carthage.' Retiring to the island of Cercina off the African coast, he was joined by his son and waited for the day when his seventh consulship should come.

Octavius and Cinna. In Italy Sulla had left Pompeius Strabo in command of an army in the north and Metellus to finish off the Samnites. But no sooner had he sailed from Brundisium in 87 than trouble broke out in Rome. The consul Cinna, with whom were a tribune Carbo and Q. Sertorius, a personal foe of Sulla but a man of real ability, proposed that the exiles should be recalled and the Italians admitted to unrestricted citizenship. His colleague Octavius opposed him. Both sides collected gangs of ruffians, and after most savage street-fighting Cinna was driven out of the city. Octavius now summoned Pompeius Strabo to his help ; but though he came, he was playing for his own hand and would do little for Octavius. Cinna and Sertorius on the other hand induced the troops at Nola to march on Rome, and in the meantime Marius had landed in Etruria and gathered armed gangs of slaves. The three surrounded Rome with their troops. Octavius recalled Metellus from the Samnite country, and sanguinary but indecisive fighting went on round Rome. Disease broke out ; both armies suffered severely, and Strabo himself died. Octavius would not give Metellus a free hand, and the latter finding the situation hopeless sailed off to Africa.

Meanwhile disease and famine were doing their work in Rome, and Octavius had no hold over his troops. Negotiations were opened, and the envoys had no choice but to throw themselves on the mercy of the besiegers, only begging that there should be no bloodshed. Cinna consented, but Marius listened in ominous silence and, when the gates of Rome were opened, refused to enter till his sentence of outlawry was revoked. Then he let

loose his ruffians.   Octavius, L. Caesar and many a
distinguished victim fell to his fury.   Sulla's wife and
children barely escaped with their lives.   For five days
the slaughter went on, till Sertorius fell on the murderers and cut them down.

Cinna and Carbo, 87–84 B.C.   Force was supreme.
Without pretence of election Marius and Cinna named
themselves consuls for 86.   But the former enjoyed his
seventh consulship for a few days only.   On Jan. 13th, 86,
he died, worn out and disgraced, a monster of revenge
and cruelty.   Cinna nominated Flaccus in Marius's place
and sent him out to supersede Sulla with the result which
we have already seen.   Then for two years, 85 and 84,
Cinna ruled with Carbo as his colleague.   There were no
elections, no pretence of constitutional authority.   Debts
were cancelled, slaves enfranchised, Italians distributed
among all the tribes.   The Samnites still in arms received
votes with the rest and kept quiet, naturally reserving
their efforts for the day of Sulla's return.   All was well
with the revolutionary party in Rome save for the one
anxiety of what would happen when Sulla returned;
and for that Cinna made no provision.

At last in 84 came a despatch from Sulla.   He told
the Senate that he had conquered Mithradates and was
coming back to restore constitutional government.   The
Senate, composed since the massacre mainly of Cinna's
friends, tried to negotiate with Sulla, offering him a safe-
conduct to Rome.   He replied grimly that he would
bring his own escort and wrote that he would respect
the grant of full citizenship to the Italians but must
punish those who had persecuted his friends.   Cinna did
not lack personal bravery.   He determined to meet Sulla
in Greece but was killed by his men at Ancona in the
autumn of 84, while trying to induce them to sail to
Greece.   With his death the unconstitutional rule of the

last two years came to an end.   Consular elections were
held, and Scipio and Norbanus chosen consuls for 83.

The return of Sulla, 83 B.C.   In the spring Sulla
landed at Brundisium with forty thousand veterans at
his back.   The consuls were sent against him, but Sulla
advancing slowly defeated Norbanus in Campania and
shut him up in Capua.   Scipio allowing himself to be
drawn into negotiations found that his men went over

Lucius Cornelius Sulla

in a body to Sulla.   Thus in the first campaign Sulla had
gained at little cost all South Italy except Samnium and
was ready for the more serious work of next year.   He
had been joined by those of his friends who had escaped
the Marian massacres, among them Metellus and Crassus,
and above all by Cn. Pompeius, son of Strabo, who had
raised three legions from his father's old soldiers and his
own clients and had already given Carbo's men plenty
of work in Picenum.

For 82 Carbo and young Marius named themselves consuls; but Sertorius, who was made Praetor, despairing of the cause retired to Spain, where we shall hear of him later. Young Marius was sent south with a hastily raised force to meet Sulla, who had advanced by now into Latium; while Carbo, rallying the last of old Marius's veterans and raising troops in North Italy, took up a position on the Adriatic coast near the southern limit of Cisalpine Gaul. Marius was easily defeated by Sulla at Sacriportus and with difficulty escaped to the neighbouring stronghold of Praeneste, after sending to Rome the disgraceful order that the surviving Senatorial leaders in that city should be murdered.

We must leave him closely besieged in Praeneste and follow the course of the war elsewhere. Sulla advanced to Rome. But it was no time for paying off old scores, and he merely made necessary arrangements for maintaining order and then marched north against Carbo. Pompeius, Metellus and Crassus had hemmed in Carbo; but the arrival of Norbanus who had escaped from Capua enabled him to move southwards. An indecisive engagement with Sulla at Clusium stopped his further advance, and attempts on his part to send troops to raise the siege of Praeneste were frustrated by Pompeius. Carbo saw that the game was up and fled to Africa.

The Samnites and the Colline Gate, 82 B.C. But by this time the Samnites were on the war-path under Pontius Telesinus, a descendant perhaps of the hero of the Caudine Forks. Joined by the remnants of the revolutionary troops they marched on Praeneste. But Sulla hastening from Etruria was before them and headed them off from the besieged city. Then they tried a bold stroke and, like Hannibal at the siege of Capua, marched on Rome. Pitching his camp outside the Colline Gate, Pontius prepared for the assault and sack of the city on the morrow. All the morning the weak garrison looked anxiously for Sulla's army. At mid-day he came and, giving his tired legions time only for a hasty meal, hurled them on the foe. Sulla himself with the left wing was defeated and gave up all for lost; but Crassus fighting on into the night won a success with the right wing. Then during the darkness part of the Samnite host went over to Sulla, and the rest were cut to pieces as they tried to retreat in the morning. Sulla summoned the Senate to meet him in the temple of Bellona outside the walls, and as he addressed it shrieks were heard from the Campus Martius. 'It is nothing,' he said, 'a few criminals are being punished.' He was executing all the prisoners and deserters alike. With battles and massacre the Samnite people was practically wiped out of existence. Praeneste soon afterwards fell. Marius killed himself; the garrison was put to the sword; and Sulla had at last stamped out all armed resistance in Italy.

In Sicily and Africa the Marian leaders still held out. But Pompeius quickly cleared the island and in a six-weeks' campaign crushed the enemy, killing Carbo and defeating the Numidians, who had sheltered the fugitives. For this he was granted a triumph, and Sulla half in irony saluted him with the title of Magnus which Pompeius afterwards adopted as his cognomen.

Sulla Dictator, 81 B.C. Sulla was now undisputed master of Rome, and to legalize his position the Dictatorship was revived after an interval of over a century; the office moreover was conferred upon him not for six months only but for as long as he should think fit. He took the title of Felix, the Fortunate, and then set to work on the punishment of his enemies and the rebuilding of the constitution.

Punishment. He had had much provocation; his friends had been murdered, his property confiscated, and

he now took care in a cold-blooded and deliberate way
that it should not happen again. He was going to kill
all men of any mark who were responsible for the late
disorders. Lists were published (*proscribere*) containing
the names of suspected persons, and all whose names
appeared in these proscription-lists were hunted out by
ruffians, of whom L. Sergius Catilina was one of the most
conspicuous. Their lives were taken, their property confiscated to the state and sold by auction. For six months
the reign of terror lasted; nearly one hundred Senators
and sixteen hundred Equites perished and some three thousand of lower rank; and many fell victims to the private
enmity and greed of the executioners. Among those who
were in danger was young C. Julius Caesar, the nephew of
the great Marius, whose life was spared by Sulla with the
words, 'In that young trifler there is more than one Marius.'

In Italy wholesale executions and confiscations of land
took place, and the few Samnite survivors were reduced
to the rank of serfs living in open villages. The land of
the rebels or proscribed was distributed in allotments
to Sulla's veterans; the slaves of the proscribed were
liberated and given the franchise, forming under the
clan-name of the Cornelii, which they took in honour of
their liberator, a body of voters who might be relied on to
carry out his wishes.

Rebuilding the Constitution. Sulla was Dictator till
79 and before that year provided Rome with something
like a new constitution. He was a strong Conservative
and looked back to the time, a century or so earlier, when
the Senate had ruled Rome. But whereas that rule had
been exercised on sufferance and without any basis of
legal authority, he intended now to make the Senate
supreme not only in fact but also by constitutional right.

(*a*) **The Senate.** He added three hundred new
members to fill up the gaps caused in the last few years

and allowed them to be selected from his old officers and others of Equestrian rank. He provided that in future election to the Quaestorship should carry with it admission to the Senate[1] and that membership should be for life. In this way he both increased the independence of Senators, by putting them out of reach of expulsion at the hands of the censors, and also gave them a claim to govern as being indirectly elected by the people. To the Senate thus constituted he gave the monopoly of initiating legislation ; no measure could be submitted to the Assemblies, which had not been previously sanctioned by that body. The privilege of supplying jurymen for the Judicia was now restored to the Senate. Again every magistrate was made responsible to the Senate for his acts ; and the Senate had the right of prolonging (*prorogatio*) appointments beyond the term of one year and of assigning provinces. Thus in legislative, judicial and administrative matters the Senate was made constitutionally the supreme authority.

(*b*) **The Tribunes.** The Gracchi, Saturninus, and other reformers had shown the power of the Tribuneship. By the rule that no legislation might be introduced without Senatorial consent, the tribunes naturally lost their power of initiating legislation. They were further limited strictly in their right of veto and power of calling public meetings ; while by a subtle stroke the Tribuneship was made a bar to higher office, so that no man of ability or ambition might enter what would be politically a blind alley.

(*c*) **Other Magistrates.** It has been pointed out that all magistrates were made responsible to the Senate and that the Senate assigned them their province. Yet there was a risk that a great general or popular leader might upset the balance. Sulla made binding the succession

---

[1] See pp. 33 and 125.

of offices (*cursus honorum*), quaestorship, praetorship, consulship, with an interval of two years between each, and revived the law which forbade the holding of the same office twice within ten years. No popular favourite could then be advanced too quickly nor continued in power too long. To meet the requirements of the state he increased the number of Praetors to eight and of Quaestors to twenty.

More important than this he divided clearly civil and military offices. For one year a man was to be Praetor or Consul in Italy with no military duties in the ordinary course. For the next year he was to be Pro-praetor or Pro-consul in command of a province with a military force under him. Italy and its citizen population, up to the Apennines and the Rubicon, was the sphere of civil government; beyond that lay the provinces and military command. To restrain these military governors the law of Treason (*Maiestas*) was strengthened, forbidding the governor to leave his province or wage war without consent of the Senate.

So much for Sulla's constitution. Not much of it stood the test of time. His system of provincial appointments was found to work well on the whole and became the lasting basis of provincial administration. In assigning the Judicia to the Senate he had increased the number of the Quaestiones Perpetuae to eight. These standing courts, each trying one class of offence and with their procedure very clearly defined, helped very greatly in getting the administration of justice into shape at Rome. But for the rest the power of the Senate, the key of the situation, depended only on the will of Sulla and his army. When he was dead, that same power of the sword would perhaps be turned against the Senate and the whole fabric collapse like a house of cards. It is likely enough that Sulla knew this truth. But he had no great care for what happened when he was gone.

In 79 Sulla, perhaps contemptuous of his own power, resigned the Dictatorship and for a year lived at Puteoli, writing his memoirs and devoting himself to luxury. In 78 he died at the age of sixty. He had been Emperor in all but name.

DATES
        87. Sulla sails East.
        87. Marius and Cinna take Rome.
        86. Death of Marius. Flaccus sent to supersede Sulla.
    85–84. Cinna and Carbo rule Rome.
        83. Return of Sulla.
        82. Sacriportus and Praeneste.
        82. Battle of the Colline Gate.
    81–79. Sulla Dictator.
        78. Death of Sulla.

CHAPTER XX

COLLAPSE OF SULLA'S CONSTITUTION.—FOUR WARS

SULLA died leaving the supreme authority to the Senate. But its position was entirely artificial. There were political opponents of its rule, a democratic party who wished for the restoration of the power of the Tribunes and the Assembly, and a party of Equestrian capitalists who were excluded from the Judicia and their share in public life. Underneath there was a seething fire of social discontent. Sulla's proscriptions had left behind them a multitude of ruined men, sons of once wealthy fathers, but themselves stripped of everything. His veterans too soon found that farming was less profitable than war; and with the enfranchised slaves, the Cornelii, they were on the look-out for any upheaval which might improve their chances. All this material for a revolution Sulla had kept in check by his own power, which was real. The Senate's paper authority could do little when he was gone. And as a matter of fact the Senate within a few years was confronted by a series of wars, with which nothing but a very capable government could have dealt. The task of dealing with them had to be entrusted to great generals with unconstitutional powers. So once more the power of the army was seen in all its nakedness as the one real force in Rome; and each new law which conferred an extraordinary command was another nail in the coffin of Republican government.

The trouble began within a few weeks of Sulla's death. An attack was made in Etruria, 78 B.C., against Sulla's veterans by the dispossessed farmers, and Lepidus and Catulus, the consuls, went to suppress it. When the fight was over, Lepidus with a revolutionary programme and a demand for a second consulship marched on Rome. But he was a man of no weight, and the time was not yet ripe. Catulus and Pompeius remained loyal. Lepidus was defeated at the Mulvian Bridge outside Rome and fleeing to Sardinia died there. Perpenna, his accomplice, took the bulk of his army to Spain, where they joined Sertorius.

Sertorius in Spain, 83–72 B.C. Sertorius had retired to Spain in 83, as we have seen, and had been joined by many of Sulla's opponents. Easily defeating the small Roman forces in the province and left undisturbed by Sulla, he had set to work to Latinize the country with the purpose of making a new Italy there and re-making the Roman world from Spain as a centre. By his clear-headed and able administration he had won the confidence of the Spaniards and had striven to educate them in Roman methods, filling the chief posts in his government with Roman exiles, but giving the natives an increasing measure of self-government as they showed themselves fit for it. In 79 Metellus had been sent against him but at first could do little, and the arrival of Perpenna with the remnants of Lepidus's army made matters worse. Pompey had refused to disband his army after Lepidus's defeat, and Rome looked to him as the only man capable of crushing Sertorius. It was true, he was only twenty-nine and could not legally be Consul for another fourteen years. But Sulla himself had allowed him a triumph six years before, and he had no intention of remaining in obscurity. In despair the Senate gave him an extraordinary command in Spain and thus began its own downfall.

Pompey reached Spain in 76 and found that Metellus had won a large part of Southern Spain from the Sertorians. His arrival caused the enemy to draw together, and Perpenna, who had been assuming an equality with Sertorius, now put himself under his general's orders. Pompey did not fare very well at first, and in the campaign of 75 he was saved from defeat twice by the opportune arrival of Metellus, who was able to move more freely while Sertorius was facing Pompey in the north. In 74 Pompey received large reinforcements, while on the other hand Mithradates had made an alliance with Sertorius and supplied him with ships and money. The insurgents were driven back very slowly towards the north-west; and though no decisive blow could be struck, Perpenna began once more to set himself in opposition to his general. Forming a conspiracy he assassinated Sertorius in 72, and with this murder the rebellion collapsed. Pompey after quieting Spain still kept his army under his command, as he saw the opportunity of using it nearer home.

The Slave-war of Spartacus, 73–71 B.C. Two slave-wars in Sicily we have already mentioned. The horrible system of slave-worked estates was now to set South Italy in a blaze. In 73 some gladiators broke out of their

training-school at Capua and took refuge in the crater
of Vesuvius. They were joined by brigands and slaves
and soon numbered seventy thousand desperate men
under the leadership of a Thracian brigand, Spartacus.
They scattered the levies brought against them and defeated the praetor Varinius who tried to oppose their
march into Lucania. In 72 two consular armies were
sent against them without much result. Campania and
South Italy were paralyzed, and Spartacus could have
effected his purpose of cutting his way through to his
Thracian home, if his men had been willing to submit to
discipline. But they ranged through the peninsula
plundering at will, and the chance was lost. In 71
Crassus with eight legions took the field and restored
discipline in his army by decimating a division which ran
away. Then gradually he drove Spartacus before him
and penned him in Bruttium, building a wall thirty miles
long across the isthmus. Dissensions broke out between
the different nationalities in the slave-army. Spartacus
was forced by his men to fight a pitched battle, and his
army was scattered. Pompey, who had returned from
Spain, joined Crassus in hunting out and crucifying the
fugitives, and the road between Capua and Rome was
lined with six thousand crosses.

The Year 70 B.C. There were now two armies in
Italy, those of Pompey and Crassus, and the generals
announced their intention of standing for the consulship
of 70. Neither was qualified. Pompey was under age
and had not held the necessary subordinate offices. Crassus
had been praetor in 71, and a two-years' interval was
required by law before he could become consul. But
the Senate had no choice with legions near at hand, and
the two were elected without much opposition. Already in
Rome the anti-senatorial party had shown its strength;
and the conduct of the wars against Sertorius and

Spartacus had shown the incapacity of the Senate. In 75 the consul Cotta had removed the bar which kept tribunes out of higher offices; and the appointment of Crassus to his late command was a recognition of the capitalists' party. It is true, he was a Senator, but his real influence came from his position as financier and banker with half the leading men of Rome in his debt ; and the impartial administration of Lucullus in Asia, of which we shall read later, was hitting the financiers hard. Pompey too had his grudge against the Senate, which viewed his irregular promotion with alarm and would have kept him out of office if it had dared.

The two consuls now undid much of Sulla's work. The Tribunes were restored to their old position, and full power of legislation given back to the Assembly. The Judicia were handed over to a mixed body composed of Senators, Equites and Tribuni Aerarii, of whom the last were probably representatives of the next grade of wealth below the Equites. Finally the power of the Censors to revise the list of the Senate was restored. In this way the rule of the Senate, as Sulla designed it, came to an end eight years after his death. The pretence that the ruler of legions was not the master of Rome was exploded.

The year however saw the rise of a man who might under more favourable circumstances have built up a party of moderate men, whose honesty and ability could have saved the state. M. Tullius Cicero, born in 106 at Arpinum, the birthplace of Marius, came to the front in this year by his prosecution of Verres. This interesting scoundrel had been by turns a Marian and a Sullan and began his career of extortion in Cilicia. Appointed to the governorship of Sicily in 73, he had for three years devastated the island. The farmers he ruined by his enormous requisitions of corn, which he sold for his own profit ; justice and local offices he sold for the same purpose; and he swept temples and private houses of every work of art he could lay hands on; for he was a connoisseur in art. Flogging and crucifixion were the penalties for opposing his will, and his cruelty respected neither native nor Roman citizen. Cicero had the weight of Senatorial influence to contend against and the eloquence of Hortensius, till then the unchallenged leader of the Roman bar; but proceeding at once to the evidence, he presented his case so convincingly that Verres, without waiting for the verdict, withdrew into exile.

The Pirate War, 79–67 B.C. At the end of the year Crassus persuaded Pompey that both armies should be disbanded, and Pompey withdrew into private life for two years before he got another chance of distinction. Then the inability of ordinary commanders to cope with the pirates of the Eastern Mediterranean gave him the greatest opportunity he had yet enjoyed. Pirates had been the scourge of that sea since the days of Homer. Athens in her prime had held them in check, and at a later date Pergamum and Rhodes had policed the seas. But in the first century B.C. the pirates had grown into an organized state with head-quarters in Cilicia, nominally a Roman Province, and in Crete, sailing in squadrons under their own admirals and reinforced by refugees of all nations. Their position made them allies of Mithradates, and their activities not only crippled trade but almost entirely cut off the Roman corn-supply from over the sea. In 79 Servilius had dislodged them for the moment, but the outbreak of war with Mithradates in 74 roused them to redoubled efforts. M. Antonius, father of Mark Antony, who was sent out with special powers to deal with them in 74, was an ignominious failure and died in Crete in 71. After this the daring of the pirates was greater than ever. They harried the coasts of Italy, burnt corn-ships at Ostia, and actually carried off two

Praetors from the Appian Road. Metellus in 68 conquered Crete ; but the nuisance went on, and owing to
the continued interference with trade distress in Rome
became acute.

Something had to be done, and a tribune Gabinius
in 67 proposed in the Assembly that for the Pirate War
a man should be nominated, who should have *an unlimited command over the seas and fifty miles inland for
three years* with a vast force of men and ships and money,
and that all provincial governors should be bound to
assist him when required. No name was mentioned, but
no one other than Pompey was thought of. In spite of
Senatorial opposition the measure was passed and the
command given to Pompey. In forty-one days he had
cleared the sea west of Sicily, and another forty-nine
sufficed for him to drive the pirates back to Cilicia and
to take their stronghold. His prisoners to the number
of twenty thousand he settled in the depopulated towns
of Asia Minor and elsewhere; and they proved by their
subsequent good behaviour that their piracy had been
the result of Roman slackness rather than of their natural
depravity. Pompey had done his work well in the short
space of three months. But another and a greater work
was waiting for him.

Second Mithradatic War, 74–63 B.C. The war of
which we have now to tell is as important as Sulla's Mithradatic War, though it has not a chapter to itself. But it
is closely bound up with the overthrow of the Senate
and must fall into its place in that story. Sulla's arrangements for Asia Minor had been only provisional, and he
had been prevented by home affairs from finally settling
with Mithradates. Indeed Murena, who had been left
in the East with the two legions of Fimbria, had continued to fight and had only ceased hostilities after a defeat
on the R. Halys and peremptory orders from Sulla to keep

quiet[1]. For several years Mithradates trained his army
on Roman lines, welcomed fugitives from Rome and
cultivated the friendship of Sertorius, while he leagued
himself with the pirates of Cilicia and his son-in-law
Tigranes of Armenia.

The occasion of this war as of the first was the death
of a king of Bithynia, another Nicomedes. He bequeathed
his country in 75 to the Romans; the Senate at once
declared it a province, and Mithradates saw all hope of

Western Asia

expansion to the North and West cut off. War broke out
in 74, and Cotta and Lucullus were sent to the East, Cotta
operating in the neighbourhood of the Propontis while
Lucullus was to advance from Cilicia. Mithradates at
first overran Bithynia, defeated Cotta at Chalcedon and
destroyed his fleet, and then proceeded to blockade
Cyzicus. But Lucullus moved cautiously from Cilicia
and shut in the king on the narrow isthmus on which

[1] This series of skirmishes is called the "Second Mithradatic War"
by some writers and the later war the third.

Cyzicus stands. All the winter the Pontic army suffered terribly, but in the spring managed to escape by sea with great loss. Lucullus followed up his success by raising a fleet and defeating the king on the Aegean. These blows caused Mithradates to retire eastwards, and Lucullus following surprised him in 72 at Cabira near the R. Lycus and inflicted so severe a defeat upon him that the king fled as a suppliant to Tigranes, who for the moment kept him as a prisoner.

For the next two years Lucullus was engaged in conquering Pontus and in relieving the Province of Asia from the load of debt which Sulla had left on it. By striking off arrears of debt and forbidding money-lenders to exact higher interest than 12 per cent., he enabled the province to clear off its debts in four years; but he hopelessly offended the Publicani whose profits he interfered with. As yet he was too successful to be superseded, but the capitalists in Rome waited for their chance.

In 70 he demanded from Tigranes the surrender of Mithradates, but the king of Armenia angry at the demand took up arms in defence of his father-in-law. Lucullus accordingly in 69 left his legates to hold Pontus and crossing the Euphrates advanced to the siege of Tigranocerta, the new capital which Tigranes had lately built. To the king the small Roman force of fifteen thousand men seemed too many for an embassy but too few for an army; but they routed the Asiatic hordes without difficulty and the city surrendered. Next year, 68, Lucullus advanced into the mountains against Artaxata the old capital. But though he won victories, winter was coming on and his legions refused to go further. He was forced to retire into Mesopotamia, where he heard that Mithradates had raised new forces and driven his legates out of Pontus. On the top of this, one of his legates Triarius was cut up with seven thousand men at Ziela in the early part of 67. Lucullus now received the unwelcome tidings that his political opponents in Rome had taken advantage of the change in his fortunes to supersede him. Glabrio, the proconsul of Bithynia, had received orders to take command, and Lucullus soon after retired from public life to the pleasures of an epicure.

The Manilian Law, 66 B.C. Lucullus was superseded while Pompey was fighting the Pirates. Glabrio did little or nothing, and it was not unnatural that the Romans on the conclusion of the Pirate War looked to the man, who had done so well already and was still in the East with an enormous force, to finish off the struggle with Mithradates. A tribune Manilius proposed that Pompey should have the provinces of Asia, Bithynia and Cilicia with similar powers to those which had been given him for crushing the Pirates. Cicero spoke in favour of the motion, and Pompey was given the chance of putting the finishing touches to the hard work which Lucullus had done.

Tigranes had quarrelled again with Mithradates, and Phraates king of Parthia joined the Roman side. Pompey advancing from Cilicia surprised and totally defeated Mithradates in Lesser Armenia in 66. Nicopolis, 'the city of victory,' was founded on the site of the battle, and the old king took refuge in the Crimea where he met his death in 63. Meanwhile Pompey turned on Tigranes but on the humble submission of that king left him in his kingdom, making him surrender all his conquests and pay an indemnity of six thousand talents. After some fighting near the Caucasus and a year spent in quieting Pontus, Pompey moved south to Syria, which he made a province in 64. In Palestine he deposed the Maccabean ruler Aristobulus and set up that prince's brother Hyrcanus as king under the supremacy of Rome. But he did not wish to offend a fanatical people by hard treatment and, after insisting on penetrating into the ' Holy of Holies '

in the Temple, he left the Jews in peace. A year more
he spent in distributing rewards and punishments among
the inhabitants of Asia Minor and then returned to Italy,
having secured peace on the Eastern frontier and having
added a huge slice of territory to the empire.

Gnaeus Pompeius Magnus

But the two great commands which he had enjoyed
had accustomed men to the idea of putting a large part of
the Roman world and of the Roman forces in the hands
of one man for a long period. They had proved to men

that Senatorial control and the regular arrangements for war were incapable of meeting any serious emergency. Pompey landed in Italy in 62 to find that the forces of disorder had been busy in his absence.

Coin of Mithradates VI, 75 B.C.
Obv. Mithradates. *Rev.* Stag feeding

		DATES		DATES
I.	Sertorius in Spain	83–72	Lepidus's rising ..	78
	Metellus in command ..	79–76		
	Pompey in command ..	76–72		
	Assassination of Sertorius ..	72		
II.	Spartacus's Slave War ..	73–71		
	Crassus crushes the slaves ..	71		
III.	War with Pirates ..	79–67	Pompey and Crassus consuls	70
	Failure of M. Antonius ..	74–71	Overthrow of Senatorial supremacy ..	70
	Metellus conquers Crete ..	68	Cicero prosecutes Verres	70
	Pompey finishes the war ..	67	Lex Gabinia	67

	DATES		DATES
IV. War with Mithradates	74–63		
Lucullus's victory at Cyzicus	73		
Cabira	72		
Reorganization of Asia	72–70		
Capture of Tigranocerta	69		
War renewed in Asia Minor	68–67	Lex Manilia	66
Pompey conquers the East	66–63		
Death of Mithradates	63	Pompey returns to Italy	62

CHAPTER XXI

CICERO, CATILINE AND CAESAR

THE principal features of the ten years 70–60 B.C. in Rome are on the one hand the attempt of Cicero to unite all men of ability and honesty in support of the Republic; and on the other the rise of Caesar, the one strong man who was capable of brushing aside all formalities and laying the foundations of a new Rome. In order to understand a rather difficult period, we must try to get some idea of the forces at work.

The Conservative party. The Senate was weak and discredited, with the magic of a great past to lend it a fictitious importance. Its less respectable members used their position to enrich themselves with the plunder of provinces; the more honest were represented by M. Porcius Cato, honest and stupid and pig-headed like his ancestors, incapable of seeing the needs of the Rome of his day. The Equites took their lead from Crassus, who was angry with Pompey for robbing him of part of the glory of putting down Spartacus and envious of his rival for his Eastern successes.   But there was little help in Crassus, who could not lead by himself but looked to his money-

Marcus Tullius Cicero

bags as a means of rising to power on the shoulders of someone else.

The one real hope for Senate and Equites alike, if they had known it, lay in Cicero, a man of sound character and great eloquence, who by his defence of S. Roscius, a victim of the proscriptions, had won credit in Sulla's life-time and by his attack on Verres in 70 had won the regard of all decent men. His eloquence was at once his great asset and his undoing. Coupled with his vanity it made him a leader where he should have been a subordinate; and he had not either the nerve to keep steadily on in a crisis or the thick skin to endure attacks. For the present his policy was to unite all the good elements of Italy and of Rome in support of a moderate form of Senatorial government, and by the integrity of this administration to set up an authority of character and talent which should be stronger than the money of a Crassus or the army of a general. He thought that in Pompey the state had a general who was at once loyal and independent; and he hoped to rally all the conservative elements of the state—the Optimates, a name which has already been loosely used for the Conservative party—in a *concordia ordinum* or union of the two great ranks of society, the Senate and the Equites, round the successful general.

The Democrats. On the other side was the democratic party, the Populares, who had been able to lift up their heads since 70 B.C., when the tribunes and the Assembly had recovered their powers. They were specially interested in the land-question and the pressure of debt, which grew urgent as Sulla's veterans threw up their farms and swelled the city mob.

C. Julius Caesar, now thirty years old, was finding himself as their leader. He had narrowly escaped death in the proscriptions owing to his relationship to Marius. He had afterwards gone to Rhodes to study oratory and on his way there had fallen into the hands of pirates. Jesting with his captors he told them that when ransomed he would come back and crucify them all, and on regaining his liberty duly carried out his promise. He returned

to Rome in 74 and through his liberality and charm of
manner began to be the centre round which the democratic
leaders gathered. He supported the Gabinian law in
opposition to the Senate, but had already in his mind the
idea of balancing Pompey's power from the democratic
side. With this end he lavished money on games, while
he was Curule Aedile in 65. He found the money of Crassus
useful for the purpose, while Crassus hoped with Caesar's
help to get control of Egypt, which was giving trouble at
the time, and with it the management of the corn supply
of Rome.

Anarchists. The Democratic party had however an
undesirable left wing of extremists or anarchists. Nothing had been done to lighten the distress which had
followed the Social and Civil wars, the ten-years' horror
of 90–80 B.C. The Sullan veterans, who had been rewarded
with land, could not make their farms pay and came to
Rome looking for a more suitable, that is, a more sanguinary employment. The ruffians, who had gained by
the proscriptions and confiscations, had quickly squan-
dered their ill-gotten gains. The children of the proscribed,
reduced suddenly from wealth to penury, swelled the class
of desperate men ; and the successes of Spartacus had
unsettled every slave in the peninsula. There was fine
material for a conflagration, and a leader was not wanting.

Catiline. L. Sergius Catilina, a member of an old
Roman family, was a man of great physical strength ;
and having considerable powers of mind and a gift for
attracting rogues to him, he became the hero of spend-
thrift young nobles and broken-down soldiers and all who
looked to violence as a means of mending their fortunes.
Unscrupulous and reckless, he was stained with such
crimes that he shocked even the Romans of his own day,
who were not very particular. He was useful to Sulla
during the proscriptions, had been Praetor and in 67

Pro-praetor in Africa, where he had committed himself
deeply by misgovernment and extortion, and on his return
in 66 was prosecuted by P. Clodius. Being prevented
from standing for the consulship of 65, as the trial was
undecided at the time of the elections, he is said to have
formed a conspiracy with his accuser Clodius and a certain
Piso to murder the consuls and proclaim Crassus as Dictator
and Caesar as Master of the Horse. That Catiline may
have formed some wild-cat scheme is likely enough; and
he may have sounded members of the soberer wing of the
Democrats as to what assistance they would give him.
But Caesar was much too clear-headed to get entangled
with any of Catiline's schemes, and Crassus the banker had
too much to lose.

At any rate nothing came of the plot. Catiline,
acquitted now by arrangement with Clodius, prepared to
stand for the consulship of 63, and again rumour said
that Crassus and Caesar were behind him. In alarm the
Senators looked for a candidate and were at last driven
to support Cicero, whom under other circumstances they
would have passed over with contempt as a *novus homo*
and a native of Arpinum. Cicero, with Italian support
as well, was easily elected, and C. Antonius by a few votes
beat Catiline for second place. Antonius was a doubtful
character. But Cicero secured his loyalty by promising
him that he should have the rich province of Macedon
next year, and he was then free to meet the attacks of
both wings of the Democratic party and to rally the rest
of the state against them.

Rullus and Rabirius, 63 B.C. The respectable democrats opened the proceedings with an attempt to set up
a power which should be a counterpoise to that of Pompey.
Crassus and Caesar put up a tribune Rullus to propose
an agrarian law. Land was to be bought up in Campania
and elsewhere throughout Italy for distribution in allot-

ments, and the proceeds of the recent Asiatic conquests were to be used for the purpose. For carrying out the scheme ten commissioners were to be appointed with power over the whole resources of the state for five years, 'ten kings' as Cicero styled them. But the city mob had no desire to work on farms, and Cicero had no doubt of Pompey's loyalty. The bill was withdrawn. Later another tribune came forward to prosecute an old man Rabirius on the charge that thirty-seven years before he had assisted in the murder of Saturninus. Caesar was appointed one of the judges, and Rabirius was convicted but appealed to the Comitia. The Comitia was dissolved and the trial ended by the lowering of the flag on the Janiculum, the old-time warning of an Etruscan invasion. But the democrats had made clear the principle that no agitator—Saturninus or another—could be condemned to death except by the people. Soon after this Caesar was elected to the office of Pontifex Maximus, a post of no political importance but one of dignity and valuable to him as a democratic leader.

The Catilinarian Conspiracy, 63 B.C. At length the extremists made their effort. Catiline was a candidate for the consulship again in the autumn of 63 and meant this time to secure election by force. At the same time he was mustering troops in Etruria under an old Sullan officer Manlius. He made no secret of his designs; and Cicero told the Senate that slaves and veterans were to be let loose on Rome, the city burnt, the consuls and all honest men massacred, and *novae tabulae* or the cancelling of all debts proclaimed. The Senate postponed the elections till Oct. 28 and armed the consuls with the Ultimum Decretum.

The revolt broke out at Faesulae under Manlius, but Catiline still remained in Rome. After the elections were held and he was again defeated, he called a meeting at

Cicero denounces Catiline

the house of M. Porcius Laeca, at which two of the conspirators agreed to call on Cicero in the morning and
murder him in his own house.   Cicero getting wind of the
danger—and he had before this been going about with a
breast-plate under his robes—refused admittance to the
assassins and denounced Catiline in the Senate to his
face (Nov. 7).   The arch-conspirator now made off to
Etruria leaving Lentulus and Cethegus to direct proceedings in Rome ; they were to have everything in
readiness for a rising on Dec. 17.   Cicero had not
seized Catiline, for he had wished to entrap all the conspirators and not to strike the leader alone ; and now
he was waiting for Lentulus to supply him with a proof
of guilt beyond dispute. Fortunately the conspirators
made overtures to some ambassadors of the Gallic tribe
of Allobroges, who were in Rome, and they reported the
matter to Cicero.   By arrangement the ambassadors were
seized when they had treasonable letters from Lentulus
in their possession.   Lentulus and three others were taken,
and being unable to deny their signatures they were placed
under arrest.

Two days later, on Dec. 5, their fate was decided.
Cicero consulted the Senate, and every one approved of
the death-penalty, till Caesar moved as an amendment
that they should be imprisoned for life.   He was swaying
the Senate to his opinion, when Cato uncompromisingly
supported the severer proposal.   His speech decided the
question.   The four prisoners were strangled in the Tullianum, and Cicero announced their fate to the people in
the one word—*Vixerunt*.   In Feb. 62 Catiline was brought
to bay at Pistoria in Etruria.   Petreius, commanding in
place of Antonius, who shirked responsibility by pleading
illness, after a hard fight defeated and killed Catiline and
three thousand of his followers.

Cicero was now hailed as the saviour of his country, and

he was never tired of alluding to his vigorous action. It was the great moment of his life. For once he had drawn together the stabler elements of the state in defence of order, and for a time the party of Crassus and Caesar was in disgrace. But he was soon to feel the reaction. That the shelter of the Ultimum Decretum was no excuse for taking life had been the contention of the prosecutors of Rabirius, and Cicero's action alienated for ever the moderate democrats who might have supported him. At the same time Pompey was annoyed. Cicero had saved the state of which he himself would have liked to be the saviour ; and the campaign which ended at Pistoria was the very work on which he could have wished to employ his veteran troops. The union of all the best men in Italy began to break up as soon as Catiline had breathed his last.

Return of Pompey, 61 B.C. Caesar went off to Further Spain in 61 to take up the duties of Pro-praetor, and in the same year Pompey entered Rome and celebrated a magnificent triumph for his successes in the East. It had been a relief to all parties that he had disbanded his army on his landing in Italy ; but so far from showing gratitude the Senate took pains to annoy him. Resentment at his share in the legislation of 70 B.C. and at his special commands in the East made the Senators critical. When he applied according to custom for the ratification of his acts in Asia and allotments of land for his soldiers, Cato and Lucullus, who had himself done much of the work for which Pompey was honoured, questioned each separate act and inquired into each minute detail, while Pompey chafed and fumed. The Senate also quarrelled with the Equites. The Publicani had anticipated great results from Pompey's Eastern conquests and had bought the taxes of Asia at a high price. Now the results had not equalled their expectations, and they applied to be let off their bargain. Cato again led the opposition, and the breach between the two orders widened.   Thus Cicero's idea of a Senate united with the Equites under the leadership of Pompey had crumbled away to nothing. To some extent the fault lay with Pompey.   He was a good soldier and looked well after his troops, but in the city he was a wet blanket.   His pompous manner did not go down with any one, and he was too conceited to stand permanently aloof.

The Coalition of 60 B.C.   Affairs were at a dead-lock, when Caesar returned from Spain, having made enough money to pay off his debts to Crassus and having learnt in a short campaign that he had a genius for military leadership.   At once with a master-hand he smoothed out the tangle.   Forfeiting a triumph in order to stand for the consulship, he proposed to Pompey and Crassus that they should unite with him for common ends.   Pompey was to have the ratification of his acts and the rewards for his troops which he desired, and to seal the bargain he was to marry Julia, Caesar's daughter.   Crassus and the Equites were content with the promise of the revision of their taxing-contracts.   Caesar himself would carry with him the Democratic party, and he stipulated that he should be consul for 59.

The bargain was struck, and the Coalition, the ' three-headed monster,' took charge of Rome with Caesar as consul, 59 B.C.   Cicero had been invited to join the Three but could not bring himself to leave the side of the Senate. But the Senatorial colleague of Caesar, Bibulus, exemplified the incapacity of the Senate for seeing when it had to deal with a big man.   He tried every means of thwarting Caesar ; he used the Tribune's veto ; he proclaimed a Justitium or cessation of all business on the ground that he was going to see unfavourable omens.   Veto and omens Caesar brushed on one side ; he fulfilled his promises to Pompey and Crassus and then made provision for his

own future.   The Senate had tried to arrange that his
Proconsular appointment should be the care of the woods
and forests of Italy.   Caesar told Vatinius, a tribune, to
propose for him the Proconsulship of Cisalpine Gaul and
Illyricum for five years with Legati of Praetorian rank
and the power of raising an army.   The *Lex Vatinia*, 59,
parallel to the Gabinian and Manilian laws, was passed,
and the Senate, making a virtue of necessity, added Gallia
Narbonensis.   Caesar had now the chance which had been
given to Pompey; but his province was at the gates of Italy.

Removal of Cato and Cicero.   Pompey and Crassus
were to keep Rome in order, but it was thought well to
get rid of Cicero and Cato.   Cato was easily disposed of.
The king of Egypt had died leaving his dominions including Cyprus to Rome.   However one son Auletes had
tried to seize Egypt, and, as he had paid a huge bribe to
Rome, he was left to maintain his hold if he could.   Another son had seized Cyprus and sent no bribe.   Cato was
offered the task of annexing the island and did not refuse.
The work kept him out of Rome till 57.   In the case of
Cicero, Caesar made one more effort to win his support,
giving him the choice of several posts including one on
his own staff if he would come to Gaul.   But on his refusal
Caesar took other measures, natural enough, but not very
creditable to their author.   Clodius, the supposed con-
federate of Catiline in 65, was the scandal of Rome.   He
had dressed up as a woman and obtained admission to the
mysteries of Bona Dea, which only women might celebrate.
He had, according to rumour, intrigued with Caesar's wife ;
and though Caesar did not believe it, yet he divorced her,
saying that ' Caesar's wife must be above suspicion.'   The
main fact about him now was that he hated Cicero.   Caesar
allowed him to be adopted into a plebeian family that he
might be eligible for the Tribuneship.   Then as Tribune
Clodius attacked his foe.   He carried a law that anyone

who put a citizen to death without appeal should be banished, and Cicero went into exile. Clodius plundered his town and country houses and proclaimed that anyone who proposed his recall would be regarded as a public enemy.

Then at last Caesar hurried off to Gaul where his presence was urgently needed.

DATES

65.	Caesar Aedile.
65.	Catiline's supposed plot.
63.	Cicero Consul.
63.	Rullus and Rabirius.
63.	Catilinarian Conspiracy.
62.	Catiline killed at Pistoria.
61.	Pompey returns to Rome.
60.	The Coalition or "First Triumvirate."
59.	Caesar and Bibulus Consuls.
58.	Cicero and Cato removed.
58.	Caesar goes to Gaul.

CHAPTER XXII

CAESAR IN GAUL

SIXTY years had passed since Gallia Narbonensis became a Province, and in that time the south of Gaul had been largely Romanized. Traders and farmers brought civilization with them, and even beyond the limits of Roman territory roads and bridges and towns showed that the same influences were making themselves felt. But no satisfactory provision had been made for the defence of the frontiers; while the Aedui, the most friendly of all the tribes to the Romans, had lost some of their vigour by contact with civilization and were hard pressed between their neighbours the Arverni and Sequani. The Gauls had no real union among themselves but were a

collection of tribes dwelling in cantons, the common
people putting themselves under the protection of some
noble, who by reason of his prowess in war was held in
honour even in peace.   Justice and Religion were in the
hands of the priests or Druids chosen from the noble
families ; human sacrifice was part of their ritual, and their
worship centred round the powers of Nature.   The Belgae,

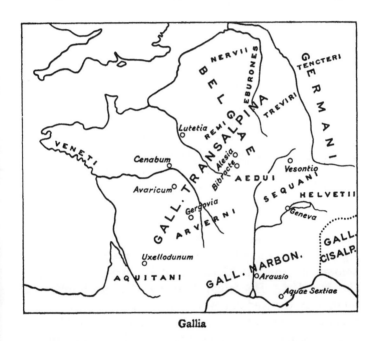

Gallia

a collection of tribes more nearly related to the Germans
than to the Gauls, occupied the north-east, more savage
than the Gauls proper owing to their greater distance from
civilization.

The great danger to Gauls and Romans alike lay in
the Germans beyond the Rhine ; and the rivalry of Gallic
tribes gave their dangerous neighbours an opportunity of

interference. About 72 B.C. the Sequani, engaged in a
quarrel with the Aedui, had called in Ariovistus the chief
of the German tribe of the Suebi to their aid. He had
come only too readily, but refused to return to his own
country at the end of the war. Pressure from the Germans
acted in other ways too. The Helvetii, cramped for room
between the Alps and the Jura and exposed to German
raids, had made up their minds to migrate in a body to
Western Gaul. They burnt their towns and were on the
move in the spring of 58, asking leave of the Romans to
pass through Gallia Narbonensis.

The Helvetii and the Germans, 58 B.C. It was this
piece of news which had hastened Caesar's departure from
Rome. There were two roads down the Rhone valley
from Geneva by which the Helvetii might come: an easy
road along the south bank and then through the Province,
a difficult road on the north bank through the narrow pass
between the Jura and the river. Caesar had only one
legion in the Province but could not allow the invasion
of the Helvetii to upset the whole of Gaul. Breaking
down the bridge at Geneva he left one of his Legati,
Labienus, to guard the south bank, hastily raised two
legions in Cisalpine Gaul, and with three more which he
summoned from the Illyrian frontier hurried back to meet
the invaders. He found that by the good offices of
Dumnorix the Aeduan, who unlike his brother Divitiacus
was a foe to the Romans, the Helvetii had obtained leave of
the Sequani to pass along the north bank and were already
crossing the Arar (Saône). Caesar was in time to cut up
the rear-guard composed of the Tigurini and forced the
invaders to turn northwards. But as he followed them,
his supplies began to fail owing to the intrigues of Dumnorix, and he was forced to fall back on Bibracte (near
Autun), the capital of the Aedui. The Helvetii, thinking
he was in full retreat, fell on him there but were routed

after a fierce fight, and the survivors submitted, 58 B.C. They were ordered to return to their own country and to hold it against the Germans.

This victory produced a great impression, and deputations from all Gaul came to congratulate Caesar. But noticing some hesitation in their manner he had an interview with Divitiacus, from whom he learnt the truth. The Gauls were thoroughly afraid of the Germans and begged Caesar to save them. He at once marched into the country of the Sequani and occupied their capital Vesontio (Besançon). But he found it necessary to quiet a panic among his officers, some of whom had not realized that they were in for serious fighting and were alarmed now at the description of their formidable foes. He then had an interview with Ariovistus, mounting some of his faithful tenth legion to act as his body-guard ; but Ariovistus maintained that he had as much claim to a footing in Gaul as the Romans, and in the end made a treacherous attack upon the escort. A few days later Caesar managed to bring on a pitched battle some distance to the east of Vesontio, in which the promptness of young Crassus decided the day. Only a few of the Germans escaped with Ariovistus across the Rhine. The German danger was over and the Rhine the recognized frontier of Gaul.

The Belgae, 57 B.C. Caesar had in one year accomplished the ostensible purpose of his Proconsulship and as in succeeding years wintered in Cisalpine Gaul to keep an eye on home affairs. He had no intention however of resting content with what he had done. In the early months of 57 he learnt that the Belgae had formed a confederacy for a general rising and were attacking the Remi who would not join them. Hurrying north with an army of eight legions he occupied a strong position on the river Aisne, waited till the impatience of the enemy loosened the bonds of their confederacy, and then crushed each tribe in turn. While assailing the Nervii, a northern tribe and the most warlike of all, he came near to a disaster. His army was preparing a camp among the forests round the river Sambre, when suddenly the enemy appeared on all sides. Hastily the men formed as best they could. But two legions were surrounded, and the situation was saved only by the steadiness of the tenth legion and Caesar's own bravery, who seized a shield and rushed into the fray, seeming to be at every point where his presence was most needed. With the submission of the Nervii the resistance of the Belgae was at an end. A wedge of Roman conquest had been driven through the centre of Gaul.

The Veneti and Aquitani, 56 B.C. At the beginning of 56 Caesar was detained longer than usual in the south by a conference with Pompey and Crassus at Luca. The importance of this meeting will be seen later; but for the present it is enough to say that Caesar gained an extension of his command for another five years till March 49 B.C. Meanwhile at the close of 57 young Crassus had moved towards Brittany and received the nominal submission of the Veneti in that district. Fighting however broke out in the early spring, and it was found that land-operations were hampered by the nature of the country. Building a fleet of light rowing galleys at the mouth of the Loire Caesar gave Decimus Brutus the task of destroying the stout sailing ships of the Veneti. He provided his crews with long scythes with which they cut through the enemy's rigging and rendered their ships helpless, and the Veneti submitted. Crassus in the meantime had subdued Aquitania, and the resistance of Western Gaul was ended.

Germany and Britain, 55–54 B.C. Gaul was now conquered, but there was still danger of interference from Germany and from Britain. From Germany the Usipetes and Tencteri, driven forward by the pressure of the Suebi, crossed the lower Rhine. Caesar moved down the valley of the Meuse and by means of treachery massacred the invaders, men, women and children. Then to frighten the Suebi he crossed the Rhine by a wooden bridge which he built in ten days. But as he met with little opposition, he withdrew, after ravaging the country, and broke down the bridge behind him. The Germans had received their lesson to leave Gaul alone. But Britain was a refuge for irreconcilable Gauls and a source of danger to the mainland. Crossing the Channel from near Boulogne in the summer of 55 Caesar landed with two legions probably near Deal, a standard-bearer of the Tenth setting the example by leaping overboard with his ' eagle ' in the face of the natives who lined the shore. The Britons offered little real resistance. But a storm disabled many of Caesar's ships, and his cavalry-transports were unable to make the shore ; and as the season was now advanced, and the natives were gaining confidence and harassing the camp, Caesar returned to Gaul and made preparations for another invasion next year.

In 54 he landed at the same point as before and without opposition. He had with him four legions, and advancing twelve miles he captured a native stronghold. But a storm which destroyed many of his ships compelled him to return to the coast and send instructions to Labienus for the building of a second fleet. Then after making his way slowly through forests, where the enemy hung on his flanks and harassed his march, he crossed the Thames probably a little above Kingston and advanced against Cassivellaunus the native commander. Caesar stormed his stronghold, possibly at St Albans, but went no further. He took hostages for the good behaviour of the islanders, and his purpose was effected by the impression which he had made. He returned to Gaul at the end of the summer, and it was a century before Roman troops were again seen in the island.

Revolt of the Belgae, 54–53 B.C.   Even before Caesar sailed in 54, the Treviri under Indutiomarus had shown signs of restlessness, and Dumnorix the Aeduan had been killed for attempted desertion.   The truth was that the rapidity of Caesar's movements had paralysed the Gauls at first, and they had submitted before they were really conquered.   Now they were recovering confidence and were ready for a new war.   In Caesar's absence Indutiomarus had prevailed on Ambiorix, chief of the Eburones, to organize a rising ; and the conspirators only waited till Caesar should have gone as usual into Cisalpine Gaul for the winter.   They were helped by the fact that a scarcity of corn had compelled Caesar to disperse his legions in separate camps over a wide area.   As soon as Caesar had gone south, Ambiorix surrounded the camp of Sabinus and Cotta, which was in the territory of the Eburones, and representing that the whole of Gaul was in revolt offered to conduct the Romans to the camp of Labienus. Sabinus weakly agreed, and the whole force was cut to pieces on the way.   Q. Cicero, brother of the orator, had his camp among the Nervii.   He was wise enough to see through Ambiorix's offer of a safe conduct, but could with difficulty keep the enemy at bay and get a message through to the commander-in-chief asking for help.   At once Caesar hurried north with two legions and relieved Cicero in the nick of time.   But the whole of the Belgic territory was in a ferment.   Caesar was forced to borrow a legion from Pompey, and raising two others he fell upon the Nervii in the spring of 53, while Labienus crushed the Treviri. A second time the Rhine was bridged and punishment inflicted on the Suebi who had helped the rebels.   The Eburones were chastised with exemplary severity, though Ambiorix escaped ; and for the moment peace was restored.

Revolt of Vercingetorix, 53–52 B.C. The revolt of
the Belgae had shown the possibility of isolating and
cutting up detachments of Caesar's army ; and news from
Rome filtered through into Gaul that the Coalition with
Pompey and Crassus was breaking up and that Caesar's
position was none too secure. The Belgae had no wish
to try the fortune of war again, and it was well for Caesar
that the two great risings in Gaul were not combined
in one. But through the western half of the country
preparations were set on foot; and under the lead of Vercingetorix, chief of the Arverni, one last effort was made
to throw off the Roman yoke. They waited till the winter
of 53 when Caesar was in Cisalpine Gaul and his legions
in winter-quarters to the north of the Loire ; and then the
revolt broke out with the massacre of all the Romans in
Cenabum (Orleans). The news was spread among the
Gauls by shouts from man to man along the hill-sides,
and the centre and west of Gaul rose to arms. Caesar
was cut off from his troops ; but collecting a small force he
made his way through the snows of the Cevennes with his
wonted rapidity and unexpectedly fell on the Arverni.
His sudden appearance drew Vercingetorix southward
from the Loire, and Caesar was able to slip round the
enemy and join his own legions. Then moving south he
marched against Vercingetorix.

The Gallic chief's plan was to starve Caesar by laying
waste the country and burning the towns. But the
Bituriges persuaded him to spare Avaricum their capital
some 50 miles south of the Loire, and Caesar crossing the
river took it by storm. Thence making his way up the
valley of the Allier into the territory of the Arverni he
made an attack on Gergovia which Vercingetorix was
holding. A repulse here caused Caesar to retire north
to join Labienus, who had advanced against Lutetia (Paris)
and who now came south to meet his leader. The momen-

tary success of the rebels caused the Aedui to join the revolt. Caesar was forced to hire some mercenary cavalry from the Germans and for some time was in danger of being cut off from the Province and Italy. But fortune soon turned again. Vercingetorix was driven into Alesia not far from Bibracte. Caesar surrounded the town with two lines of fortifications, one to keep in the defenders and the other as a protection against the army of two hundred and fifty thousand Gauls who came to the relief of the town. Two battles against the two forces of the Gauls finished off the siege. Alesia surrendered, and Vercingetorix in 52 threw himself on Caesar's mercy, only to die six years later in the conqueror's triumph. No more serious fighting was necessary. The suppression of risings among the Belgae in 51 and the capture of the town of Uxellodunum near the Garonne left Caesar the undisputed master of Gaul.

Caesar had shown severity and in certain cases more than severity. He now set to work to repair the ravages of war. No cruel conditions were imposed. A moderate tribute was exacted, but the tribes were allowed to retain their local customs and in great measure to govern themselves under the supremacy of Rome. The more restless and energetic of the men were enrolled in Caesar's army, and the country, gradually becoming Romanized, settled down into the regular ways of civilized life.

Caesar was now ready to turn his attention towards Rome. His eight years of fighting had given him a trained army, which knew and worshipped him, but knew little of Rome. He had learnt too in his absence how to make a new country ; and in learning that he had learnt perhaps that there was something beyond the petty rivalries and narrow aims of Roman politics—that he might have to make a new Rome.

DATES

72. Ariovistus called in by Sequani.
58. Migration of Helvetii.
58. Bibracte. Helvetii sent back.
58. Vesontio. The Germans driven out.
57. Belgae subdued.
56. Veneti and Aquitani subdued.
55. Invasions of Germany and Britain.
54. Second Invasion of Britain.
54–53. Revolt of Belgae.
53–52. Revolt of Vercingetorix and Gauls.
51. Gaul finally subdued.

CHAPTER XXIII

BREAK-UP OF THE COALITION

Recall of Cicero, 57 B.C. Caesar started for Gaul
early in 58. Pompey and Crassus had been left to govern
Rome in the interests of the Coalition, while Clodius was
to manage the city-mob through the political clubs
(*sodalicia*), which he controlled. But the old jealousy
between Pompey and Crassus broke out afresh; and
Clodius, without Caesar to keep him in order, began to
rule the streets with his gangs of ruffians. The result
was that Pompey's position became very uncomfortable.
He was getting no advantage out of his alliance with Caesar
and felt the need of someone to keep Clodius in check.
With Pompey helpless the elections for 57 went all against
the Coalition, and the consul Lentulus Spinther began the
year by proposing the recall of Cicero. Pompey welcomed
the proposal. But Clodius had no intention of allowing his
enemy to return if he could help it, and his *operae* or gangs
made the streets unbearable. In the end a tribune Milo,
a man of the same breed as Clodius, got together an opposition gang and beat Clodius at his own game. The
recall of Cicero was carried with the help of Italian voters.

Cicero landed at Brundisium, and thousands turned out to welcome him, as he followed the Appian Road to Rome. Soon after his arrival he showed his gratitude to Pompey by proposing for him the control of the corn-supply for five years with Proconsular power throughout the Empire.

The Conference at Luca, 56 B.C. The Optimates were beginning to lift up their heads after Cicero's return. The Senate thought of revising the Agrarian law of 59, which gave land to Pompey's veterans; Cicero in his defence of Sestius made a strong attack on Vatinius, the proposer of Caesar's command in Gaul; and Domitius Ahenobarbus, who hoped to be consul in 55, openly gave out that he would propose the recall of Caesar. These hopes all came to nothing. Caesar in 56 met Pompey and Crassus at Luca on the frontier of Cisalpine Gaul and discussed the whole situation with them. He had still much work to do in Gaul and did not wish to have a serious conflict at home forced upon him for the present. It was agreed that Pompey and Crassus should be consuls in 55, after which Pompey was to command in Spain and Crassus in Syria for five years. Caesar himself obtained the extension of his proconsulship till March 49 and was to be consul in 48. The presence of nearly two hundred Senators in Luca lent weight to the agreement of the Three. The Coalition was firmly re-established, and Cicero admitted that he had been a ' born donkey ' to expect anything else.

Crassus and the Parthians, 54–53 B.C. The presence of some of Caesar's troops under young Crassus was needed to secure the election of the consuls ; but with their help everything passed off well. Cicero sent his brother to serve on Caesar's staff, and Pompey gained some popularity by building the first stone theatre in Rome. At the end of 55 Crassus started for his province. The conquests of Pompey had brought the Romans into

The Roman Forum

close contact with Parthia; but they had not accepted the Euphrates as the natural frontier in this direction. Crassus crossed that river in the summer of 54 but returned for the winter to Syria, where he was joined by his son. Next spring 53 B.C. in spite of warnings to march round the desert through the northern hill-country, he struck across the Euphrates into the sandy wilderness. After a few days the Parthians swooped down on the weary legions. Riding like the wind and shooting their arrows as they rode, they found Crassus's infantry the easiest of preys. Young P. Crassus with his little band of cavalry was unable to drive them off and advancing too far from the main body was surrounded and slain with his whole detachment. The infantry then began a retreat towards Carrhae (Haran). Crassus was lured into an interview with the Parthian chief, and he and his staff were murdered. C. Cassius with ten thousand men cut his way back to Antioch. But ten thousand remained prisoners in the hands of the Parthians together with many Roman standards. The rest of the force perished.

The death of Crassus was a blow to the Coalition. He was a buffer between his two partners, and with his removal the rivalry between them with all its possibilities became clear. Unfortunately in 54 B.C. the great personal link between the two had been snapped by the death of Julia, Caesar's daughter and Pompey's wife, who had done much to smooth relations between the two.

Pompey in Rome. Pompey did not leave Rome for his province after his consulship but sent his Legati Afranius and Petreius to take charge of Spain with the help of the legions which he had raised. He thought that his presence in Rome would give him an advantage over Caesar and that he would have the control of affairs in his own hands. He made a poor job of it. The gangs of Clodius and Milo renewed their rioting. During a whole year they made it impossible to hold the consular elections for 53; and again at the end of that year, when Milo was standing for the consulship and Clodius for the praetorship, the elections had to be postponed till the beginning of 52. In January of that year these two arch-ruffians met on the Appian Road, and Clodius was killed in the fray. His body was brought to Rome, and feeling ran so high that a funeral-pyre was raised in the Forum, and in the ensuing tumult the Senate House itself was burnt down. So serious was the disorder that the Senate placed itself under Pompey's protection and procured his election as Sole Consul for 52. Milo went into exile, Cicero breaking down in the attempt to deliver the speech which he had prepared in his defence.

Open breach between Pompey and Caesar. Men were now wondering what was to happen when Caesar's command in Gaul expired; and the difficulties, with which he was face to face owing to the Gallic revolts, gave some hope that Pompey and the Senate would be too strong for him. Pompey in the course of his consul-ship carried laws providing (i) that all candidates for office must appear in Rome, (ii) that praetors and consuls should not go to their provinces till five years after their year of office in Rome. Now it had been agreed at the Conference of Luca that Caesar's Gallic command should expire in March 49 and that he should be consul in 48 with the expectation of some other provincial appointment at the end of that year. He was anxious that there should be no interval during which he held no official position. For he knew that his enemies would prosecute him on one charge or another as soon as they could; and just as no man might stand for office while he was being prosecuted, so on the other hand no prosecution could be brought against a man while he was still in an official position. He therefore expected to be allowed to stay on in Gaul till the end of 49 and then to enter on his consulship without having previously canvassed in Rome. With regard to the personal candidature Pompey with his usual indecision had made Caesar an exception to the rule, though its whole object had been to thwart Caesar's plans. But at the end of 51 a proposal was made to supersede Caesar in March 49; and though at Pompey's request the motion was postponed, he promised to support it at a later date.

Early in 50, on the pretext of avenging Crassus, both Pompey and Caesar were requested to contribute a legion for war in Syria. Caesar complied, but Pompey gave the one which he had lent his rival in 53. Caesar's army was in this way reduced by two legions, which were not sent after all to the East but kept at Capua under Pompey's orders. The breach between the two rivals was clear enough, and Caesar began to look about for some one to represent him in Rome. He bought up the services of C. Curio, one of the ablest and most dissolute of the rising generation, who had lately been elected tribune. Curio in March 50 with Caesar's approval, who was confident of his own ability to beat Pompey in any fair field, proposed that Pompey and Caesar should resign their commands simultaneously. The motion was carried, but Pompey refused to agree and proposed that Caesar should resign in November 49, which would still allow an interval for prosecution. At the end of the year Curio joined Caesar in Cisalpine Gaul but returned to Rome on Jan. 1, 49 with a new offer from Caesar, that he should retain one province with one legion till the consular elections. Among the tribunes of 49 were two of Caesar's party, M. Antonius (the Mark Antony of Shakespeare) and Q. Cassius, brother of Crassus's legate. They insisted that Caesar's proposal should be read to the Senate. It was rejected; and in defiance of their veto a motion was carried that Caesar should be declared a public enemy, unless he at once disbanded his army; and the consuls were armed with the Ultimum Decretum. The two tribunes fled from Rome saying that their lives were in danger. Caesar addressed his soldiers telling them that he was forced to take up arms to maintain the liberty of the state against a clique of nobles. Though he had but one legion with him he crossed the Rubicon, the small stream which formed the northern boundary of Italy, and advanced on Ariminum.

The civil war had begun. Caesar had behind him a compact province and a splendid army devoted to him. Of all his officers none but Labienus and Q. Cicero deserted him. Pompey had nominally the rest of the Roman Empire. But twelve years of peace had made both him and his veterans less efficient, and he could not get to his best troops who were in Spain. The support too of the Senate, while it seemed to lend strength to his cause, really meant a division of authority most detrimental to military operations.

DATES

57. Cicero recalled.
56. Conference at Luca.
54. Death of Julia.
53. Death of Crassus.
52. Pompey Sole Consul.
51-50. Proposals for Caesar's return.
49. Caesar crosses the Rubicon.

CHAPTER XXIV

THE CIVIL WAR AND RULE OF CAESAR

A. War in Italy, 49 B.C. Caesar, when he crossed the Rubicon, had sent word to his troops in Gaul to move southwards as quickly as possible. His rapid movements paralysed his Senatorial opponents as much as they had paralysed the Gauls. While Pompey was coming to the conclusion that Rome could not be defended and was concentrating his forces in Apulia, Caesar had already moved down the Adriatic coast. He made one more ineffectual effort for peace, offering to disband his army if Pompey would go to his province in Spain. He then came upon Domitius Ahenobarbus who was trying to rally Pompey's personal adherents in Picenum. Sweeping him back from Auximum he shut him up in Corfinium. Pompey could send no help. Domitius made secret preparations for flight, and his men went over to Caesar in a body. Caesar dismissed the officers without harm; the men enlisted in his army. Pompey meanwhile, completely cut off from his legions in Spain, had resolved to fall back on the East, where the memory of his earlier conquests would still gain him adherents. He retired to Brundisium, whither Caesar followed him; and succeeded in embarking his troops and conveying them in safety to Greece. Caesar left Antony to secure Brundisium and South Italy against a return of the Pompeians and himself paid a brief visit to Rome. He had secured Italy by a two months' campaign; and his clemency to prisoners had given the lie to the rumours of coming massacres with which his enemies had scared the minds of the common people. On his way to Rome he met Cicero. For a while the latter wavered, but at last threw in his lot with the Pompeians and went off to Greece. Caesar met with but a cold reception from the Senate, but he had more important business than talking to do. He merely provided for the security of Italy, disappointing those who hoped for a cancelling of debt. Then sending Curio to secure Sicily and if possible to invade Africa, he himself started to join his legions in Gallia Narbonensis and to advance against Pompey's legates Afranius and Petreius in Spain.

B. **War in Spain, 49 B.C.** Caesar took his risks

Gaius Julius Caesar

wisely.   There was danger in leaving Italy, while Rome
was ill-disposed towards him; and Cato from Africa or
Pompey from Greece might return to Italy in his absence.
But Antony in Italy and Curio in Sicily were likely to be
able to hold the enemy in check; and if he himself could
conquer the Pompeians in Spain, he would then have a
united West behind him and no danger of a serious rising
in his rear, when he turned against the main body of the
enemy in the East.   Sending on troops to secure the
passes of the Pyrenees, he left D. Brutus and Trebonius to
blockade Massilia, whither Domitius had betaken himself
from Corfinium, and hastened to Spain.   The Pompeians
fell back to the line of the Ebro at his approach; and
Caesar came upon them at Ilerda on the river Sicoris, a
northern tributary of the Ebro.   He was greatly hampered by floods and at one time was cut off from his
supplies by the carrying away of his bridges across the
Sicoris.   The Pompeians thought that they had him at
their mercy.   But he crossed the stream higher up in
coracles; and Afranius and Petreius, finding that he was
surrounding the town, set off south-east across the hills
which lay between the Sicoris and the Ebro.   Caesar's
legions followed them and by splendid marching reached
the pass in the hills before the foe.   After four days the
Pompeians surrendered for want of food; and the governor
of Further Spain soon afterwards submitted.   Caesar
without a pitched battle had secured the West and received
the surrender of Pompey's legions.   Once more he dismissed his prisoners, allowing those who wished to enlist
under his command.   He now marched back to Massilia
which had surrendered to his Legati; and from there he
returned to Italy to find that he had been made Dictator
for the purpose of holding the consular elections.

Curio in the South had been less successful.   He had
driven Cato out of Sicily and so secured the Roman corn-

supply. But on crossing to Africa he had been surprised
by the king of Numidia, an ally of the Pompeians, and had
been killed together with most of his army. But for the
present the enemy made no use of the success which they
had gained.

C. **War in Greece, 48 B.C.** Caesar on his arrival in
Rome nominated himself as one of the consuls for 48 and
passed laws for the relief of the financial distress, the
restoration of the children of the proscribed, and the
enfranchisement of Cisalpine Gaul up to the Alps. Then
after a stay of eleven days in Rome he started for Brundisium to fight Pompey in Greece. The more disciplined
part of Pompey's army had already been defeated without
its leader in Spain. But with the Senators and Equites
and their adherents, who followed after him, and with
Romans living in the East, he had a force of nine legions
supplemented by various contingents of cavalry and light-
armed troops from all the nations of the East and a fleet
from Rhodes, Phoenicia and Egypt. He had no expectation that Caesar would cross to Greece before the spring
of 48. But as usual Caesar was too quick for his enemy.
He was at Brundisium with twelve legions, reduced by
campaigns to thirty-five thousand men in all, and transports for only a part of that number. But on Jan. 4 he
landed in Epirus near Oricum, eluding Bibulus, who had
been set to watch the coast and could only vent his rage
by destroying some of the transports on their return.
However Caesar was isolated in an enemy's country with
not more than 5000 men and with little prospect of Antony
being able to bring the remainder of his troops across to
him from Brundisium. Advancing north he captured
Oricum and Apollonia and was approaching Dyrrhachium,
when Pompey arrived from his head-quarters at Thessalonica to save that important harbour. At last in
March Antony put to sea. But a south wind carried him

past Caesar and past Dyrrhachium itself; and he was
obliged to run into a haven on the Illyrian coast and make
his way by land to join his commander.   Caesar's army
was now suffering from lack of supplies, and he felt that
he must try to bring Pompey to a decisive battle.   His
force was inferior in numbers to that of Pompey; but he
tried to enclose the enemy with a line of siege-works
fourteen miles in length and to cut him off at once from
Dyrrhachium and the interior.   The work went on amid

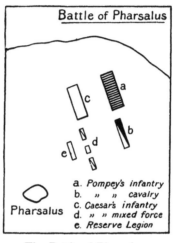

The Battle of Pharsalus

incessant fighting; but at last the Pompeians broke
through at a point to the south, where the walls were
unfinished, and inflicted a severe defeat on Caesar.
He retreated to Apollonia and thence over the hills into
Thessaly, whither the enemy followed him, disputing
already about the division of the spoils they were to win
and the punishment of the Caesarians.

Caesar was in a difficult situation, but could rely on
his men and on his own genius to pull him through a
pitched battle.   Pompey on the other hand with hot-

headed Senators on his staff, who knew nothing of warfare, could not prevent his friends from forcing his hand.   The battle which decided the fate of the Roman world was fought at Pharsalus in South Thessaly, Aug. 9, 48 B.C. Pompey with his great superiority in cavalry hoped to ride over Caesar's small body of horse and then to fall on the rear of his infantry.   But Caesar, conscious of the danger, had strengthened his cavalry by posting six cohorts of light infantry between the squadrons of horse and the Tenth legion in reserve behind them.   In the battle the Pompeian horsemen failed to break through the composite force opposed to them ; and the reserve legion charging on them, with *pila* used as pikes and not as missiles, drove them off the field.   On their flight the rear of Pompey's legions, who were already closely engaged, was exposed to attack, and a rout began.   Fifteen thousand were killed ; the remainder fled to the hills where they surrendered in a body next morning.   A few irreconcilables escaped to Dyrrhachium, where Cato had been left in command, and eventually reached Africa to rally their forces for another fight.   But the rank and file of the Pompeians including M. Junius Brutus, for whom Caesar had a great affection, and C. Cassius, commander of the Aegean fleet, took service under Caesar.

D.   War in Egypt, 47 B.C.   Pharsalus was the decisive battle of the war, but much still remained to be done.   Pompey had ridden off the field, when his cavalry was defeated, and joining his wife and son in Mytilene sailed for Egypt.   Ptolemy Auletes was now dead and had left his kingdom to his daughter Cleopatra and young Ptolemy, a mere boy.   Civil war had followed ; and now the young king, thinking that Pompey's presence would bring further trouble on Egypt, gave orders for his assassination.   The great man on his arrival was invited to come ashore in a small boat and was stabbed in the back as he stepped on to the beach. His head was then struck off before the eyes of his wife and child. Caesar coming in pursuit of his rival reached Alexandria in the autumn of 48. He was genuinely sorry that a man, who had done loyal service to the state and with whom he had been closely connected, an excellent soldier and a man of unblemished character, should have come to this end. Many times Caesar had tried to negotiate with Pompey and to avoid the clash of arms ; but vanity coupled with an honest though short-sighted purpose of maintaining Senatorial government had made Pompey refuse. Now Pompey was gone, and Caesar had no longer a jealous rival to fight against ; he was clearly fighting against the Senate and all it stood for.

In Egypt Caesar stayed nine months, either fascinated by Cleopatra or seeing in Egypt the link between Europe, Africa and the East, from which he might conquer them all. During the time he was in great danger. He had but three thousand men, and Ptolemy raising an army attacked him unexpectedly, while the mob of Alexandria joined in. Fighting went on round the harbour of that town, and Caesar had once to save his life by swimming. The arrival of a relieving army, which made its way through Palestine in the early part of 47, freed him from his difficulties. A battle was fought on the Nile in which the Egyptians were defeated and Ptolemy drowned. Caesar gave Cleopatra and a younger brother the nominal sovereignty of the country. But as the Romans obtained much corn from Egypt, a Roman garrison of two legions was left there and a Roman administrator. From Egypt Caesar marched into Syria against Pharnaces, son of Mithradates, who had taken advantage of the civil war to attack the Roman legate in Asia. A campaign of five days settled matters, and Caesar sent home his famous despatch, ' Veni, vidi, vici.'

E.   **Italy and Africa, 47–46 B.C.**   Caesar now returned to Italy.   He had been made Dictator a second time and Consul for five years and had been given the Tribunician power for life, as soon as the news of Pharsalus arrived. But in his absence things had been going badly.   In Spain Q. Cassius's misgovernment had caused a rising against him.   In Africa the Pompeians had rallied.   Under Cato and other republicans they had gathered fourteen legions and a large force of Numidians and had set up a rival Senate at Utica.   The republican fleet was harrying the coasts of Italy; and in Rome Mark Antony, no pattern of respectability himself, had had to deal with two insurrections which aimed at the cancelling of all debts. Caesar reached Rome at the end of 47 and to the surprise of all restored order without any massacres or proscriptions.   He gladly welcomed Cicero, who came to make his peace, and then began preparations for ending the Civil War by the conquest of Africa.   But his legions were weary of fighting and on receiving orders for a new campaign broke into mutiny.   Caesar met them and granted their discharge at once, addressing them no more as fellow-soldiers but 'Quirites,' civilians.   At the word which marked their severance from the chief whose labours and glory they had shared, the mutineers were quelled ; they professed their allegiance to Caesar and begged to be taken back into his service.

But the mutiny had delayed his start.   As he crossed to Africa, a storm dispersed his fleet, and he was left for some days at Leptis on the coast of Africa with no more than three thousand men.   His ships however arrived in the course of time bringing troops; and in April 46 he forced on a battle by attacking Thapsus.   The republicans were easily defeated ; and Caesar's men, tired of continual fighting, cut down fifty thousand of the fugitives, while he lost but fifty.   Cato retired to Utica and committed

suicide.　He was an honest but obstinately short-sighted
man, and he owes his reputation among posterity, partly
no doubt to his resolute championship of a losing cause,
but partly to the fact that Lucan wrote a striking line
about him :

Victrix causa deis placuit sed victa Catoni.
The gods favoured the victorious cause, Cato the vanquished.

Marcus Porcius Cato

Utica now surrendered ; Numidia was punished by loss
of its independence, the eastern half being incorporated
with the Province of Africa, the western half added to
Mauretania.　Caesar then returned to Rome and celebrated a fourfold triumph over Gaul, Egypt, Pontus and

Numidia ; for the conquest of his fellow-countrymen no triumph was possible.

He was now appointed Dictator for ten years and Praefectus Morum or Censor for three, and he began his work of governing Rome and Italy. The political clubs, which in Clodius's hands had been a source of anarchy, were abolished; and every association which might have political aims was required to be licensed for the future. The distributions of free corn were carefully limited, and the number of recipients reduced to one hundred and fifty thousand. To his veterans and to poor citizens he made grants of land but scattered them over Italy, that with only a few in any one place they might the more readily settle down in the life of the district ; and he encouraged settlements outside Italy, sending colonies to Carthage and Corinth which grew once more into busy towns. He also reformed the Roman Calendar. The old Roman year had consisted of 355 days, and the shortage of 10¼ had been made up from time to time by 'intercalating' an extra month. Carelessness however had allowed matters to get so far wrong that the calendar said August when the sun said June. To put matters right Caesar called in an astronomer, Sosigenes of Alexandria, by whose advice he made the year 46 B.C. to consist of 445 days. Then beginning the year on Jan. 1 instead of March 1, which had been the old New Year's Day, he adopted the year of 365 days with an extra day in February every fourth year. The error in this Julian calendar was very slight, 3 days in four centuries ; and in our calendar the error has been corrected since 1752, when the system introduced two centuries earlier by Pope Gregory XIII was adopted in England. Now we do not reckon 'century' years as leap-years, unless they are divisible by 400.

Munda, 45 B.C. One more campaign awaited Caesar. The sons of Pompey, Sextus and Gnaeus, with Labienus

and others had fled from Africa to Spain, where the misbehaviour of Caesar's legate enabled them to raise a revolt.
Caesar took with him his sister's grandson, C. Octavius,
and reached the south of Spain while it was still winter.
A short campaign ended with the hardest fight of all the
Civil War at Munda near Corduba. Labienus was killed,
and many of the rebels refusing to surrender were cut down.
Cn. Pompeius escaped badly wounded but was slain soon
after. S. Pompeius fled to cause trouble in after years.

Caesar's power and work. On his return from Spain
Caesar was made Dictator for life and Consul for ten years,
with power to nominate all magistrates and to command
all the forces of the state. Marks of distinction were given
him, the triumphal laurel wreath and embroidered robe,
and the title of Pater Patriae; his head appeared on the
coinage; the month Quintilis was re-named July; even
divine honours were decreed him, and his descent from
Venus through Iulus, Aeneas's son, was admitted. But
it is more to the point to see on what his power was really
based and how he used it. We have seen that from the
days of the Gracchi the power of government was slowly
but surely passing into the hands of the master of the
legions, the Imperator. The title was that with which
soldiers saluted their victorious general; and the Imperium
carried with it the right to choose Legati to whom the
general entrusted his powers. Caesar recognized that his
power was an Imperium based on the army, and he meant
that the real business of the Empire should be carried on
by his Legati responsible to him. During his command in
Gaul he had naturally appointed his staff-officers to command in his name, when he was in another part of the
country. During the Civil War the real control of Italy
had been in the hands not of the consuls or the Senate
but of his Legatus Antony. The regular magistracies he
used as marks of distinction, complimentary posts with no

important duties attached to them. In his treatment of the Senate he followed the same line ; consulting it if he pleased, but deciding matters of real importance on the advice of a small cabinet of those whom he could trust. The Assembly, no longer the representative of all the citizens since the extension of the franchise to all Italians, served only to register the laws and approve the candidates whom Caesar recommended.

Caesar was supreme. He had seen the incompetence of the old régime and the need of one strong man at the centre. He was that strong man. Public works to improve the resources of Italy and to lead the city-mob once more towards useful employment, colonies and settlements over the sea for those who would emigrate, rules for the employment of a certain proportion of free labour on Italian farms, a beginning of bankruptcy laws—such were some of the means by which he tried to restore healthy life to Italy. In the provinces he gave citizenship freely to leading men ; and by promoting in provincial towns the municipal organization which prevailed in the towns of Italy, he gradually developed among them the power to manage their own affairs in an orderly and business-like fashion.

Death of Caesar, 44 B.C. Caesar, with a contempt for forms which had lost their meaning, had swept aside as so much lumber many things which less able men might have spared. He knew that he ruled, and he was too great to disguise the truth. It was to be expected that he would make enemies. Men to whom republican forms were dear were ready to conspire with those who had some personal grudge against the ruler. In Feb. 44 Antony at the Lupercalia had jestingly offered Caesar a crown ; and though he put it aside, the disapproval of the populace made itself heard. A conspiracy was formed against him in which C. Cassius, who thought himself slighted over some appointment, and M. Brutus, a republican on principle, whose imagination was roused by tales of his regicide ancestor five centuries before, were the leaders. Caesar knew of his danger but refused to take precautions and set on one side even the warnings of his wife Calpurnia. On March 15, 44 B.C. the conspirators pressed round him in the Senate House, while Tillius Cimber presented a petition for the recall of his brother from exile. 'The envious Casca' dealt the first blow from behind. Caesar for a while defended himself, till he saw Brutus, whom he had treated as his son, among his assailants. Then with the words, 'Et tu, Brute,' he drew his cloak before his eyes and fell pierced with twenty-three wounds at the foot of Pompey's statue.

So died the greatest of Romans who did

> bestride the narrow world
> Like a Colossus.

As a general he made for himself a devoted and irresistible army; and by his unerring instinct for the point at which to strike, his clear estimate of the risks, and the rapidity and decision of his movements, he swept his foes before him. In the hour of victory he showed mercy beyond the standard of his contemporaries; and Italy, won almost without bloodshed, found that he came not to massacre and proscribe, but to heal the wounds of civil strife. As an orator Cicero praised him highly; and as an author he has left the pattern both of military history and clear writing. As a statesman he saw what needed doing and did not shrink from doing it. The government which had done well enough for Rome as a city-state had ended in anarchy when it tried to deal with an Empire. Caesar saw in the Imperium the power which was needed and through it gave a strong centralized government to the Roman world. As a man he dwarfed his contemporaries— a very king of men.

Dates

Denarius of Julius Caesar

CHAPTER XXV

THE SECOND CIVIL WAR

Antony in Rome. Some time before his death Caesar had made various appointments for 44 and 43. Antony was Consul with him for 44, M. Brutus and C. Cassius Praetors, and these two were to have the provinces of Macedonia and Syria respectively in 43. For 44 Trebonius was governor of Asia, D. Brutus of Cisalpine Gaul ; Plancus commanded Transalpine Gaul, and Lepidus had Gallia Narbonensis with Hither Spain. It will be seen that the murderers of Caesar controlled most of the provinces near to Italy. But Antony as Caesar's colleague in the Consulship had a strong position. He did not know how ever the strength of the conspirators and felt it necessary to walk warily. Immediately after the murder he secured the support of Lepidus, who was on the point of starting for his province with an army, by the promise that he should be Pontifex Maximus. Then on March 17 he met the Senate and agreed that, while the assassins should not be punished, yet all Caesar's measures should remain in force. He had already obtained Caesar's private papers and at the funeral read his will to the people. The reading of this document, which gave the populace Caesar's gardens across the Tiber and a largess of £3 to every citizen, so inflamed the passions of the mob that it turned against the murderers or Liberators, as they styled themselves, and burnt the house of Brutus. The Liberators fled from Rome; and Antony felt strong enough to re-assign the provincial appointments, nominating his own friends in the place of Cassius and the Bruti.

Octavian. At this point the heir of Caesar, his great-nephew C. Octavius, landed at Brundisium with his friend M. Vipsanius Agrippa. As the adopted son of Caesar he took the name of C. Julius Caesar Octavianus. Octavian was only nineteen years of age; but he was extraordinarily cautious and self-controlled, and he had the support of the veterans of Caesar. He began by professing friendship with Antonius and paid to the people the largess, which Caesar had ordered in his will and Antony had not paid. To the Senate he showed deference. Cicero, who had begun his Philippics against Antony, thought that the young man would be a useful ally, easily to be discarded when his assistance was not needed. Octavian meanwhile collected as many of Caesar's veterans as he could. Two of Antony's legions went over to him, and he adopted the pose of champion of the Senate against all its foes.

By the end of 44 Antony was besieging D. Brutus in Mutina, in the attempt to deprive him of Cisalpine Gaul.

The Senate declared the aggressor a public enemy and
sent the Consuls Hirtius and Pansa with Octavian to
relieve Mutina.   In April 43 a series of engagements took
place round Mutina ; Antony was defeated, but Hirtius
and Pansa were both slain and Octavian left in command
of the troops.   He had shown Antony that he was to be
reckoned with, but had no wish nor power to do more at
present.

Marcus Junius Brutus

The Triumvirate, 43 B.C.   Octavian returned to Rome
and threw off his mask of deference to the Senate.   He
insisted on his election as Consul and then went north
with eight legions to meet Antony, who had joined Lepidus
in Gaul and was now coming south with an army of seventeen legions.   D. Brutus, caught between two armies,
found that his men deserted him and was himself killed
at Aquileia.   Antony and Octavian by Lepidus's good
offices were brought together at Bononia, and the fate of
Rome was decided.   The Three were to have a commission

for five years as *Tresviri reipublicae constituendae* ; Lepidus
was to command Spain and Gallia Narbonensis, Antony
to have the rest of Gaul, Octavian to rule Sicily, Sardinia
and Africa.   But for the present Lepidus was to hold
Italy, while Antony and Octavian went against Brutus
and Cassius in the East.   These arrangements were duly
ratified by the Assembly, which had no choice in the
matter; and then the Three entered Rome.   They had
no intention of making Caesar's mistake of allowing their
enemies to live and become their murderers.   In a cold-
blooded way they made out their lists of victims, each
surrendering his own friends or relations to the vengeance
of the other two, till the proscribed numbered some three
hundred Senators and two thousand Equites.   Cicero
paid with his life for his fearless attacks upon Antony.
He had attempted to escape by sea ; but his boat was
driven back by the winds to Formiae and he was over-
taken there by the executioners.   His head and his hands
were hung on the Rostra, and Antony's dissolute wife
drove her needle through the tongue which had assailed
her husband and herself.   Others of the proscribed fled
to Sicily, where Sextus Pompeius resisted successfully the
attempt of Octavian to land on the island.

   Philippi, 42 B.C.   In the spring of 42 Antony and
Octavian crossed into Macedonia.   Brutus and Cassius,
who had gone to their provinces of Macedonia and Syria
in the previous year, had gathered a force of one hundred
thousand men at Sardis in Asia Minor but had wasted
time and were still in Asia, when their enemies with an
equal force reached Greece.   The two armies came into
touch near Philippi.   Cassius wished to avoid a battle, as
he knew that the enemy was already in want of provisions.   But the troops insisted on fighting.   Octavian
with the left wing was defeated by Brutus, while Antony
on the right repulsed Cassius ; the latter, thinking that

Denarius of 41 B.C. *Obv.* Antony. *Rev.* Octavian

Gaius Cilnius Maecenas

all was lost, slew himself. Brutus twenty days later, though his opponents were almost starved, was foolish enough to give battle again and being defeated, committed suicide. The survivors of his army joined Sextus Pompeius in Sicily. But the Republican cause was lost, and the chief credit for its downfall rested with Antony.

Treaty of Brundisium, 40 B.C. Octavian had shown himself a poor general and for the future relied upon Agrippa to lead his armies, while in political matters he took the advice of C. Cilnius Maecenas. His task was now to hold the West and defeat Pompeius, while Antony was to secure the East and fight the Parthians. Lepidus's day of usefulness was over ; he was nominally in charge of Italy, but events soon happened there which made Octavian assume control. The need of the latter to provide allotments for his soldiers caused him to evict civil occupiers in the interests of the legionaries. Risings broke out which were supported by L. Antonius the consul and Fulvia, Antony's wife. Agrippa in 41 drove the rebels from Rome and shut them up in Perusia in Etruria, which surrendered next year. Fulvia fled to her husband, and Antony landed in Italy, 40 B.C., ready to fight. But the soldiers forced their leaders to come to terms. By the Treaty of Brundisium Antony was to command the East, Octavian Italy and the West, while Lepidus was given Africa alone. The agreement was sealed by the marriage of Antony, whose wife Fulvia was now dead, with Octavian's sister Octavia.

It seems strange that Antony, the victor of Philippi, should have been content to leave Octavian with the stronger half of the Empire. But soon after Philippi he had met Cleopatra at Tarsus and, succumbing to her charms, had thrown away his real chances of Imperial power for the phantom hope of an Eastern Empire with an Eastern wife. But he was nevertheless suspicious of

Octavian and thought that Sextus Pompeius might be a useful ally.   At Misenum it was arranged that Pompeius should have Sicily, Sardinia, Corsica and Achaea for five years.   The conference took place on board Pompeius's ship, and the captain asked his master whether he should cut the cable and ' make him master of the Roman

Marcus Vipsanius Agrippa

world.'   Pompeius replied, ' You should have done it first and asked me afterwards.'

Antony now went back to the East, where the Parthians, led by a renegade son of Labienus, had overrun Asia Minor.   His Legatus Ventidius Bassus in his absence expelled the Parthians from Syria and in 38 followed up his success by a victory at Gindarus. But with Antony's return operations ceased. He was losing both his taste and his ability for serious warfare.

War with Sextus Pompeius, 38–36 B.C. In the West meanwhile a naval war had broken out between Pompeius and Octavian, who had seized Sardinia and Corsica. Agrippa was suppressing a revolt in Aquitania, and during his absence Octavian suffered a defeat. Agrippa on his return at the end of 38 saw that a good fleet was needed, and for two years practised his crews in the Julian Harbour, which had lately been formed near Baiae by connecting Lakes Avernus and Lucrinus with the sea. During this time Antony, fearing the probable success of Octavian in the war, arrived at Tarentum with three hundred ships. But by the influence of Octavia and the diplomacy of Maecenas peace was patched up and the Triumvirate renewed for five years.

In the summer of 36 Agrippa's fleet was ready. It was high time that Pompeius should be crushed. For six years he had encouraged every disorder in the Mediterranean, and his ships were as great a danger as the pirate fleets of Cilicia, which his father had suppressed. Lepidus from Africa and fleets from Tarentum and the Julian Harbour converged on Sicily. But a storm broke up the first attack. The second attempt succeeded. After a preliminary victory of Agrippa at Mylae and the defeat of Octavian on the east coast, Pompeius was finally crushed at Naulochus near Mylae, 36 B.C., and fleeing to the East was put to death in the following year by Antonius. The same year saw the fall of Lepidus. Dissatisfied with his inferior position he demanded from Octavian his old share in the Triumvirate. But his men deserted him, and Lepidus threw himself at Octavian's feet. He was deprived of all his power, but allowed still to enjoy the empty dignity of Pontifex Maximus.

Antony, Cleopatra, and Actium. The Coalition of Three became now a Coalition of Two. Octavian was given the Tribunician power for life but refused other honours. With the help of Maecenas he set himself to obliterate the memory of the proscriptions, while Agrippa reduced Alpine tribes to order and secured the peace of Italy. Octavian was posing as the champion of the Republic and the saviour of Rome in opposition to the lawless Antony. The latter had done his best to ruin his own cause. On his departure from Tarentum in 37 he had left Octavia in Italy, and the news of his relations with Cleopatra soon scandalized Rome. Her name appeared on his coinage, her children were given Roman provinces, and she took her place at his side in a triumphal procession as Queen of the East. In 32 Octavian published Antony's will, which had been betrayed to him. In this the sons of Cleopatra were named as his heirs, and Octavian accordingly denounced him in the Senate. Antony had alienated the sympathies of all respectable men, and Octavian had not been slow to make capital out of his misbehaviour. The Senate declared war, and Octavian could meet his rival as the champion of Rome against the East, of civilization against barbarism.

Antony gathered his forces in the west of Greece, one hundred thousand men and five hundred galleys with towers on their decks. Accompanied by Cleopatra he took up a position at the mouth of the Gulf of Ambracia. If he had invaded Italy at once, he would have had a fair prospect of success. But he allowed Octavian time to call in legions which were fighting on the northern frontier, to collect a fleet of light Liburnian boats and to cross into Epirus. Agrippa blockaded the enemy's fleet in the Gulf of Ambracia; and the generals of Antony proposed to retreat inland; that they might draw the foe after them and decide the struggle by a land battle. But

Cleopatra would not leave the coast. On Sept. 2,
31 B.C. Antony issued out from behind the headland of
Actium, which juts out at the entrance of the gulf, to
fight his way through to Egypt. A fresh breeze threw
his galleys into disorder and exposed them to the attack
of the Liburnian ships. In the confusion Cleopatra's
squadron sailed away for Egypt, and Antony with the
fight still in progress gave orders to follow her. The
whole fleet lost heart, and many ships were set on fire

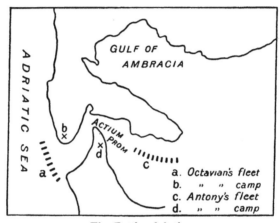

The Battle of Actium

by the burning missiles with which Agrippa attacked
them. The rest surrendered. A few days later Antony's
land force deserted by its leader submitted.

Octavian without further fighting secured the East
and in the next year advanced on Egypt. The forces
which Antony had been able to collect were easily routed,
and believing a message that Cleopatra was dead,
Antony stabbed himself. Cleopatra then tried her arts
on the conqueror; but receiving no encouragement she
killed herself by the bite of an asp, brought to her, it is

said, in a basket of figs. With her death the kingdom of Egypt was abolished. The country was placed under a Praefectus of Caesar, and no Senator permitted to enter its borders.

This was the end of the Civil War. Octavian or Caesar, as he now styled himself, celebrated his triumph in 29 B.C. and then set himself to heal the disorders produced by the long struggle and to secure by peace the position which he had won in war.

DATES

43.	Siege of Mutina.
43.	The Triumvirate.
42.	Philippi.
41.	Siege of Perusia.
40.	Treaty of Brundisium.
38–36.	War with S. Pompeius (Naulochus).
31.	Battle of Actium.
30.	Death of Antony and Cleopatra.

CHAPTER XXVI

AUGUSTUS

OCTAVIAN was master of the Roman world after the battle of Actium, and while he was a much smaller man than Julius Caesar, he had two great advantages over him. The Empire had seen the horrors of civil war for thirteen years and knew that Octavian's rule was the only alternative to anarchy; on the other hand the new ruler could profit by the mistake which his great-uncle made in not disguising his power. Octavian now built up a system, in which all the real power was his and was exercised through his representatives, but which disguised the truth under the forms of Republican government. In 27 he resigned his powers into the hands of the Senate and

People and received back from them the *Consulare Imperium* for ten years and the *Proconsulare Imperium* in all those provinces where a military force was needed. At the same time he was given the title of *Augustus*, by which we know him, and that of *Princeps*, First Citizen or Champion of the State, the title by which he preferred to be known. A final arrangement was made in 23 B.C., the year from which the Empire or Principate is commonly dated. In that year he resigned his consulship but was given the Imperium in Italy as well as the provinces—for five years nominally, though it was of course renewed as often as it expired—which gave him control over all magistrates. He chose however to disguise the nature of his rule by professing to base it on the Tribunician Power which he held, and he dated the years of his government by his tenure of that power. We must endeavour to see the nature of his rule as it took shape in its different departments.

The Provinces, Finance and the Army. The Republican system of Provincial government broke down from the inability of the Senate to keep the governors in control. Corruption and oppression had been the rule, and in the end the great commanders had turned against the home government. Under the Empire provinces were divided into two classes: Imperial provinces which needed armies and were directly under the Emperor, and Senatorial provinces held by no more than a police force and administered under the Senate's control. The Imperial provinces, which were mainly on the frontiers, were governed by *legati pro praetore* or, in the case of smaller districts or dependencies, by *procuratores* and *praefecti*, all alike directly appointed by the Emperor and responsible to him; no raising or use of an army was allowed without his sanction. Appointments were prolonged in the case of good governors; temptation to extortion was prevented by granting suitable allowances to governors and by

Gaius Julius Caesar Octavianus Augustus

putting all the finances of the province under a separate
procurator responsible directly to the Emperor. This
central control made a permanent and continuous policy
of provincial administration possible and led to the
growth of a class of able and efficient administrators, who
looked to employment in the provinces as their natural
career. Senatorial provinces were governed by Proconsuls
and, though not directly under the Emperor, were naturally
assisted by the example of well governed Imperial provinces and the fact that there was no army in them to
be provided for. A large part also of their financial
administration was transferred to Imperial procurators.
Careful surveys were made of the resources of each province, and the system of tithes was generally replaced by
money taxes on land and property. Under the new
conditions the prosperity of the provinces increased very
rapidly, and to the provincials at least the establishment
of the Empire was clear gain.

The revenue from Senatorial provinces was paid into
the *Aerarium* for the ordinary purposes of government;
but that from the Imperial provinces together with the
income from mines and state lands was assigned to the
Fiscus or Imperial treasury. With its better management the *Fiscus* could show a balance, which the *Aerarium*
failed to do; and it became necessary to transfer the cost
of the corn-supply and of the public roads to the Imperial
department.

The Army system of the Republic was closely connected
with its provincial system. The provincial governors
were in ordinary circumstances the generals, and the same
lack of control marked both departments. The legions
had been enrolled not by the state but by the general; war
had to be paid for out of the proceeds of victory; and the
soldier looked to his general alike as the object of his
loyalty and the rewarder of his service. Augustus,

though he could not prevent an army from supporting its general against the state, yet took every means to lessen the danger. The military oath was taken to the Emperor, the war was fought under his auspices, the generals were his *legati* or representatives, and none but the Imperial family were allowed to celebrate a triumph. The standing army was a force of twenty-five legions, and the cost was met out of the *Aerarium Militare*, which received 5 per cent. on legacies and 1 per cent. on all sales made in the markets.

The armies were stationed on the frontiers. But Augustus, following the example of the generals of Republican times who had been attended by a picked body-guard, enrolled nine cohorts each one thousand strong, of which he stationed three outside Rome and the rest at his country residences in Italy. These Praetorian guards had special privileges in the shape of higher pay and short service—twelve years instead of twenty—and were all of Italian birth. Tiberius, the successor of Augustus, brought together all the Praetorian cohorts into one permanent camp just outside Rome with the object of overawing the populace. While other troops lay at a distance from the city, the Praetorian cohorts gained in time to come great political importance ; and on the death of an Emperor their choice was often decisive in the appointment of his successor.

For the protection of the city an old office was revived. When the consuls in early times left the city for the Latin Festival, a *praefectus urbi* had been appointed to keep safe the city in their absence. Augustus was often absent and appointed a City Prefect to act as Mayor while he was away; and the office under later Emperors became permanent. He had city-cohorts or police under him for the maintenance of order, while a corps of *Vigiles* dealt, or failed to deal, with the numerous outbreaks of fire.

Magistrates and Comitia. The number and duties of the magistrates (except for the Censor) nominally remained what they were in Republican times. But with the chief departments of the administration in the hands of Augustus's representatives there was little for them to do; and the position came to be valued as an honorary distinction. Even so, many candidates for office were practically nominated by Augustus, who furnished them with a *commendatio* which could not be overlooked; and he also issued authorized lists of candidates for the chief elections. The Comitia met at first to legislate and to elect. But under the circumstances the meetings became a matter of form, and the elections were soon handed over to the Senate.

The Senate and Equites. Augustus was very careful to maintain the outward dignity of the Senate while he kept the real power in his own hands. In 28 B.C. he revised the list and expelled the provincials admitted by Julius, reducing the number of members to six hundred, who were carefully selected to represent the better elements of Rome and Italy. A higher property qualification was demanded, and the privilege was restored to the Senate of trying and sentencing its own members. But the power of government was all in the hands of one man. The ex-magistrates who composed the Senate were practically the nominees of the Emperor; and though Augustus sometimes issued his edicts in the form of *Senatus Consulta*, they were none the less his orders. The Senate fell back to its original duty of giving advice when asked. With its weight of experience its advice was still valuable; and especially on social and moral questions it reflected the considered judgment of the educated classes.

Maecenas, the great adviser of Augustus, who was no doubt responsible for much of Augustus's policy, had remained an Eques throughout his life. Augustus took

steps to give the Equites a career of their own, different
from that of the Senators and with less dignity but in
some ways more useful.   He created a body of five thousand official Equites, at the head of which his heir was
enrolled as *princeps iuventutis*.   To this body he entrusted
the Judicia and chose from it the procurators and prefects,
who, in charge of small provincial districts or managing
the Fiscus and the corn-supply, did much of the hard work
of administration.

Other influences.   We have now seen that Augustus
had the reins of government in his own hands and ruled
without seeming to rule.   He wished to appear as the
Princeps, the First Citizen in a free state, and encouraged
every influence, which would divert men's minds from
the fact that he controlled every department and at the
same time point to him as the natural champion and
leader of Rome.   With Maecenas's help he encouraged
literature ; and Vergil and Horace with a train of lesser
lights have made the Augustan Age the golden age of
Latin literature.   Their writings opened to men a new
career in the world of letters where the dangerous subject
of politics was excluded.   But at the same time they
spoke of the early ages, when life was simpler and men
enjoyed the reign of peace and justice; and they spoke
of the new ruler, born of the Julian race, descended from
Aeneas and Venus, as the restorer of those happier times.
Augustus made efforts by the restoration of temples to
recall the Romans to the worship of the old gods.   But
the religious revival of his time turned in another and
more useful direction.   The worship most deeply rooted
in Roman minds was the worship of ancestors, the Lares
of the family.   It was only a step from this to worship
the Lares of Rome, the household gods of the city ; and
none but the Emperor was the father of his country.
The dead Julius had his worship as *Divus Iulius* ; and

while Augustus would not permit direct worship of himself, yet altars sprang up through the provinces in honour of *Roma et Augustus*. The genius of the city was incarnate, as it were, in the person of the Emperor, and loyalty to him was a religious duty.

The Frontiers. In the earlier years of his reign the reduction of outlying districts or the protection of the frontiers often called for the Emperor's attention. Spain had never been completely conquered, and Augustus went in person against the Cantabrians of the north-west in 26 B.C. But it was not till seven years later that they finally submitted to Agrippa. In the East the defeat of Crassus and the mismanagement of Antony had left a crop of disorders to be dealt with. But in 20 B.C. Phraates king of Parthia voluntarily gave up the standards of Crassus and recognized the Euphrates as the western boundary of his kingdom. A fringe of client states, which were in the course of time taken over by the Romans, protected the frontier. Among them may be mentioned Judaea which was a prosperous kingdom under the rule of Herod the Great, a personal friend of Agrippa. In after years it was put under a procurator and became a part of the province of Syria.

The Northern frontier was a source of great trouble. By taking the Rhine as the boundary in this direction an awkward angle was left between the upper waters of this river and of the Danube, at which an enemy could press right in to the Helvetian territory and prevent the army of the Rhine from co-operating with the army of the Danube. The attempt was now made to substitute the Elbe for the Rhine as a boundary, which with the Danube would give a fairly straight frontier from the mouth of the Elbe to Vienna. This great undertaking required many years' fighting and ended in disaster. The south-eastern end of the proposed line was dealt with first.

Tiberius and Drusus the stepsons of Augustus, children
of Livia by her former husband, won Noricum and Rhaetia
in 16 and 15 B.C. After this an attempt was made at
the north-western end between the lower reaches of the
Rhine and the Elbe. Drusus defeated the Chatti and
Cherusci and half subdued the district but in 9 B.C. was
killed by a fall from his horse. Tiberius took over the
command and fought with success for two years. It then

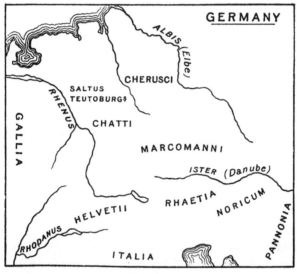

Germany

remained to win the middle of the line by the conquest
of the Marcomanni. Ten years were spent in securing
the country which had already been won. But when in
6 A.D. preparations for the new undertaking had been
completed, a serious revolt broke out in Pannonia and
Dalmatia. Tiberius with Germanicus the son of Drusus
was sent to deal with the rising, and it took three years'
desperate fighting before peace was restored. The year

9 A.D., which saw the end of the revolt in Pannonia, saw also a serious disaster in Germany. Quintilius Varus with three legions was enticed by Arminius the leader of the Cherusci into the Saltus Teutoburgiensis to the east of Cologne, and his force was cut to pieces. The country rose and massacred the Roman garrisons. Augustus was overwhelmed by the blow. He went into mourning and would wake at night to cry, 'Give me back my legions, Varus.' But he realized that his project for a new frontier had failed, and he warned his successor not to aim at further extensions of the Empire.

Succession. In theory the Emperor held his power by gift of the Senate and People, who would resume their old authority on his death. In practice it was impossible to let loose again the forces of anarchy; and the Principate passed to the man whom the Emperor had most clearly associated with himself in his work. Augustus from the first gave careful thought to the question of his successor, only to find that hope after hope failed him. He had married three times but had no children, except one daughter Julia by his second wife. In the early years of his Principate he had adopted his sister's son Marcellus, a young man of great promise, to whom he gave Julia in marriage. But Marcellus died in 23 B.C. He then gave his daughter to his faithful minister Agrippa, whom he made his colleague in the Imperium and Tribunician Power. Agrippa died in 12 B.C., and for a while Augustus looked to C. and L. Caesar, the children of Agrippa and Julia, as possible successors. But his third wife Livia was a strong and resolute woman, who urged the claims of Tiberius Claudius Nero her son by a former marriage, the successful general on the Northern frontier. C. and L. Caesar both died suddenly, and it was hinted that Livia had procured their death. A younger son of Agrippa and Julia proved unmanageable and was banished. Julia scandalized Rome by her profligacy and was banished also. Augustus was now compelled to fall back on Tiberius whom he did not like. Tiberius had been a sharer in the Tribunician Power since 4 A.D. and was made colleague in the Imperium in 11 A.D. He was an able general and, being named heir in Augustus's will, was at once recognized as the Emperor Tiberius on Augustus's death in 14 A.D.

DATES

23 B.C.	Establishment of the Empire.
16 B.C.– 9 A.D.	The Northern Frontier.
9 A.D.	Defeat of Varus.
14 A.D.	Death of Augustus.

THE FAMILY OF AUGUSTUS

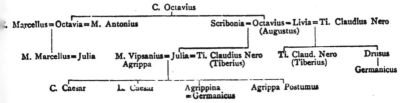

CHAPTER XXVII

TIBERIUS TO DOMITIAN

TIBERIUS was already in possession of the Imperium and Tribunician Power. In virtue of his Imperium the troops took the oath of allegiance to him, and by the latter power he convoked the Senate, which after a show of discussion conferred on him the full power of Emperor without limit of time. Inheriting the nature of the Claudii which did not make for sanity, he had lived in an atmosphere of suspicion, unhappy in his married life, watched by spies, neglected in exile at Rhodes for seven years, and afterwards distrusted by Augustus till circumstances compelled his recognition as successor. For fourteen years while his mother Livia was alive he restrained himself, governing well and promoting the welfare of the provinces, though his character showed through the mask at times. But at the end of his life he was a monster of cruelty and lust, shunning men's eyes and giving himself up to infamous orgies in the island of Capreae.

In 14 A.D. the legions on the Rhine mutinied for higher pay and better conditions of service and offered to make their commander Germanicus Emperor. Augustus had compelled Tiberius to adopt Germanicus as his successor; but he remained loyal to his uncle and induced the troops to return to their allegiance, keeping them occupied for two years in raids and conquests east of the Rhine. Then Tiberius recalled him, out of jealousy according to the popular belief, but more probably because Tiberius like Augustus before him regarded conquest beyond the Rhine as impracticable. Germanicus returned to Rome a popular hero and was then sent East with general powers over all lands east of the Hellespont and specially to set

up a friendly king over Armenia. But at the same time
Cn. Piso, whose wife was a rival of Agrippina Germanicus's
wife, was made governor of Syria. Relations between the
two men were unfriendly. Germanicus fell ill at Antioch
and died 19 A.D.; and Piso, suspected of having poisoned
him, committed suicide on his return to Rome. Tiberius's
unpopularity was greatly increased by Germanicus's
death, and he in his turn became more morose and suspicious.

The law of Treason (*Lex Maiestatis*) was now given a
wider interpretation. Chance words and acts of disrespect
were made the ground of prosecution; and as Rome had
no Public Prosecutor, a swarm of private informers
(*delatores*) was on the look-out to win rewards by twisting
private conversations or harmless acts into treason
against the Emperor. They were aided in their work by
L. Aelius Sejanus, Prefect of the Praetorian Guard, an
unscrupulous man of Equestrian rank, who persuaded the
Emperor to concentrate all the Praetorian cohorts in a
camp on the Esquiline and aimed at succeeding to the
Principate himself. In 23 A.D. he poisoned Tiberius's son
Drusus without arousing the Emperor's suspicions. Three
years later he persuaded the Emperor, sensitive as he was
to his unpopularity, to retire to Capreae off the Campanian
coast; and after the death of Livia in 29 A.D. he procured
the banishment of Agrippina and her two sons. But he
over-reached himself and aroused Tiberius's suspicions.
In 31 A.D. a long letter of the Emperor was read in the
Senate, which ended unexpectedly with a demand for the
punishment of Sejanus. The favourite was at once executed
and his friends cruelly persecuted. Tiberius lived on for
six years, during which time Agrippina and her elder son
died of starvation. Her younger son Gaius, nicknamed
Caligula—from *caliga* the soldier's boot, because he had
been born in his father's camp in Germany—was named

by the Emperor as his successor together with Tiberius's grandson, the son of Drusus. In 37 A.D. the Emperor tried to leave his retirement and visit Rome, but his courage failed him and he died at Misenum on his way back.

Caligula, son of Germanicus, was hailed with delight as the new Emperor, and the Senate without delay conferred on him full powers. He began well by banishing informers and professing to recognize the independent authority of the Senate. But he had notions of sovereignty which he had learnt in part from Eastern princes and especially from Herod Agrippa, with whom he had been educated in Rome. Now absolute power brought out all the worst in him, and his four years' rule 37 to 41 A.D. was a horror of savagery and lust which drove him mad. Claiming to be a god, he extended his palace by a great bridge from the Palatine to the sacred Capitol and spanned the Bay of Baiae by a bridge of boats. He could brook no rival. The son of Drusus must die, who had been made his co-heir by Tiberius; and the statues of men of old were overthrown, who might seem to challenge his greatness. He gave extravagant shows in which he forced even Senators to fight as gladiators, and he claimed like Jupiter to take what wives he would. As his money failed, he revived the Treason laws, and a reign of terror and confiscation followed worse than that of Tiberius. Once he thought of conquering Britain but got no further than Boulogne, where he ordered his men to pick up shells, which were sent to Rome as spoils of the ocean. At another time he made his horse a consul and just before his death he outraged Jewish feeling by ordering that his own statue should be set up in the Holy of Holies. But he was known to be planning the massacre of all Romans of note; and in 41 the Praetorians put an end to the mad brute by assassinating him in the palace.

Caligula had named no successor, and the Senate

debated the question of restoring the Republic. But the judicial murders of the last two reigns had left few men of note alive, while the threads of government had passed into the hands of permanent officials, the Freedmen of the Imperial Palace, and the real power in Rome rested with the Praetorian Guard. Both Civil Service and Household troops required a head, and one was found in Caligula's uncle Claudius, the brother of Germanicus. He had been the butt of the Imperial family; was awkward, shy, and pedantic, but not without some literary talent; and he was hard-working and had some idea of what Rome ought to do for the world. In 43 A.D. he turned his attention to Britain. Roman civilization had made its way into the S.E. of our island since Julius Caesar's time and disputes between native princes gave an excuse for interference. Aulus Plaùtius with four legions landed in Kent and pushing north captured Camolodunum (Colchester). Claudius himself arrived in time to see the fall of the city but returned after sixteen days, leaving Plautius and his subordinate Vespasian to subdue the southern half of the island. Their chief opponent was Caractacus, who held out among the Welsh hills till he was betrayed to the Romans in 51 A.D. and sent to Rome.

At home Claudius held the Censorship in 47 and 48 A.D. and placed some chiefs of the Aedui on the roll of the Senate, a wise step towards recognizing that the Empire was more than a dependency of Italy. But his wife Messalina with the help of freedmen ruled the Emperor. She had borne him a daughter Octavia and a son Britannicus but was a woman of shameless character; and in 49 Claudius was told of a mock marriage between her and a certain Silius and put her to death. Agrippina, daughter of Germanicus and widow of Domitius Ahenobarbus, took her place and persuaded Claudius to adopt her son Domitius, who was henceforth known as Nero. The claims of

Britannicus were ignored; Nero was given the Imperium in 51 and married to Octavia. The Praetorian Guards were won over by bribes, and in 54 A.D. Claudius was poisoned.

Nero was at once saluted by the Guards as Emperor, and the Senate ratified their choice. To the chagrin of his mother, who was jealous of their influence, he placed himself under the direction of Burrus the Praetorian Prefect and Seneca the philosopher and for the first years of his reign, his *Quinquennium*, gave promise of being a good ruler. He promised to check the freedmen and to divide the functions of Emperor and Senate as Augustus had done. But he was soon intoxicated with absolute power and at the mercy of his passions; there was not even a sound Public Opinion to check him; while Burrus and Seneca contended with Agrippina for such authority over him as could be obtained. After a time he fell under the sway of Poppaea Sabina, wife of his friend Otho. She persuaded him to kill Agrippina; and after he had failed to drown his mother in a ship cleverly constructed to capsize, he sent soldiers who killed her in her house 59 A.D. Burrus died in 62 and Seneca was driven into retirement on a charge of treason. Nero then divorced Octavia and later on put her to death.

With Poppaea Empress, Nero had nothing to restrain him and he found in Tigellinus, the new Praetorian Prefect, a creature who helped him downward in cruelty and debauchery. He had a real taste for poetry and music and he scandalized Roman feeling by appearing on the stage, where he sang odes of his own composition to the lyre after the fashion of Greek contests. In 64 A.D. a fire broke out and, burning for six days, destroyed half the city. Nero was wrongly suspected of starting the conflagration and cast the blame on the Christians, whom he persecuted cruelly, burning many as living torches to light his chariot races. He rebuilt the city with wide arcaded streets and

Bust of Nero

set up for himself on the Esquiline a palace called the Golden House, enriched with treasures from the whole Empire. But the exactions necessary to meet the cost of his building, coming on top of the scandal of his appearance on the stage, led to the conspiracy of Piso against him in 65 A.D., in which Lucan the poet, nephew of Seneca, took part from literary jealousy. Some of the officers of the Praetorian Guard were involved, and in the general alarm Tigellinus was able to strike down many noted men including Seneca and the chief Stoic philosophers, whose decent lives were a reproach to the vicious court.

During Nero's reign Cn. Corbulo defeated the Parthians and placed a descendant of the Herods on the throne of Armenia in 59 A.D. In Britain Suetonius Paulinus defeated in 61 A.D. Boadicea, Queen of the Iceni, who had sacked Camolodunum and Londinium; and South Britain settled down quietly under Roman rule. For the last years of his life Nero was often away from Rome performing at games in Greece; but he found time to order the death of Corbulo. At last in 68 A.D. the storm broke. Vindex, a Gaul who had risen to be governor of Gallia Lugdunensis, raised an army to assert the independence of Gaul and made overtures to Galba, governor of Hither Spain. Verginius Rufus, the general in Upper Germany, crushed Vindex. But Galba moved on Rome, professing to be the champion of the Senate and People. The German legions deserted Nero, the Praetorians wavered, and Nero in panic at last nerved himself to commit suicide.

Galba entered Rome Jan. 1, 69 A.D.—a man of 73 who owed his success to the universal contempt felt for Nero. But he was distrusted for his association with Vindex and he had no personal popularity. The Praetorians were disaffected and hailed as Emperor Otho, a former friend of Nero. Galba was killed and Otho took his place. Meanwhile the legions on the German frontier had declared for Vitellius their general, an elderly glutton, who entrusted the command of his men to two subordinates Caecina and Valens. They crossed the Alps, and Otho, though he might have waited for troops from the Eastern provinces, hurried north at the head of the Praetorians. He was defeated in April at Bedriacum near Cremona and killed himself.

Vitellius arrived in Rome in summer and was accepted as Emperor but did not long enjoy his triumph. The year 69 A.D. points to the change which had taken place in the Roman world. Rome as the head of government now meant little. The Comitia had no power, the Senate's authority was shadowy, magistracies were empty titles carrying only some municipal duties inside the city, all real power was centred in the Emperor, who through the Civil Service—Freedmen and Equites—might govern effectively but whose real power rested on his command of the legions. When by madness, cruelty, or shamelessness, he had outraged all decent feeling as Tiberius, Caligula, and Nero had done, there was no sanctity in his position as head of Rome which would hinder any other military commander in aspiring to the Imperial purple. But old habits are strong, and for fifty years more the pretence that the Emperor ruled by consent of the Senate could be maintained.

On the death of Otho the armies of the East made Vespasian Emperor. He had served in Britain and was sent by Nero to crush the rebellion, which had broken out in Palestine in 66 A.D. owing to misgovernment on the one hand and religious fanaticism on the other. He and his son Titus had set about reducing the country systematically and were gradually closing in on Jerusalem. Now Vespasian left Titus to complete the work and secured Egypt, the granary of Rome, while the legions of Pannonia invaded Italy. A second battle of Bedriacum went against Vitellius and he agreed to abdicate. But the Praetorians attacked Vespasian's supporters and massacred them on the Capitol, which they burnt. Vespasian's brother was killed and his second son Domitian only just escaped. But Vespasian's troops soon arrived, slaughtered the Vitellians and killed Vitellius himself. Vespasian was acknowledged Emperor; and under Domitian, who ruled in his absence, Rome suffered the horrors of a captured city.

In Gaul fighting was still going on. Civilis, an able native commander in the Batavian cohorts of the Roman army, had taken up arms nominally on behalf of Vespasian but really with the idea of making a separate empire of Gaul. The Treviri alone of the Gauls joined fully in the project, and an Emperor of Gaul was set up at Trèves. But the time was not yet ripe for any civilized state apart from Rome. Cerealis in 70 A.D. defeated the insurgents and soon the West settled down to quiet. By the spring of this year Titus laid siege to Jerusalem, which was crowded with fugitives whom he had driven thither before him. Slowly the outer city was reduced, while the Jews resisted desperately and quarrelled murderously among themselves. After three months the Temple was taken and burnt; but it was not till September that the upper city was stormed and the remnant, who had survived famine and the sword, surrendered. Titus set up his arch at Rome in honour of his victory, and the siege was memorable for its horrors. A million Jews are said to have perished and 100,000 to have been sold as slaves.

In 70 A.D. T. Flavius Vespasianus entered Rome. He had lived outside the narrow life of the city and the vicious atmosphere of the court and represented the spirit of Italy rather than of Rome. The world needed peace and he aimed at preventing wars of succession by establishing the Flavian dynasty. His elder son Titus was given the Imperium and Proconsular power, while Domitian received the title of *Princeps Juventutis*; from the Senate he re-

Arch of Titus

ceived the unlimited right of recommending candidates for magistracies and could in that way improve the composition of that body of ex-magistrates. But he was a blunt soldier and had little sympathy with the Senate's pretence of authority. This fact brought him into collision with Stoic philosophers who professed Republican sentiments; and Helvidius Priscus among others lost his life on that account. Vespasian restored the discipline of the army and by strict economy and control of the Treasury officials paid off some of the debts of the State and put the finances on a sound footing; but the heavy taxation made him unpopular. He is remembered as the builder of the Coliseum at Rome but he did more useful work in the provinces. To Spanish towns he gave the Latin citizenship; in the East he incorporated dependent principalities in the Empire as provinces; at the angle between the Rhine and Danube he occupied the Black Forest; and he strengthened the Danube frontier, where the Dacians were giving trouble; in Britain he appointed Agricola as governor with a view to the final conquest of the island. His reign shows that he was alive both to the dangers to the Empire from without and to the need of a strong and liberal policy within.

Titus, who succeeded his father in 79 A.D. died two years later. In his reign a great eruption of Mt Vesuvius buried the towns of Pompeii and Herculaneum. He was a universal favourite, but his extravagance would have exhausted the Treasury and he was perhaps fortunate in dying before he could outlive his popularity. His brother Domitian who was Emperor from 81 to 96 A.D. had been kept in the background but now showed that he meant to use his power to the full. The Flavian dynasty encouraged the worship of the Imperial House, but Domitian went a step further and insisted that he should be addressed as *Dominus et Deus*. He paid little attention to the Senate

but by lavish expenditure on shows won popularity with
the people, while he kept a tight hand on provincial
governors.   In the Rhine-Danube angle he continued his
father's activity and drew a line of fortifications to include
the Black Forest and adjoining regions and he suppressed
a rebellion of the legions quartered at Mainz, who had
proclaimed their own commander Saturninus Emperor.

In 85 A.D. the Dacians further down the Danube crossed
the river under their king Decebalus and over-ran Moesia;
they were driven back, but an attempt to seize their
capital Sarmizegethusa resulted in the destruction of a
large Roman force. After two years' preparation another
Roman army crossed the Danube and got within striking
distance of the capital.   But Domitian rashly provoked
the hostility of the neighbouring Marcomanni and Quadi
and suffered defeat at their hands.   He was forced to make
peace with Decebalus, agreeing to supply him with Roman
engineers, and returned to Rome with the sense of failure.
He had seen that danger threatened Rome on the Danube
frontier but was not a big enough man to cope with it
successfully.   In his reign Agricola, who commanded in
Britain, defeated the Caledonians in a pitched battle
84 A.D., while the Roman fleet rounded the north of
Scotland.   But the English half of the island alone was
effectively conquered.   Agricola was recalled, perhaps
through the Emperor's jealousy but more probably
because his conquests were not worth their cost.   Domitian at any rate was embittered by his own failures, and
the end of his reign was a time of universal suspicion and
terror in Rome.   The *delatores* were busy again; Stoics
suffered for their Republican leanings, Christians for their
refusal to join in the Imperial worship; and among the
victims were members of the Emperor's house.   At last
in 96 his wife and freedmen joined in a conspiracy and
Domitian was assassinated.

During the first century of the Empire except for the year 69 the legions were on the frontiers and the Praetorian Guards the only considerable force at home. It was not a time of great wars, though signs of danger were not wanting. In the East Augustus's policy had been to leave a fringe of dependent states between the provinces and the Parthians, who were east of the Euphrates. But the incapacity of native princes soon caused a change. Eastern Asia Minor was gradually split up into provinces; the fate of the Jews has already been noticed. But the chief difficulty was in Armenia, whose hills bordered both on Parthia and on a Roman province. Princes friendly to Rome were placed on its throne and dislodged by the Parthians; and though Corbulo in 59 A.D. won a military success, it was left for Vespasian to extend direct Roman control as far as the Euphrates and to secure some definite peace in Armenia. On the Rhine-Danube frontier there were warnings of danger for the future; for at either end of the line civilized provinces were within reach of the barbarians, and in the centre the angle between the two rivers brought the frontiers dangerously close to Italy. Punitive expeditions into Germany secured respect for the barrier of the Rhine; under the Flavian Emperors the Black Forest district was occupied by Roman settlers and defended by earth-works and forts stretching from Rhine to Danube; and Domitian's war with Dacia aimed at least at securing the provinces south of the Lower Danube. But there was real danger both from the Dacians and from the Marcomanni who had settled in Bohemia. They were enraged but not subdued by the Roman operations.

The Provinces were happier under the Empire than under the Republic. Peace was established, the governors were well paid and retained their posts for several years if they showed ability. Even the worst Emperors put down mis-government and oppression. Provincial towns received gifts of citizenship, and Claudius is said to have admitted Gallic chieftains to the Senate. Impartial justice, fixed tolls and duties, and a uniform standard of coinage made the exchange of goods an easier matter. With fewer opportunities in war and politics, trade offered an outlet for men's activities; and good public buildings and general contentment testified to the well-being of the Provinces. This was especially true of Asia Minor and the East, where trade had never been looked down upon as it was in Rome. Spain and Gaul were more affected by Roman thought and literature, and already poets and soon Emperors came from the Western Provinces. Local customs were seldom disturbed by the Romans, and provincial towns had their own magistrates and institutions, though they began to rely more and more on the central authority. Municipal office too brought heavy expenses on its holders and by the end of the first century was beginning to be a burden rather than an honour. Amid all their prosperity there was a danger of over-centralization. Rome and Italy had lost their vitality and all power was centred in the Emperor. So too from the provinces men of note made their way to Rome; provinces and towns relied on the central government and invited its interference in their local affairs at the cost of their own energy and independence.

The position of the Emperor had become clearer in the course of the century. Augustus had tried to cloak his power as master of the legions under Republican forms. Later Emperors were less careful. They marked out their successors, as he had done, by high office during their own life-time, and the new Emperor received from the Senate the Proconsular Imperium and the Tribunician Power. But Claudius owed his position to the choice of the Praetorians, and the events of 69 A.D. made it clear that the Senate had no power but to ratify the choice of the soldiers. Under Tiberius the elections were transferred from the Comitia to the Senate, and as Senatus Consulta took the place of the laws passed by the Popular Assembly under the Republic, the people lost all share in government. But the Senate did not gain in real power; their legislation was controlled by the Emperor's will, while the Imperial provinces were governed by his Legati, whose policy and authority depended on him. The Senate was used as a court of justice under the Empire, but here too its decisions were often guided by the Emperor, and he alone was the court of appeal for all cases arising in the provinces or departments under his control. The Executive officers looked to the Emperor as their head; he nominated an increasing number of magistrates and governors, and the posts to which the Senate appointed were posts rather of dignity than of importance. Thus legislation, judicial and executive powers were in the Emperor's hands. Nor was there a Civil Service strong enough to control the ruler. The early Emperors used their educated slaves or freedmen to act as clerks and heads of departments. They were often Greeks and men of ability; but while they could use their position to play an important part in court intrigues and to enrich themselves, they did not yet constitute a bureaucracy capable of thwarting their patron. His power was absolute, provided always that he had the support of the soldiers. It was only rarely that the legions of the frontiers rose in revolt. The Praetorian cohorts were concentrated by Tiberius in one camp near the city wall and served as the Imperial bodyguard. But they had to be kept in good humour by special pay and privileges and were at the same time the main defence and danger to the Emperor.

DATES		DATES	
14–37 A.D.	Tiberius.	54–68 A.D.	Nero.
37–41 A.D.	Caligula.	69 A.D.	Year of the four Emperors
41–54 A.D.	Claudius.	69–96 A.D.	Flavian Dynasty.

CHAPTER XXVIII

NERVA TO COMMODUS

THE murderers of Domitian had looked out for a successor likely to be acceptable to Senate and Praetorians, and Nerva, a senator sixty years old, became Emperor. He swore to respect the lives of senators, and his successors took the same oath. His accession was hailed as the restoration of liberty, but the Senate was incapable of using real power, and the contentment which marked most of the next century was due to the fact that the Emperors were mainly men of good character and ability who observed the decencies of life and gave to the Senate respect but not authority. Under Nerva began the endowment schemes, *alimenta*, for encouraging agriculture and at the same time maintaining poor children. Money was lent to farmers on easy terms, and the interest was used to support destitute boys and girls.

Nerva, who died in 98 A.D., had adopted M. Ulpius Trajanus, a Spaniard and a distinguished general in command of the legions of Upper Germany. Trajan's advancement hardly implied the rule of a provincial over Romans, but it is evidence of the extent to which Spain had been Romanized and it made for wider views. A soldier and coming from the provinces, he knew little of the prejudices of Roman society and could regard the Empire as a living concern with varied interests and not as a mere contributor to the glory of Rome. He treated the Senate with respect and made the Praetorians understand that he was their master; he put down *delatores* and allowed freedom of speech; but in the Senatorial provinces and even in Italy as well as in the Imperial provinces he interfered frequently, sending commissioners to put the finances of cities in order and to arrange the affairs of provinces. Governors consulted him frequently. Pliny as governor of Bithynia applied to him for direction as to the treatment of Christians; and the Emperor replied that no efforts should be made to discover them, but if convicted, they were to be punished. All this made for good government but it destroyed local initiative; and it became increasingly difficult to find men willing to take municipal office in provincial towns, while at Rome the thousand and one questions submitted to the Emperor increased the numbers and importance of the Civil Service which was needed to deal with them.

Trajan's reign was marked by two great wars. The first was against the Dacians and was perhaps inevitable, as the Danube frontier was a danger to Rome and the indecisive campaigns of Domitian had aggravated the situation. The course of the war can be traced on the Column of Trajan still standing in the Forum. In two campaigns 101–102 A.D. he compelled Decebalus to submit to terms, but the Dacian king took up arms again in 105 and invaded the country south of the Danube. Trajan gradually drove back the Dacians, captured Sarmizegethusa and hunted the remnants of the Dacian force through forests till Decebalus was brought to bay and slew himself. Dacia was made a province and protected by a ring of forts; a stone bridge was built over the Danube; and Trajan, who realized that the defence of the upper Rhine was closely connected with that of the Danube, constructed roads from one river to the other. In the wars against the Parthians, 114–116 A.D., Trajan seems to have been led on by love of conquest. The vexed question of the sovereignty of Armenia was brought to a head by Chosroes king of Parthia, who deposed Trajan's nominee. Trajan refusing all offers of negotiation reduced Armenia to the status of a province. In 116 he descended the Euphrates,

Column of Trajan

captured Ctesiphon the Parthian capital, and made Mesopotamia a province.   But insurrections in his rear caused
him to retreat, and in 117 he died on his way back to Rome.

Trajan was followed by his cousin Hadrian, a Spaniard
too, who had served with distinction in Dacia and was in
command of the Syrian army in 117.   He was one of the
greatest among the Roman Emperors and his reign marks
the change from local patriotism to the sense of a wider
nationality embracing all the peoples of the Empire.
'A searcher out of all strange things,' a Greekling, as he
was called, a poet and artist, filled with Hellenic ideas,
he was a man of moods, swayed at times towards suspicion
or passion.   But he represented also the best of old Rome,
mastered the details of business, laboured for the good of
his dominions, and realized in his own words that the ruler
exists for the State and not the State for its ruler.   He
reversed Trajan's policy of conquest and withdrew in the
East from Mesopotamia and Armenia.   Dacia he was
forced to hold by its nearness to the heart of the Empire
and he strengthened the line between Rhine and Danube
by a palisade and stone forts.   A similar defence protected
Roman Britain, though the Tyne-Solway wall is probably
of later date.   Enclosing the Empire as it were in a ring
fence, he kept the legions in the provinces in which they
were recruited and then set to work to organize the Empire
as a unity behind its defences.   Local self-government and
citizenship were given to many provincial towns; Italy
was treated almost as a province and divided between four
commissioners of consular rank; the Senate was treated
politely but set on one side; and the Equestrian order,
freed from its military associations, became a purely civil
body, from which Hadrian chose capable members to
serve him in the provinces or to act as members of his
Council or as his secretaries of state.   The latter had
generally been drawn from the ranks of Freedmen and were

the heads of the departments of the Civil Service.   The
most important were the Finance Minister (*a rationibus*),
dealing with all questions of revenue and expenditure; the
Provincial Secretary (*ab epistulis*), who handled the corre-
spondence with foreign states, provincial governors, and
military officials; and the Clerk of Petitions (*a libellis*).
The transference of these duties to Equites marks the full
recognition of the Civil Service, whose work was done by
men who felt themselves the instruments of the Emperor's
personal government.   Hadrian devoted much thought
to the finances of the Empire and substituted direct
taxation for the oppressive system of tax-farming by
Publicani.   To his Council he summoned the best lawyers
of his time and endeavoured to bring Roman law into
harmony with the more humane feelings and higher
morality of the age.   The Praetor's Edict, a body of rules
modifying and applying principles of law, which had been
handed on from one praetor to another and developed in
the course of centuries, was now arranged and systematized
by Salvius Julianus.

For much of his reign Hadrian was absent from Rome,
travelling through the provinces and learning their needs
and possibilities at first hand.   In 133 a revolt broke out
in Palestine under a false Messiah, Barchochebas, which
was suppressed after heavy loss of life, and the Jews were
driven finally out of their own land.   In 138 Hadrian died.
He had first chosen a worthless friend Verus to succeed
him; but Verus died, and Hadrian chose in his place
T. Aurelius Antoninus, an elderly man of high character,
who was at the same time compelled to adopt both his own
nephew, who took the name of M. Aurelius Antoninus,
and the young son of Verus.

Antoninus Pius was a pattern of all private virtues but
not a great ruler.   Hadrian's centralized system needed
a strong man to control it.   Now the tax-collectors

worked only too well, and Egypt in particular suffered heavily; the cultivators turned brigands to avoid exactions and villages were left deserted. Italy was restored to its position outside the provincial system, the Emperor never went beyond the limits of the peninsula, and he found his real happiness in celebrating the 900th anniversary of the founding of Rome in 147 A.D. He continued Hadrian's legal work, and the influence of Stoicism helped to give greater effect to principles of equity. In Britain he built a turf rampart between the Forth and Clyde. In the East trouble was brewing, which broke out after his death. In 147 he associated M. Aurelius with himself as joint Emperor, passing over young Verus. But when Antoninus Pius died in 161, Marcus made Verus his colleague.

The reign of the philosopher-prince was a time of war. The Parthians had over-run Armenia, and Verus was sent to take command against them in 162 A.D. While he spent his time at ease in Antioch, Statius Priscus recovered Armenia and placed a prince friendly to Rome upon the throne. Further south there was more fighting on the Lower Euphrates, where Avidius Cassius forced the passage of the river, burnt Seleucia and Ctesiphon the two chief cities of Parthia, and made part of Mesopotamia a province 165 A.D. But the armies on their return brought with them a pestilence, which devastated the Empire and spread to the legions which were engaged in another and more serious struggle. The tribes of the Upper Danube had long been dangerous. In 167 the Marcomanni from Bohemia and the Quadi from Moravia with the Iazyges from the plains of Hungary swept over the Danube, over-ran Rhaetia Noricum and Pannonia, and beseiged Aquileia. Verus died in 169, but for eight years Marcus was engaged in a desperate war. He succeeded in averting the danger for the time but was unable to complete the conquest of the barbarians, as he was called away in 175 to put down

Bust of M. Aurelius Antoninus

Avidius Cassius, who had proclaimed himself Emperor in Syria; and fighting was still going on against the Marcomanni when Marcus died in 180 A.D. War and famine had greatly reduced the population, and barbarians had been hired to fight barbarians. In the devastated provinces too Marcus settled thousands of barbarians in a condition of serfdom, the beginning of the system of replacing a declining population by barbarians from the north. Marcus is famous for his "Meditations" written by the camp-fires, revealing the soul of a man strong to do his duty and to accept the burden of war and responsibility, from which he would gladly have been free.

Commodus his son was made joint Emperor in 177 and ruled alone on Marcus's death, an example of the danger of autocracy where one of the noblest Emperors was followed by one of the basest. After a reign of twelve years, in which he disgusted the world by his cowardice and mad profligacy, he was put to death by his favourites.

In the Age of the Antonines the Roman Empire reached its climax. Rulers of ability and good character had developed a system of administration which had in it the weakness of over-centralization, but which at least in their day was welding the Roman world into a unity. After their time disruptive forces from within and the pressure of barbarians from outside raised new problems and brought new developments. Two centuries of peace, almost unbroken in the lands which bordered on the Mediterranean, had given the Roman world a steady government, a common language and loyalty, free inter-course and trade between one part and another, and in the main a common administrative system and common laws. As a result the provinces had become Romanized though in varying degree. Spain and Gaul in particular had learnt Roman habits of life and thought and had made them their own. The Eastern provinces with a civilization older

than that of Rome had less to learn, but the strength of
Roman government had given them the stability which
they needed for their development; while even the barbarians, who began to serve in the army or settle in the
territory of Rome, learnt something of her spirit, so that
when Rome fell before the invaders in 410 A.D., her
influence though hidden for the time was not destroyed.
It was part of the fabric of the world. The long peace
encouraged the development of industries and arts; the
commercial cities of Asia Minor and Egypt and Greece
enjoyed a prosperity greater perhaps than ever before.
With seas and roads alike secure and trade unhampered
by restrictions, riches poured in and fine public buildings
rose as evidences of material well-being. Universities
flourished, and Greek culture, though it could not produce
the equals of the great writers of old, had a wider field in
which to make itself felt.

To the East the Roman world was indebted for new
religious influences. Western religion was bankrupt.
Philosophy had killed the worship of Olympus; the worship of Emperors was only a sort of patriotism and became
absurd when the Emperor was a mad brute. Stoicism
held before men's eyes a high standard of duty and morality,
but though it strengthened the strong, it had no help for
the weak. Oriental religions, which the State welcomed
if they did not conflict with Emperor-worship, were based
on the contrast between light and darkness, God and the
world. They recognized the need of perfection and the
possibility of it with immortality as the prize. The Phry-
gian worship of the Great Mother Cybele had its *Tauro-
bolium*, where the initiate was drenched with the blood
of an ox and reborn to new life. The Egyptian priests of
Isis by impressive ritual and liturgy made real to the
minds of the worshippers the promises of happiness in
another world. From Syria came the cult of Mithras, god

of light, worshipped in underground chapels and represented as a young god sacrificing a bull. Here gathered
men of every age and rank and country realizing in their
worship something of the continual struggle between right
and wrong, in which they saw the hope of victory. Later
Emperors turned the creed to political use by posing as a
kind of incarnation of Mithras; at present it was the chief
religion of the Roman soldiers. Christianity was spreading;
but as it could not permit the worship of Emperors, it
suffered persecution as a form of treason. It went too
deep in its demand for purification and self-surrender, as
well as in the certainty which it offered, to suit a world
which was not entirely dissatisfied with itself.

DATES

96– 98 A.D. Nerva.
98–117 A.D. Trajan.
101–106 A.D. Dacian Wars.
114–116 A.D. Parthian War.
117–138 A.D. Hadrian.
138–161 A.D. Antoninus Pius.
161–180 A.D. M. Aurelius Antoninus.
167–175 A.D. War with Marcomanni and Quadi.
180–192 A.D. Commodus.

CHAPTER XXIX

THE SEVERI TO AURELIAN

THE murder of Commodus was followed by confusion,
in which the Praetorian Guard took the lead. Pertinax,
who was first appointed Emperor, offended the Guards by
trying to restore discipline and was murdered. The
Empire was then put up to auction and bought by Didius
Julianus who offered the Praetorians £200 a man. But
the legions of Pannonia were close at hand and proclaimed

their general L. Septimius Severus Emperor. He had to deal with two rivals, Pescennius Niger who commanded the Syrian army and Clodius Albinus from Britain. The latter he induced for the moment to rest content with the title of Caesar and the prospect of succession. Then turning on Niger, who had advanced as far as Byzantium, he routed him at Nicaea and by 195 A.D. had secured the East, punishing Byzantium by razing its walls and thereby robbing the Mediterranean of one of its defences. He then settled with Albinus, whom he defeated near Lyons in 197. Septimius Severus was an African by birth, the first Emperor from the country which was now the centre of intellectual activity, as Spain had been a century earlier. He owed his position to the legions, and his reign marks the establishment of undisguised military autocracy, in which the army gained in political power but got out of hand and decayed as a fighting force. He disbanded the Praetorians, who had supported Julianus, and filled their place with soldiers picked from the legions. Thus Italy lost her old privilege of supplying the household troops and had to submit to another indignity in the shape of a legion permanently quartered in the peninsula. He is said to have advised his sons to shower favours on the soldiers and to treat civilians with contempt; legionaries received increased pay and were allowed to wear the gold ring, hitherto the mark of a knight; centurions were given equestrian rank and veterans exempted from all municipal burdens. The Prefect of the Guard became the head of the Imperial service and the court of appeal for all cases outside the radius of a hundred miles from Rome, the Prefect of the City having jurisdiction within that limit. The Praetorian Prefect also had charge of the importation of supplies to the capital and of the commissariat department for all the Imperial armies. The Senate he neglected entirely and where possible appointed knights to the command of legions. The Aerarium, nominally controlled by the Senate, became merely the municipal treasury of Rome; the Fiscus or Imperial treasury with the Patrimonium Caesaris received the revenues and met the expense of governing the empire, while a new department, the Privy Purse or *res privata principis*, founded on confiscations, became a useful means of buying loyalty or paying for extravagance.

Septimius Severus was not a great soldier. He strengthened the wall in Britain from Tyne to Solway and the defences between the Rhine and Danube. But the need of such defence was a sign of weakness and had the effect of tying down the frontier troops to lines which they were incapable of holding. In the East he won successes on the Euphrates and raised the city of Palmyra to the rank of a colony. Under its leading family, the Odae-nathi, it served as a bulwark on the Eastern frontier but was destined soon to be a rival of Rome.

Severus died in 211 A.D. He had been strong enough to keep order, but his son Caracalla combined madness with all the possible vices. Murdering his brother Geta, he proceeded to a general massacre in which 20,000 are said to have perished. He is however to be remembered for the *Constitutio Antoniniana* which dates from the first year of his reign, by which Roman citizenship was conferred on all freeborn members of the Empire. It was the completion of the levelling-up process, which had been going on for more than two centuries with grants of citizenship to one town after another, and of the equalization of the provinces with Italy. Hadrian, as we have seen, had grasped the idea of one Empire and one common nationality within a ring-fence. Later Emperors had acted on that conception and Caracalla completed their work. But the ring-fence was now weak and equality with later Romans not greatly to be valued, though the development was natural. It meant in theory and partly as a matter of fact that Roman civilization and institutions prevailed over a great part of Western and Southern Europe and the adjoining lands. The structure of the Empire might be tottering but its life was firmly rooted throughout these lands, and much of what Rome stood for was bound to survive the dissolution of the Empire and the fall of the city. Certain incidental results followed from the equalization. The 5 p.c. succession duties, which Italians had paid instead of the land tax borne by the provincials, had now to be paid throughout the Empire; on the other hand the right of appeal, which citizens such as St Paul had claimed against provincial governors, was abolished except in a very few cases.

Elagabalus, priest of the Syrian sun-god, filled up the chief part of the interval between Caracalla's reign and that of Alexander Severus, and his rule was a time of degradation. Eunuchs, charioteers, and hair-dressers held the chief posts, and the Emperor spent his time between superstition and orgies of cruelty and vice. At length in 222 A.D. Alexander Severus, already Caesar, became sole Emperor after the murder of Elagabalus. He was a conscientious ruler without much strength, who made an attempt to restore power to the Senate. Under him various senatorial committees were appointed, which Alexander consulted on the question of new laws or provincial appointments. We may notice here a development, which was gradually taking place in the Empire and which Alexander helped forward. *Collegia* or private societies had been viewed with much suspicion under early Emperors. But later they had been found useful as trade-guilds, licensed for the undertaking of special public services and receiving in exchange exemption from other public duties. As bureaucratic control grew stronger, these *collegia*, entrusted perhaps with the monopoly of baking bread or the importation of food-stuffs, found themselves burdened rather than favoured by their special position. Alexander Severus is said to have extended the guild-system to include all industries; private initiative waned and each employment became more and more a hereditary caste. This was specially true of the *coloni* or cultivators of the soil, who received grants of land on condition of hereditary service. The Roman world was becoming artificial with no life in it, where everything was done by routine. Men did not do their work because they had aptitude for it but because they were born to it; the provinces did not manage their own affairs but referred the most trifling matters to the central government; and at the centre was no vigorous head but a set of clerks, who could look up precedents and stereotype their own mistakes. When the chief argument for a practice is that it always has been so, bureaucracy has reached the height of its ambition and has brought its country to nothing. There really was need of some strength somewhere in Rome. The Alamanni were breaking through into Rhaetia; the Parthians had been overthrown by the Persians, who claimed to be the descendants of Darius and whose horsemen clad in mail were ravaging Cappadocia and Syria; the tribes across the Rhine taking advantage of the disturbances in the East were pressing into Roman territory. Alexander gained some success at great cost against the Persians but he tried to buy off the German invaders. His men, disgusted at his lack of military spirit, murdered their Emperor in 235 A.D. and set up Maximin, a Thracian peasant-soldier of gigantic strength in his place.

Thirty years followed in which the Empire came near to breaking. The Emperors were either brutes like Maximin, grinding down their subjects by oppressive taxation and secure only by the fear they inspired, or weak and

holding their position only till a rival should be set up by
the soldiers.   With the Empire distracted by oppression
and civil war at home, foes from without were battering
at the doors.   Maximin drove back the German invaders,
but there were other and more pressing dangers.   To the
south of the Danube and its tributaries lay the path to
Italy at one end and to Greece and the Aegean at the other
with a possible outlet through the Black Sea.   Since about
170 A.D. the Goths had been pushing south-eastwards from
the shores of the Baltic towards the Black Sea, and with
their inroads the attacks of tribes, such as M. Aurelius had
had to meet, were swallowed up in a more dangerous tide
of invasion.   The Ostrogoths under their king Cniva
crossed the Danube and in spite of the resistance of the
Emperor Decius captured Philippopolis.   Then turning
north with their plunder they fell on Decius who tried to
oppose their march in the Dobrudsha marshes to the south
of the Danube estuary and defeated and slew the Emperor
in 251 A.D.   For a few years, partly by payment of subsidies and partly by hard fighting, the Roman armies held
the Northmen at bay, and their hordes tried to find an
easier way to the Mediterranean by sea.   Over-running the
Crimea they obtained a fleet and cruising along the
Eastern shore of the Black Sea ravaged the coast as far
as the Bosphorus.   Byzantium had been dismantled by
Septimius Severus, and the Goths passed through the
Straits on their raids.   Ephesus was plundered and even
Athens attacked.   It was not till the reign of Claudius,
who from his success took the name of Gothicus, that the
Goths were for the time driven back.   He was an Illyrian
trained in fighting on the Danube, and his men had pro-
fited by many years' fighting against the Goths.   Moving
to the relief of Thessalonica which was hard pressed he
compelled the Goths to leave the Aegean coast in order to
meet him.   Then driving them northward he inflicted

a crushing defeat on them in 269 A.D. near the modern town of Nish in Serbia and in the course of the year drove the invaders north of the Danube.

Further East the Persians under the dynasty of the Sassanids had overthrown the Parthians and invaded Roman territory. The younger Gordian, a successor of Maximin, drove them back to the Euphrates in 244 A.D., but their king Shapur was by no means done with. Taking advantage of Rome's difficulties in the Gothic invasion, he over-ran Armenia and occupied Antioch. The Emperor Valerian in attempting to relieve Edessa, was captured by the Persians in 258 A.D. and according to the story was used by the Persian king as his footstool and ultimately flayed and his skin stuffed with straw. The Persians now made their way through Asia Minor to the Aegean; and with the collapse of Roman power in the East an opportunity was given to Palmyra out in the desert beyond Damascus to assert its independence. The fortunes of this city will be noticed later. But it is important to recognize how near the Empire was to dissolution. With frontiers assailed in every direction, Goths breaking through to the Mediterranean, Persians streaming across Asia Minor, rival generals contending among themselves for power, the outlying districts had to look to themselves for the help which Rome could not give. Palmyra was not alone in separating from the main body. In the West under pressure of inroads of the Franks a separate Empire of the Gauls was proclaimed in 258, and Postumus was chosen to fill the position to which Civilis in the days of Vespasian had aspired. He succeeded in driving the invaders across the Rhine and strengthened the natural defence of the river with a line of forts. He fixed his capital at Trèves and copied the institutions of Rome, senate and consuls and the state-religion. But the Empire of the Gauls did not last long. With the accession of

Claudius Gothicus in 268 A.D. Rome began once more to pull the Empire together. Spain and Gallia Narbonensis came back to their allegiance and the Empire of the Gauls gradually crumbled away.

Claudius died in 270 and the same year saw the accession of Aurelian. A peasant's son from Pannonia Aurelian had considerable administrative ability; but he was above all a hard and stern soldier, who in the course of a few years drove back the barbarians and welded the Empire once more into one body. The Juthungi from the upper waters of the Danube had supplied troops to the Roman army; but now plundering Rhaetia on their way they came through the eastern passes of the Alps into Italy. Aurelian marched north through Noricum and cutting off their retreat compelled them to sue for peace. They were allowed to return to their homes but the trouble was not over. From the plains of Hungary the Vandals crossed into Pannonia, fore-runners of the race which assailed the Empire a century later. Aurelian ordered all stores and cattle to be collected within the towns of the district and fell on the starving enemy, who were forced to make peace and leave the Roman lands unmolested. But before he could return, the Juthungi had risen again in company with their neighbours from the Upper Rhine, the Alamanni. Bursting into North Italy they laid waste the plains of the Po and streamed south along the Adriatic coast. In the hour of crisis Goths on the lower Danube and Palmyra in the east added to Aurelian's difficulties, while the armies in all directions set up their generals as rival Emperors. But Aurelian kept cool. Giving orders for the walls of the Italian cities to be repaired he met the invaders at Fanum Fortunae near the Metaurus. After defeating them there he pursued them along the Via Aemiliana and annihilated them not far from the Ticinus 270 A.D. Italy was freed from the barbarians, and Aurelian after quieting the

Walls of Aurelian

disturbances which had arisen in the hour of danger at Rome commenced the building of the walls of defence with which Rome is still encircled.

Palmyra had been honoured by Septimius Severus. At the meeting-place of caravan routes across the Syrian desert it had grown in wealth and importance and its archers were the nucleus of a good army. The leading family, the Odaenathi, were ambitious and after Valerian's defeat in 258 saw in the collapse of Roman power both the need of increasing their own army and the opportunity of asserting their independence. Proceeding cautiously Odaenathus by his activity against the Persians became recognized as the ruler of the East and was given the title of Imperator. In 267 Zenobia became regent for her young son with Longinus and the Christian bishop Paul of Samosata as her ministers and threw off allegiance to Rome. Rome, hard pressed by the Goths, was in no condition to interfere, and the Palmyrène army invaded Egypt and gained most of that country and of Asia Minor. It was not till 271 A.D. that Aurelian had leisure to deal with Palmyra. In that year Egypt was recovered and Aurelian's main army moving through Asia Minor met little resistance. On the upper Orontes the Palmyrenes barred the way at Emesa but in spite of the good work of their cavalry they were defeated, and Zenobia could only hope that the hundred miles of desert which lay before Palmyra would save her city from Aurelian. In spite of difficulties and the attacks of Arab horsemen he made his way forward and laid siege to the city. A Persian relieving force was beaten off and hunger did its work. The city surrendered and was treated with moderation. But scarcely had Aurelian retraced his steps, when the Palmyrenes rose and massacred the Roman garrison which had been left in the city. This time Aurelian made an end. The city was destroyed and Zenobia herself taken to Rome to grace his triumph.

From the East Aurelian turned to settle with the tottering empire of the Gauls. But Tetricus the Gallic Emperor could not protect his country from German invaders and entering into negotiations with Aurelian deserted his troops, who were cut to pieces by the Emperor's legions in 273 A.D. Aurelian had now finished most of his military work. He had checked the dissolution of the Empire and had restored its unity; he had driven out the invading hordes; but he recognized that danger was still threatening. The lands beyond the Rhine and Danube were no longer tenable, and troops were withdrawn behind these rivers, as Augustus had advised in days long past. The fortification of Italian cities was an evidence of the insecurity of a land long unmolested by war; but the building of walls round Rome made it clear that not even the Imperial city was any longer safe from the barbarians.

Aurelian was murdered in 275 while on his way to punish the Persians for their assistance to Palmyra, and another period of disorder followed till the accession of Diocletian in 285 A.D..

DATES

193–211 A.D.	Septimus Severus. Military autocracy.
212 A.D.	Constitutio Antoniniana of Caracalla.
250–270 A.D.	Barbarian Invasions.
251 A.D.	Decius defeated and killed by the Goths.
258 A.D.	Valerian captured by the Persians.
258 A.D.	Palmyra independent.
258 A.D.	Empire of the Gauls.
268–270 A.D.	Claudius defeated the Goths.
270–275 A.D.	Aurelian.
270 A.D.	Defeat of Vandals, Juthungi and Alamanni.
271 A.D.	Zenobia, Queen of Palmyra, subdued.
273 A.D.	End of the Empire of the Gauls.

CHAPTER XXX

DIOCLETIAN AND CONSTANTINE

THE death of Aurelian, who left no son to succeed him, was followed by a renewal of the struggle between rival aspirants to the Imperial power. Among them we need only notice Probus, one of Aurelian's generals, who crossed the Rhine and checked the German tribes who had sacked the cities of Eastern Gaul. He repaired the devastation which invaders had caused both in Gaul and Illyria, and in Moesia he followed Aurelian's policy of settling in the country frontier-tribes who had been driven south by the Goths. But he could not keep his own soldiers in hand and was murdered in 282 A.D. while planning a campaign against Persia. Out of the disorder at last emerged the son of a Dalmatian slave, Diocles, who disposed of his rivals and became Emperor in 285.

Diocles, or Diocletian as he styled himself, came like Aurelian and other Emperors before him from the lands lying to the east of the upper Adriatic, and he worked out as a system of government the tendencies which as a matter of fact had been growing up under his predecessors. He is to be regarded as the organizer of a new type of Empire, the man who marked the definite change from the old system under which authority was nominally divided between the Emperor and the Senate, the man who finally dropped the disguise under which Augustus had endeavoured to conceal his true position. His predecessors had lacked either the ability or the leisure to remodel the State. Diocletian had both, and he organized Absolutism, not allowing tradition to hamper him but treating every branch of administration as clay to be modelled into any shape he pleased.

He assumed for himself the style of an Eastern Monarch. While the canonization of dead Emperors had gradually led to their assumption of divine honours during their lifetime, Diocletian, boldly insisting on ceremonial which marked him as in a different sphere from his subjects, made access to his presence a difficult matter only to be ventured upon to the accompaniment of prostrations. Rome was still the Sacred and Eternal City in name, but the Emperor's Court was at Nicomedia in Bithynia. Rome and Italy were put on the same footing as the provinces, and the immunity of the peninsula from direct taxation was cancelled. The Senatorial Order remained a kind of hereditary caste, but the Senate became nothing more than a municipal council for the city of Rome, while the old Republican magistrates became in the same way merely municipal officers. The old idea of a city-state with dependencies governed in the interests of the city was gone at last.

The real danger of the last three centuries however had been the system under which provincial governors had had large armies at their disposal, and the civil wars which had been the natural consequence. Diocletian endeavoured to meet this danger by the division of power; and as we shall see later his fourfold arrangement of Augusti and Caesars had this in view. But for the present we must notice that he first subdivided the existing provinces including Italy into 116 smaller units and then grouped them in 13 *dioceses*. The governors of the provinces were primarily responsible to the *vicarii* who were set over the dioceses, and these in turn were under four *praefecti*, who commanded the four Praefectures of (i) the Gauls including Spain and Britain, (ii) Italy with Pannonia and Africa, (iii) Illyricum and the Balkan Peninsula, (iv) the East. In addition to this the military command in the provinces was finally separated from the civil administration and entrusted to specially appointed *duces*.

In the hope of keeping out the barbarians, changes were made in the army either by Diocletian or his immediate successors. Besides the troops stationed in permanent quarters along the frontiers who garrisoned the forts and lines of defence, a field-army was organized capable of taking the offensive when required. The recruits for the large army which had to be maintained were raised partly as a charge on land-owners, a method not unlike the Feudal System of later date. But naturally the least serviceable men would be sent by the owners of property. For the picked regiments voluntary enlistment supplied the larger proportion of men, and in this way a military caste grew up of those who made fighting their profession. They were largely barbarians, whose personal bravery was better than their discipline and knowledge of tactics; and the soldiers of the Empire lost the main advantage which civilized forces have over uncivilized enemies.

The expenditure on military needs as well as on the more elaborate system of civil administration added to the already heavy burden of taxation. The coinage had been debased again and again, and as the value of money declined, requisitions for the army were now often made in kind. Assessments were made from time to time based on the nature of land and the amount of labour employed upon it, and corresponding contributions levied from each district. But apart from dishonesty, which was common enough, there were inevitable mistakes and inequalities in the assessments and great waste of the supplies collected. Distress was universal and the cost of the necessaries of life exorbitant. Diocletian in 301 A.D. attempted by his Edict of Prices to regulate the price of every commodity sold in any market throughout the Empire. But we need not be surprised that he only added to the general confusion and distress.

For his highly centralized government the Emperor needed information from all parts of the civilized world. To obtain it he organized a vast system of espionage. By the side of every provincial administrator was an agent who sent home reports on the governor to the Emperor, while his spies travelled far and wide through the provinces and gathered information for him from every source. An atmosphere of suspicion prevailed, which prevented the development of any real ability or originality in the administration.

So much for Diocletian's system, which was slowly developed as his reign went on. But would it stand the test of time? To prevent the disputes between rival claimants which followed the death of an Emperor, Diocletian, who had no son, chose as his colleague Maximian a Pannonian soldier and gave him at first the title of Caesar. While Diocletian fixed his court at Nicomedia, Maximian chose Milan. The latter was first employed in crushing a revolt of the peasants in Gaul against the heavy load of taxation but in 286 A.D. found a rival in Carausius, a British commander in the Imperial Navy. Carausius styled himself Emperor in Britain and after four years' fighting was recognized till his death in 296 by Diocletian and Maximian, the latter of whom soon took the title of Augustus. In 293 the two Augusti appointed two Caesars as their destined successors, Diocletian nominating Galerius and Maximian choosing Constantius. The Caesars were to be regarded as deputies of the Augusti, and while they might act outside their own districts, Constantius received the special care of the West and made Trèves his capital, Maximian took Italy and Africa, Galerius the Balkan Peninsula, while Diocletian retained the East for himself. In future each Caesar was to rule in that capacity for ten years and then to be an Augustus for ten years, after which he was to lay down his power. Diocletian arranged that he and Maximian should both abdicate in 305 A.D. and that when Constantius and Galerius became Augusti, Maximian's son Maxentius and Constantine son of Constantius should be made Caesars. But the abdication in 305 was followed by a period of confusion. Galerius attempted to gain the whole power for himself and his nominees. Constantine fled to his father in Britain and on Constantius's death there in 306 was saluted as an Augustus by his troops. A confused period of disputing and fighting followed, in the course of which Maximian and Diocletian both came out of retirement and endeavoured without success to make an arrangement between the rivals. Gradually the struggle resolved itself into a contest between Constantine, with the western provinces at his back united in loyalty to him through his just government, and Galerius with his subordinate Licinius, while Maxentius intervened when occasion offered. Galerius died in 311. He had been a persecutor of the Christians, and Constantine who had shown them consideration during his time in Britain, now adopted the *labarum* with the Christian monogram as his standard and marched on Rome. He defeated and slew Maxentius at the Milvian Bridge in 312 and then turned against Licinius. A hollow peace was made between the two, but hard fighting took place in 314, after which they agreed to divide the Empire between them. For nine years Constantine secured his position, and by recognizing Christianity as one of the public religions of the Empire and by helping the Christians to settle their internal disputes, he gained the support of an important section of the people. At last in 323 Licinius, who had alienated his own supporters by cruelty, took up arms. He was defeated twice at Adrianople and Scutari and after his surrender was put to death.

Constantine was now sole Emperor and in 325 A.D. presided at the Council of Nicaea in Bithynia, which condemned Arius who denied the full divinity of Our Lord. But though the arguments of Athanasius had their effect on the council, the Emperor himself inclined later to the side of Arius.   In any case it would be difficult to say how far his conversion to Christianity was genuine.   The story goes that on his march against Maxentius he saw a bright cross in the sky with the words "In this conquer."   He was probably attracted by Christianity without being able to free himself from the associations of other religions which were part of the atmosphere of the time.   Motives of policy no doubt played their part as well.   The Christians were a numerous and not unimportant body; and his own position, while Maxentius was still alive, would make him welcome a means of gaining friends.   While on the one hand he is said to have allowed his statue to be set up at Constantinople in the character of the Sun God, on the other hand he is stated to have excluded heathen cults from the new capital and he was buried there in a Christian church.   To the Christian body he left the doubtful advantage that Christianity was now the religion of the state and not of a persecuted sect.   The number of its adherents grew as their sincerity was less severely put to the test.

From 326 to 330 A.D. he was engaged in founding at Byzantium the new Eastern capital of the Empire, named after himself Constantinople.   A wall two miles long protected the tongue of land between the Golden Horn and the Sea of Marmora, and the Golden Horn itself was made an excellent harbour.   The foundation of a new capital appropriately marks the new type of government which dates from Diocletian and Constantine; and here a new system and a new state-religion could flourish unhampered by the traditions which clung to the old capital.   At the meeting-point of two seas and two conti-

nents the commerce of the Eastern and Western world
would readily come to its wharves, and the wisdom as well
as the folly of East and West meet within its walls; while
the Emperor would be near enough to the Northern

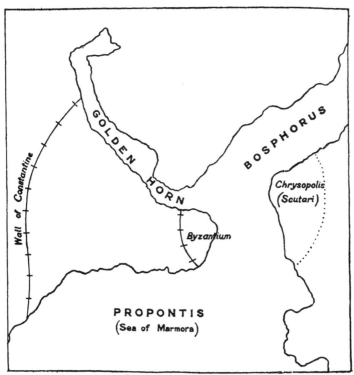

Plan of Constantinople

barbarians to control the defensive measures necessary
against them.

In 337 A.D. Constantine died, and with him the story
of Old Rome may end.   A new city, a new religion, a new
system of government, were now to play their part.
Hitherto each stage had been a development, an adaptation
of the old to new conditions.   Adaptation and extension

were the methods of Old Rome.   Now we have a new
departure.   One may call it New Rome, as Constantine
was inclined to call his capital.   But whatever the name,
the facts have changed.   Henceforth we should be dealing
with the beginnings of a new world rather than with the
end of the old.

DATES

285–305 A.D.	Diocletian. Absolute Rule.
301 A.D.	Edict of Prices.
305 A.D.	Constantine a Caesar.
312 A.D.	Constantine supports Christianity.
	Battle of the Milvian Bridge.
323 A.D.	Constantine sole Emperor.
326–330 A.D.	Building of Constantinople.
337 A.D.	Death of Constantine.

INDEX

298 INDEX

Artaxata, 188 (map), 189
Arverni, 148, 204, 205 (map), 211
Asculum in Apulia, 63 (map), 66
Asculum in Picenum, 3 (map), 161, 162
Asia, 62; province, 147, 167; taxation, 170, 189; see Pergamum, Mithradates
Assembly; see Comitia
Athens, 26, 106, 167, 168 (map)
Attalus, 140, 147
Augusti and Caesares, 292–3
Augustus, C. Julius Caesar Octavianus, 230; Mutina, 234; Triumvirate, 235–8; Philippi, 236; commands the West, 238; S. Pompeius, 240; Actium, 240–3; Empire, 243–5 (illustr.); departments of government, 244–8; literature and religion, 249; frontiers, 250–2; succession, 253
Aurelian, Emperor, 285–8
Aurelius Antoninus, M., 273–6
Avaricum, 211
Avidius Cassius, 274–6

Bedriacum, 261
Belgae, 205 (map), 207, 210
Beneventum, 63 (map), 66; colony, 67
Bibracte, 205 (map), 206
Bibulus, M. Calpurnius, 202, 223
Bithynia, 112, 166; province, 188 (map)
Bocchus, 150, 151
Boii, 40, 41 (map), 59, 81, 88
Bovianum, 54 (map), 58
Brennus, 43, 44
Bribery, 34, 130, 131, 135
Britain, 209, 256–7, 260, 264–5, 272, 274
Brundisium, 96 (map), 175, 223; Via Appia, 67; treaty of, 238
Bruttians, 55, 67, 96 (map), 99, 104
Brutulus Papius, 55
Brutus, D., 208, 222, 233; Mutina, 234, 235
Brutus, M., 14, 19
Brutus, M., 225, 231–8; Philippi, 236
Burrus, 258
Byzantium, 279, 283

Cabira, 189

Caecilius; see Metellus
Caepio, Q. Servilius, 125
Caepio, Q. Servilius, 152
Caere, 41 (map), 43, 45, 46; see Citizenship
Caesar, C. Julius, 178, 193, 195, 196, 198; Catiline, 197, 200; Spain, 201; coalition, 202, 203; Gaul, 204–13; Luca, 215; breach with Pompey, 215–8; civil war, 219–30, 221 (illustr.); works and character, 220, 227, 229–32; will, 234; Divus Julius, 249
Caesar, L. Julius, 161, 162
Calendar, 229
Cales; colony, 51, 54 (map)
Caligula, 255–6
Camillus, M. Furius, 34, 35, 42–6
Campania; Etruscans, 4, 40; Samnites, 48–50, 56, 57, 69; Hannibal, 91, 95–7; Social War, 161, 162
Campi Raudii, 153
Cannae, 92, 93 (plan), 94, 96 (map)
Capitalists, 25, 36, 133, 135, 138, 144, 147, 185
Cappadocia, 159, 188 (map)
Capua, 48; Via Appia, 52, 54 (map), 57, 65; Hannibal, 91, 94–7, 175
Caracalla, 280
Carbo, Cn. Papirius, 152
Carbo, Cn. Papirius, 173, 176, 177
Carneades, 117
Carrhae, 188 (map), 216, 250
Carthage, 62, 65, 70–2 (map); three Punic Wars, Chap. viii–xi, xiii; 121 (plan), 123, 143, 145, 229
Cassius, C., 216, 225, 231, 232; civil war, 233–8; Philippi, 236
Cassius, Q., 218, 227
Cassius, Sp., 25, 26, 28
Cassivellaunus, 209
Catilina, L. Sergius, 178, 196–201
Cato, M. Porcius, 111, 117, 120; Spain, 124, 125–9
Cato, M. Porcius, Uticensis, 193, 200–3; civil war, 220–7
Catulus, Lutatius, 78
Catulus, Lutatius, 153, 154
Catulus, Lutatius, 182
Caudium, 48, 54 (map), 56
Celtiberians, 100 (map), 124–6
Cenabum, 205 (map), 211

For EU product safety concerns, contact us at Calle de José Abascal, 56–1°, 28003 Madrid, Spain or eugpsr@cambridge.org.

www.ingramcontent.com/pod-product-compliance
Ingram Content Group UK Ltd.
Pitfield, Milton Keynes, MK11 3LW, UK
UKHW012329130625
459647UK00009B/167